*The Witness of
William Penn*

THE MACMILLAN COMPANY
NEW YORK · CHICAGO
DALLAS · ATLANTA · SAN FRANCISCO
LONDON · MANILA

BRETT-MACMILLAN LTD.
TORONTO

The Witness of
William Penn

EDITED WITH AN INTRODUCTION

FREDERICK B. TOLLES
and
E. GORDON ALDERFER

New York — 1957
THE MACMILLAN COMPANY

Contents

III. THE FINAL DISTILLATION

Introduction

I

History has dealt most curiously with William Penn, for in this rare instance the legend-makers have concocted a sentimental image considerably inferior to the true character of the man. It is difficult to avoid the impression created by the ubiquitous prints of "Penn's Treaty with the Indians," a painting constructed from errant memories by Benjamin West, the Pennsylvania Quaker lad who became court painter to George III. Benign of countenance and portly of figure, Penn stands under the great elm at Shackamaxon, eternally dispensing peace and yard goods to the Indians. The genial Founding Father image has been perpetuated through the years by schoolbook writers, antiquarians, political orators, and Quaker sentimentalists.

What the Founding Father image lacks is intelligence and tension. Penn was born in the year when Cromwell won his first important victory over the forces of Charles I at Marston Moor, and as the son of a great British admiral he grew up in the tense political and ideological struggles that continued throughout his life. His birth year, 1644, was marked by the publication of Milton's *Areopagitica*, and Penn himself would one day continue the painful struggle for freedom of conscience and expression. Tension and challenge confronted him every year of his life until his final illness. Penn was endowed with a lively imagination and a high order of intelligence, qualities which the Founding Father image quite obscures.

Social historians and muckraking biographers, it is true, modified the image created by the legend-makers, but unfortunately most of them paid little heed to his voluminous writings. Because many of his works sprang out of conditions peculiar to his times, they have

been labeled "polemics" and left to molder on the shelves of anti-
quaries. Yet there is no better mirror of the man than his writings.

As a writer William Penn is capable of a surprisingly wide variety of
moods and techniques. In *Fruits of Solitude* he is master of the
maxim, a compression of thought which radiates its energy into large
segments of human experience. Few works in the dramatic literature
of his age have greater force and interest than the trial he dramatized
in *The People's Ancient and Just Liberties*. Clarity of reason and inci-
sion of logic are demonstrated in other writings. Yet his mind is
seldom without the warmth of passion, even in the most skillfully
reasoned treatises. When Penn the critic becomes Penn the prophet,
his writings take on a dark charged beauty and an apocalyptic grandeur.
Of course, like other writers of his time, his mind occasionally becomes jaded by polemics, and then he fails to take an artistic measure
of his work. Such passages have been omitted from this present com-
pilation.

Perhaps one of the attributes that kept Penn out of the ranks of the
greatest writers of his age was that modesty which led him to rely all
too frequently on the mountainous body of learning he accumulated.
How such an active, outward personality could have found the time
and intellectual perseverance to glean such vast resources of learned
reference, both pagan and Christian, ancient and modern, remains a
mystery. His short and interrupted scholastic career certainly cannot
account for it. Yet by his twenty-fourth year—a year crowded with
imprisonment, pamphleteering, domestic troubles, preaching jour-
neys—he was able to jot down in the second part of *No Cross, No
Crown*, the testimonies of about a hundred and fifty of the ancients,
the church fathers, and modern writers. Under the circumstances it
was an astonishing achievement. His deep learning in the law and
broad knowledge of history are coupled with an ability to sweep away
the chaff and rescue the meaningful kernels in a dramatic way.

These qualities remind us of Montaigne, with whose essays Penn
was familiar. But the significant point is that they used their sources
differently. Montaigne's classical quotations are invariably short and
pointed, firmly embodied in what Montaigne himself is saying, a kind

of alter ego accompaniment to his own personality. Though Penn's quotations are purposeful enough, they appear too often in ponderous, unassimilated blocks. The comparison, of course, is not altogether apt or fair. Montaigne was a child of the pagan Renaissance. Penn's England, outside the licentious court circle, was steeped in the somberness of a latter-day Reformation.

As a writer Penn did not reach toward the stars like his two older contemporaries of the English Reformation, Milton and Bunyan, for his imagination is seldom unfettered. The "plain truth" of Quakerism was but a dull medium in comparison with the visionary grandeurs of the tinker of Bedford or the great blind poet. Moreover, Penn seldom wrote by inner compulsion alone: nearly always an immediate objective guided his hand. Yet Penn was not without a consciousness of style. If he erred in style, he erred on the side of weightiness and "plain truth"; a little more sail and a little less ballast would have helped.

Admittedly, the available editions of Penn's writings have not encouraged a re-evaluation of his work. No adequate selection of his literary output has appeared since 1825, and the occasional reprints of his separate writings have for the most part been aimed at a limited sectarian audience. And then there is the problem of selection: the range and variety of his works, the overlapping caused by frequent returns to the same ideological barricades, his long citations of authority, all require a judicious pruning, editing, and explanation which the editors have here for the first time endeavored to provide.

Once the chaff is winnowed away, Penn's writings emerge as a direct challenge to the static intellectual inheritance of the seventeenth century—the age-old marriage of Church and State, the uncharitable traditionalism of Christendom, the bigoted intolerance of both Churchman and Puritan, the licentiousness of the times, the obstruction of human rights, the spiritual deadness creeping through the body politic. Penn was in the vanguard of those who resurrected the principles of religious freedom, separation of Church and State, and government recognition of the rights of conscience. He was among the first to envision an inclusive organization of sovereign nations for the preservation of peace. He framed perhaps the most enlightened and liberal plan of government prior to the eighteenth century.

America especially will forever be indebted to him. If there is anything permanently abiding in America's history, it is the respect for human dignity and human rights. That tradition may lose its force and currency or be sacrificed on the altar of security, but the memory of it must surely endure. The Holy Experiment of Pennsylvania was the first notable modern application of that ageless search for human freedom within the bounds of a benevolent governmental discipline. That experiment was the product of a great mind whose radiant energy, in a fog-bound transitional age, revealed basic principles by which Western civilization, America particularly, could find its way to freedom. Jefferson may have been the perfect product of that evolution, but Penn was its herald angel.

II

Penn's biography presents a pattern of oscillation between the poles of mysticism and action, prophecy and administration. The pendulum seldom came to rest at dead center, but neither did it stop for long at either extreme. The drama of that pendulum movement is the glory and the tragedy of both his life and his times.

Though an active and happy lad, his mind was filled, even from his early teens, with mystic and divine impressions. Throughout his years at Oxford (from which he was expelled for associating with a small group of dissenters), on his grand tour, at the French Protestant University of Saumur, even during his law studies at Lincoln's Inn, his attitudes shuttled back and forth between those of a typical active English gentleman and those of the mystic seeker.

When finally he cast his lot with the despised Quakers, he became almost at once a traveling minister and apologist for the movement. His first pamphlet, issued hardly a year after his final conversion, flamed with Jeremiac imagery hurled with youthful abandon against the spiritual deadness of his time. In that one year alone (1668) he wrote no less than four works: the prophetic *Truth Exalted*, the doctrinal *The Sandy Foundation Shaken*, the learned *No Cross, No Crown*, and the skillfully reasoned *Innocency with Her Open Face*. And part of that year was spent as a prisoner in the Tower of London!

Then followed several years in which the mystic became the man of action. His attention turned from the Church to the State. His life in these years reached a grand climax in his famous trial at the Old Bailey in 1670. This event, so significant in the annals of British constitutional history, he dramatized with something of the old Renaissance spirit in *The People's Ancient and Just Liberties*. In the face of hostile authorities he issued *The Great Case of Liberty of Conscience* in the same year. The following year he made his first religious tour of Holland and Germany, and in 1672 married the lovely Gulielma Springett.

Again the pendulum swings back from the world of affairs, and in 1673 Penn published a treatise on *The Christian Quaker* in collaboration with George Whitehead. But two years later he was again in the midst of practical affairs, becoming involved in the administration of New Jersey, bombarding Parliament with proposals for toleration of dissenters, and justifying the scruples of Quakerism to a hostile magistracy.

By 1677 when, for the second time, he toured Holland and Germany in company with George Fox, Robert Barclay, George Keith, and George Whitehead—the top echelon of the early Quaker movement—his journal and letters reveal the same apocalyptic mysticism that marked the opening of his writing career. "Awake, O Christendom!" he cries, "for the great and notable Day of the Lord is drawing apace upon thee." No doubt his excited and uplifted spirit left an indelible impression on the minds of the religious outcasts and dissidents of those countries. Ten to twenty years later his memory was still very much alive among them as many prepared to embark to his province in the New World.

It was on this trip that Penn discovered the dynamic spiritual ferment in western Europe which made those fields "white unto harvest," and he began thinking concretely about establishing a refuge for the true Christian seekers of all nations. Among Mennonites,

Socinians, Pietists, Separatists, and a host of individual seekers in Holland and the Germanies he found "a breathing, hungering, seeking people solitarily scattered up and down this great land," and his letters and journal throb with the consciousness of a new destiny.

The new vision was not uninfluenced by the mystical groups so common in the Germany of those years who withdrew from the affairs of the world to establish separate societies of their own. On his first visit to Germany, he had gone considerably out of his way to visit the commune of Jean de Labadie. But the aging De Labadie himself rebuffed him, and by the time of his second visit Penn made up his mind that "True godliness does not turn men out of the world, but enables them to live better in it."

However, one last hope for the reformation of English society persisted in his mind. During the next year he wrote the once famous *Address to Protestants* in an effort to shock his nation into a realization of what is truly and basically Protestant and English. In the same year he engaged in the abortive campaign of his good friend the radical Algernon Sidney for a seat in Parliament, and in *England's Great Interest*, a remarkable piece of political pamphleteering, warned his compatriots not to "make a swop of our birth-right" for a mess of stale political pottage. Those causes substantially lost, he wrote *One Project for the Good of England* in a final effort to win religious toleration, but it is a relatively meek and mild document. Again in 1686 and 1687 he issued tracts urging moderation in the harsh treatment of dissenters, but the old fire of social reform had flickered out. From the time Charles II granted Penn the Charter of Pennsylvania in 1681, Penn's vision of society focused on the New World province where the "Children of Light" would gather together and live at peace.

This event is followed by years of the most intense political activity. Two years were spent in the new province putting together the framework of the Holy Experiment. Then he was called to England again, partly by Lord Baltimore's claims to southern Pennsylvania and partly by increased religious persecution in the homeland. Penn's highly influential position in the king's circle made his presence necessary at court on both counts. In 1687–1688, James II, in an effort to protect his own Catholic communion and extend its influence, issued his Declarations of Liberty of Conscience. But the resurging tide of Protestant Whiggery brought the "Glorious Revolution," and James was deposed in favor of William and Mary. Penn, who had placed his political eggs in the Stuart basket, had to start building anew. Finally, in 1689, came the Act of Toleration; Penn's battle on this front was now permanently won, but he himself remained under the deepest suspicion, and in 1692 was deprived of governmental control of his province for two years.

During most of this period Penn lived in deep seclusion, visited only by his most faithful and trustworthy friends, including the great John Locke. It was a time of humiliation, and he devoted himself to study and meditation, writing occasional epistles-general to the Friends, and jotting down some of those pregnant reflections later assembled under the title of *Some Fruits of Solitude*. If before he was the fiery challenger of political intolerance, social slavery, and spiritual deadness, or an extraordinarily busy administrator of public affairs, he now became the serene philosopher. He had seen the full swing of the pendulum in his life, and at last disengaged himself from its orbit, to view the world with a deeper and more gentle compassion.

In 1693 Penn published the highly distilled essence of his view of life in the first part of *Fruits of Solitude*, and his most stately political vision, the *Essay Towards the Present and Future Peace of Europe*— documents which reflect the final wisdom of the man of experience in the house of tranquillity. Had he been able to continue in this vein, he might yet have become one of the truly great writers of his century. But Fate cast a different die.

During these years of enforced tranquillity the storms that dashed his later life began to form. First came echoes of disaffections within the body of Quakerism. To stem the tide of complaints against the seeming rigors of the Society's discipline, Penn in 1692 wrote *Just Measures*, justifying religious discipline when it becomes necessary to prune excesses and preserve order. In some quarters the plea fell on deaf ears, and soon all kinds of charges and jealousies were heaped upon him.

Meanwhile, attacks on Quakerism from outside needed to be answered, and Penn, the best writer in the Society, was obligated to reply. Three brilliant defenses of Quaker doctrine took shape under these urgencies. In 1692 *A Key Opening a Way to Every Common Understanding* answered current perversions of Quaker idealism. It went through no less than twelve editions during Penn's life. Two years later *The Rise and Progress of the People Called Quakers* was published. It is still, perhaps, one of the most thoughtful interpretations of a Christian denomination ever written. The distinguishing feature of this work is Penn's constant care to trace Quaker concepts to the dispensation of the Apostolic Church and to record how that inward dispensation, the Light of God within, differed from other, outward dispensations. Finally, in 1696, his masterful *Primitive Christianity Revived* identified Quakerism with that mystical ferment in Western civilization which time and again rises to the surface of history and enlivens the intellectual life of Europe.

For the rest of his life Penn's creative spirit was smothered by tragedy. Something of the old beauty of mind expressed itself as late as 1699 in the maxims of *Fruits of a Father's Love* and several years later in the second part of *Fruits of Solitude,* but through much of that decade tragedy relentlessly pursued him. Though King William finally cleared Penn of all suspicion and opprobrium in 1693, the next year his beloved wife, Guli, was taken in death. Two years later, a month after he married Hannah Callowhill, his promising son Springett died.

Meanwhile, things were going from bad to worse in Pennsylvania. Though the settlers achieved a general level of prosperity, the proprietor could gain virtually no revenue from them by way of quitrents; the practice of "squatting" on unpatented and proprietary lands increased; and non-Quaker elements troubled the peace with the Indians. The dramatic if not always scrupulous democratic leadership of David Lloyd united the ingrates and the discontented under the banner of a powerful anti-Proprietary party. To make matters worse, Penn delegated administration of the province to a series of deputy governors who too often failed to understand the Quaker rootage of the colony. The disaffection of the three lower counties (now the state of Delaware) led to their eventual separation from Pennsylvania. Penn's once vast financial resources become seriously, dangerously reduced. As early as 1691 he wrote to Thomas Lloyd that he had lost some £30,000 on Pennsylvania's behalf. Constant ministerial travels and efforts in behalf of the oppressed drained his estate still more.

The decline of the Penn estate, the tangled affairs in England, his gradual loss of influence, and, in spite of all this, his arrival at a mature philosophical quietude led Penn to hope for an amiable retirement at his handsomely planned estate on the banks of the Delaware. He arrived on his second visit late in 1699 and soon moved his family to Pennsbury. But there was little rest. If provincial discontent subsided temporarily, more serious problems intervened. In 1701 King William required a contribution from the provincial assembly for defense purposes. The request was repugnant to Penn, both as a Christian pacifist and as a proprietor who successfully maintained peace with the Indians without a defense establishment. The Quaker assembly merely postponed action. Whatever effect this had on the Crown, Penn soon heard of a movement on foot in England for annexing all proprietary governments to the Crown. He returned immediately to help stave off the threat.

Fortunately the movement did not gather sufficient force. But a host of complicated troubles came to a head. William Penn, Jr., had developed into a wild, undisciplined youth, disgraced himself thoroughly on a visit to Pennsylvania, and caused his father great grief. David Lloyd's country Quaker following in Pennsylvania, as well as the Anglican party there, caused renewed political ferment. The vast Irish estates Penn inherited from his father, "my old principal verb" in money matters as he wrote to the learned James Logan, his administrative secretary in Pennsylvania, were so belabored by the severities of England's trade discrimination against the Emerald Isle that they ate up their reduced rents in administrative expense. No wonder he began to think of selling the province—but not as he wrote to Logan, "without a security to the inhabitants. . . ."

At this juncture Penn's own son-in-law, William Aubrey, "insisted rudely upon the payment of his wife's portion faster than the means of her father would allow." The extravagances of William Penn, Jr., added to the burden. Debts piled up. Meanwhile the most severe trial of all was brewing. Philip Ford, manager of Penn's estates and a trusted friend, had for years charged unreasonable commissions for the sums he handled, and compounded a ridiculously and illegally high rate of interest on the debt thus accumulated against Penn. It was sheer knavery, and forced Penn to secure the debt with a lien upon his province. When Ford died, his widow and son demanded possession or settlement. Friends were slow to raise funds for Penn's assistance; and, owing in part to David Lloyd's artful misrepresentations, some members of the Society turned against him. It was the crowning insult. He was sent to debtors' prison until at last the Fords were forced to consent to an accommodation.

Was it any wonder that in those final years of active life a certain asperity should show through his letters?

The long years of trouble and vexation took their toll. After the Ford settlement Penn continued awhile to travel as a minister for the Friends, but in 1712 paralysis struck. The mind broke down at last, and William Penn became a sweet, gentle, aged invalid with a vacant smile on his face. Now and then an apparently lucid interval broke through the fog of death moving in. Less rugged men would not have lingered so long, but his magnificent physical constitution prolonged his life until 1718. All that was left to him in those years was an inexpressibly sweet tranquillity, a proper robe for entering the life to come.

III

Penn's political influence in the court of the Stuarts has always presented to his critics, such as Lord Macaulay, a difficult and highly complex problem. Yet as the son of a famous admiral, to whom that court was indebted, it was natural enough that, in spite of his strange Quaker ways, he should gain a certain unofficial intimacy there and indeed become one of the most effective advocates outside of the king's own ministers. The result of his effectiveness at court was not only the acquisition of a great province but an opportunity to introduce to the New World those principles of freedom and conscience which became the cornerstones of American life.

Fundamentally, the answer to this riddle lies in Penn's unimpeachable integrity. The Restoration court was filled with men who would lie, perjure, and sell their souls for a pittance if it paid dividends in the king's favor or their own personal advantage. Amoral, licentious, drugged with luxury and power, skeptical and faithless, very few of the courtiers who surrounded the second Charles and his brother James bothered about scruples. Possibly the free-and-easy Charles was bored with such faithless and false adulation; possibly the unscrupulous and bigoted James "used" Penn's friendship with the Stuart house to strengthen his own hand among the dissenters in an effort to gain ascendancy for Catholicism. Very likely both the Stuarts still maintained a scrap of honor to which the undeviating honesty and forthrightly agreeable manners of William Penn secretly appealed. And Penn remained faithful to the Stuart court, even in adversity, in spite of his close friendship with such exiled Whigs as Algernon Sidney and John Locke. Penn's position must have been very like that of "one of Queen Elizabeth's great men," perhaps Raleigh, whom he quotes: " 'The advantage,' says he, 'I had upon others at Court, was, that I always spoke as I thought; which being not believed by them, I both preserved a good conscience, and suffered no damage from that freedom.' "

More than in any other age since that time, religion, or that which masqueraded as such, was an ever present concern in the minds of men. English society was split into adherents of the established Church of England, the Presbyterians, Independents, Anabaptists, radical dissenters such as the Quakers, and the Roman Catholics. Even the secretly Catholic Charles and the openly Catholic James could hardly stem the tide of Catholic persecution. The dissenters were still worse off most of the time. Following the failure of the Protectorate these religious cleavages became even more pronounced.

The great tragedy of this cleavage, to the sensitive mind of Penn, lay in the entanglement of ecclesiastical with civil government, an unnatural union used to propagate faith by force. To civil government, he readily admits, belongs the administration of the law for the protection and enhancement of practical social virtue. But when civil magistracy, in league with the State Church, assumes control of a man's conscience, it takes unto itself the things that belong not to Caesar but to God.

For a while Penn appeared to be fighting this battle almost single-handedly. But eventually those principles—separation of Church and State, tolerance of religious minorities, and the duty of government to respect individual conscience— became firmly ingrained in the social fabric.

No less courageous was Penn's battle to preserve the ancient constitutional liberties of Britain—a battle parallel and interwoven with his jousts on the religious front. Both the Protectorate of Cromwell and the restored monarchy of the Stuarts abused or neglected the traditional liberties of Englishmen, and by the time James II came to the throne the king's councilors were running roughshod over ancient liberties. Few had the courage or position to combat the trend. Luckily for British freedom, William Penn had both, and not even the scurvy dungeons of the time could dampen his zeal.

In 1670 Penn, along with William Mead, was apprehended, committed to Newgate, and indicted for preaching to "an unlawful, seditious and riotous assembly." This ominous phrase was applied, under the Conventicle Act, to a quiet meeting of Quakers outside their condemned meetinghouse on Gracechurch Street, London. In the trial that ensued, the justices on the bench, including the Lord Mayor of London, flagrantly abused virtually every long-established principle of trial by jury, including refusal to recognize the jury's first verdict, which was merely "Guilty of speaking in Gracious Street." Again the jurors were locked up, this time without meat, drink, fire and tobacco, but before they filed out Penn rose from his seat and challenged: "You are Englishmen! Mind your privileges, give not away your right!"

At least until 1679 Penn continued to believe that these and similar conditions degrading the freeborn Englishman could be reformed by legislative action. In that year his hopes soared high, as he campaigned for his old friend Algernon Sidney. Even though Sidney's early ardent republicanism had been cooled by exile, his liberalism was still in advance of his day. When the votes were tallied, Sidney received the majority of votes in his district but was counted out on a trumped-up technicality. To add insult to injury, Penn was cast out of the polling place by force and insulted by the authorities in charge. Penn's hopes for Parliamentary reform were crushed, and the disillusionment marked the beginning of the vision that culminated in the Holy Experiment.

But at least Penn clarified for his century the fundamentals of the English birthright. It was his constant aim to insist on the triune nature of political freedom—the right to life and the security of property, the consenting and representational power of the people in the making of laws, and the right of fair trial by jury.

The principle of government by consent of the governed, the great rallying point of the century to follow, has seldom been so incisively and challengingly stated as in Penn's work *England's Great Interest in the Choice of This New Parliament*. We see in that work at least the seed of the very terminology used by American revolutionary leaders almost a century later.

Though the principle of the social contract is implied in many of Penn's political writings, it is by no means to be assumed that he extended the idea so far as to include republicanism or political equality and popular self-government. Government by consent, to Penn's mind, did not depend upon an equal distribution of power among the individual units of society, for that was not in accordance with nature. The idea of consent was limited to the Law and Constitution of a people, and the true interest of a government lay in "a just and equal Constitution." A nation's fundamental laws are thus the con-

necting link between king, lords, and commons. Thus too the power
of the monarchy always should be limited by a superior and non-
personal agency, the law, which evolves by and from the consent of the
governed.

William Penn was one of the few of his age who dared to reassert
the principle of constitutional government by consent and declare
himself for a limitation of monarchical power. Some latter-day
American historians have criticized Penn for not extending those
principles to what may appear as their ultimate and natural end, the
republican form of democracy. Such criticism, however, suffers from
a disregard of historical timing. The judgment is unjust because it
applies nineteenth century Jacksonian theory to a seventeenth century
world. True, republican ideas apppeared in Penn's time; Algernon
Sidney and others believed that England could do without a king. But
these ideas by no means necessarily implied a democratic leveling of
society. Penn and other advanced thinkers assumed a natural order of
different levels among men to be implicit in God's own plan.

There is nevertheless a wide difference here from the then widely
accepted principles of Hobbes. The distinction lies in Penn's insistence
on the *moral responsibility* of the governing class, coupled with
genuine humility in recognizing that the love of God goes out equally
to all men regardless of their station.

Indeed, the very institution of government finds its source in the
cosmic pattern. "Magistracy," says Penn, "is an ordinance of God."
Therefore the magistrate is morally responsible to God for his conduct
in office. Moreover, he is the guardian of public morality in the largest
sense of the term. Penn points to the debasement of English character
by the perversion of this principle, particularly at the height of the
French influence in the Restoration: "The French have sufficiently
revenged themselves upon us, by the loose manners they have brought
amongst us . . . But I must needs say, to their credit but our reproach,
they keep their wits in their debaucheries; whilst we, by overdoing
them, lose both."

Government is therefore a means to right conduct, but though
divinely instituted it is never an end in itself. In common with such

modern thinkers as Aldous Huxley who have been influenced by the
Quaker ethic, Penn insisted that a pure and blameless objective could
never be accomplished by impure means, and he would have been
shocked and grieved by the wholesale confusion of the two in the
world of today.

When Penn outlined the governmental structure for his province in
a virtually uncharted wilderness, he was equally insistent that the law
be superior to those administering it. But though law is the prime
necessity of human society—for disobedient man, having refused to
conform to "the holy law within," must therefore be subject to "the
just law without"—its administration is subject to the vagaries of
human personality. In the final analysis, therefore, the quality of
government is dependent on the element of human morality. Alter
one factor (morality), and the other side of the equation (government)
automatically changes. The eternal equation of human society, Penn
concludes, is "to support power in reverence with the people, and to
secure the people from the abuse of power; . . . for liberty without
obedience is confusion, and obedience without liberty is slavery."

The moral algebra that ruled over Penn's theory of government also
determined the theorem that governed his conception of other social
institutions. That theorem was basically one of personal responsibility.
It is true that he believed educational opportunity should be extended
to all levels of society. But mass education in itself would not suffice.
The first principle of Penn's educational philosophy was to "Breed
up youth in morality."

His next requirement for the education of youth was, significantly,
the study of nature, including mathematics as the tool of that study.
In a time when formal education virtually began and ended in Greek
and Latin, he severely rebukes his age for its ignorance of natural law
and nature as the mirror of God. After the youthful mind begins to
ripen, human history and institutions should then be studied. The
learning of history, however, requires a mind capable of weighing the
evidence of historical action on the scales of morality.

In one respect Penn would have been heartened by modern educational theory. "Cross not the genius of your youth," he proclaims in

An Address to Protestants, "but match their talents well; for if you do
not suit their studies to their understanding, it will be drawing up hill."
Honestly recognizing the inequalities of mind and capacity, Penn
hoped in his province to provide as broad-gauged an educational
program as possible, keyed to individual talent. That program, however, fell by the wayside; those whom it was to benefit refused to
support and provide for it.

In an age noted for its excessively rigorous discipline of youth, Penn
insisted on a reasonable, kindly, compassionate attempt to understand
youth's vagaries. If correction has to be applied, it must be done without anger or passion.

In another social discipline—economics—Penn sensed that a nation's
economy is only a mirror of its moral vitality. Luxury and other
economic excess reveal a fault of character, and if society is to be truly
healthy those excesses must be pruned.

Like his friend John Locke, Penn places much emphasis on the
fundamental right of property. Although he freely granted that government should have functions beyond the mere control of evildoers, he
believed that property stewardship must remain in the hands of the
individual rather than in the all-too-grasping hands of government.
The state may prune excesses by taxation, but the right of individual
stewardship "of this great farm, the world that we live upon," must
remain inviolate.

Reduced to its basic elements, Penn's economics is a personal not a
mass discipline. Though he considered it "a reproach to religion and
government to suffer so much poverty and excess," the remedy lay not
in the force of a leviathan state but in a personal ethic which combined
frugality with generosity. Like Jefferson a century later, Penn maintained that the proper environment for nurturing this moral discipline
was the country rather than the city. He advises his children (all in
vain, alas!) to "chuse God's trades before man's"—that is, husbandry
of the soil before the trades of the town—and urges them (more than
half a century before Rousseau) to consider the evil implicit in the
modern urban setting.

We cannot here delineate Penn's New World social and political achievements. The personal tragedies of his Holy Experiment only serve to heighten our sense of the beauty and breadth of mind that conceived an experiment in social living founded upon love. How superior that conception in comparison with the relatively crabbed feudal framework of government his friend John Locke outlined for the Carolinas! How unique and loving his compact with the American Indian in comparison with the frightened, frightful, and loveless attitudes of other colonial officials! Nor is it to be forgotten that Penn was the very first to propose a legislative and executive union of the colonies—more than half a century before Franklin offered his proposal at the Albany conference.

In one other major respect the world is politically and socially indebted to the founder of Pennsylvania. More than two centuries elapsed before something akin to Penn's proposal for an international parliament to settle disputes and preserve world peace was haltingly ventured in practice. His *Essay Towards the Present and Future Peace of Europe* may be considered a direct philosophical ancestor of the world court, the League of Nations, and the United Nations.

What distinguished Penn's vision of peace from that of his pacifist Quaker contemporaries was his sincere conviction that a large-scale social peace was as possible, as worthy an objective as the inner personal "peace that passeth understanding"—the peace that makes it impossible for the individual to take up arms.

His pacifism is fundamentally a concept of justice among nations. Peace, he declared, "is maintained by justice, which is a fruit of government, as government is from society, and society from consent." On the international as on the national scale, government is primarily "an expedient against confusion; a restraint upon all disorder; just weights and an even balance."

Penn conceived his international organization as a balance of forces, with aggressors compulsively restrained by the will of the majority. The great difference between modern efforts and Penn's proposal lies in the fact that Penn provided for an inclusive representation—inviting "enemies" of the prevailing balance of powers and even the hated infidel Turks to full membership. National representation was to be granted strictly on the basis of "the value of the territory." He suggested that England have perhaps six delegates while Germany would have twelve and England's archenemy, France, ten.

One of Penn's biographers, Samuel Janney, relates the story that a copy of Penn's remarkable essay "supposed to be the same that Penn presented to Queen Anne was produced at the Peace Convention held within a few years at Paris, where it was received by the members with great interest. . . ." We cannot help speculating what course human history would have taken, had the delegates then and there put Penn's proposal into operation. But at least the seed of international arbitration on a permanent basis was sown.

IV

If Penn was a man of action, a champion of liberty, a landed proprietor, a social philosopher, he was, above all these, a man of faith. The "evidence of things unseen" was the substratum of reference by which he constantly tested himself.

There was one great difference between Penn and his spiritual ancestors of the Puritan Reformation. The Puritan considered the earthly pilgrimage a journey through a vale of tears, dark, tormenting, essentially devoid of hope to all but a handful of the Elect, and with only the most tenuous connection between life and afterlife. But to Penn's mind hope was always present; the light of God was everywhere, available to all men in spite of its being hid by human institutions. All life was directly sustained by the timeless spirit of God.

Thus nature is not to be feared and loathed as the handmaid of the Serpent; on the contrary, "The world is certainly a great and stately volume of natural things, and may be not improperly styled the hieroglyphics of a better." In his loving acceptance of the natural world, Penn is more akin to Montaigne and the Elizabethans than to the Puritans. Much the same attitude prevails in his respect for the human body, which he calls "the most curious structure of the world, a living, walking Tabernacle." And in an age when marriages were generally made for social and economic gain, Penn advises, "Never marry but for love: But see that thou lovest what is lovely."

Where Penn saw a constantly equated relationship between nature and God, the Puritan conceived of the divine and the natural as essentially hostile. Purity to William Penn signified a direct emanation of the divine in the human world, not a phenomenon predetermined in the origin of things. In this respect Penn bridged the philosophical gap between the Elizabethan age and the age of reason, but without the lustiness of the one or the presumptuousness of the other.

To Penn's way of thinking, reason was a tool, not the goddess she became in the age to follow. Reason was simply an endowment of pragmatic common sense, and Penn believed that its value lay only in interpreting the tangible and measurable. True, in *The Christian Quaker* he endeavors to prove by reason the universality and sufficiency of the Inner Light, but since the Light operates beyond and above reason, the latter has neither the force nor depth of mystical or spiritual experience. The one looks through the glass of nature darkly; the other, face to face with the infinite Mind that supports nature.

In a way, the Quaker doctrine of the Light Within announced the end of the Puritan age and the beginning of the brighter and freer age to come. As no other concept did, it laid bare the inadequacy of "literal knowledge, historical faith and outward religion." It vastly expanded the reference shelf of truth to include not only the inner experience of the non-priestly classes of all conditions in Christendom but also the moralists and philosophers of the ancient pagan world. Penn himself compares the principle with the "Great Light" of Pythagoras, the "divine mind" of Anaxagoras, the Socratic "good spirit," Plato's "perfect principle of truth," and Plotinus's "root of the soul." In recognizing the correspondence between the Inner Light and the ultimate principle of the ancients, Penn rediscovered the interconnection between the philosophical history of the pagan world and the religious history of the Judaic-Christian tradition.

With this blossoming of the Inner Light principle, a new kind of freedom became intellectually and spiritually possible. Penn did not, however, relegate Christ to the mere position of prophet. To Penn, Christ was the very center and embodiment of faith, "the Word-God"; and the opening passage of St. John's Gospel was to him literally true:

"the Word was made flesh." The freedom of the human spirit consists in obedience to the Word of God, made available to man by direct inspiration, by inner consent, and by resignation to the divine will.

Penn's battle for spiritual freedom centered upon the imperfections and incompleteness of the Reformation, the corruption of Christianity as a moral force, and the refusal of Western man to accept the purity of original Christianity. In this he is part of a minority tradition stemming back at least to Constantine's imperial acceptance of the faith. During the medieval era the tradition of primitive Christianity was in part preserved by individual mystics under the aegis of the Church and in part by heretical sects. The tradition was sustained during the Reformation era by mystical dissenters and by those more radical reformers generally grouped under the heading of Separatists. The tradition of primitive Christianity, in the sixteenth and seventeenth centuries, concentrated in the Netherlands and the Germanies, spread to England during the Puritan revolution, and became the spiritual mainspring of early Quakerism.

In the doctrines of Calvin, Luther, Zwingli, and the established Church of England Penn saw a dangerous determinism which, in its final effect, canceled out the inward reformation of man taught by Christ, and left little room for the reformation of society. In his doctrinal writings against this deterministic trend Penn marshaled every resource at his very extensive command. For those who can still appreciate doctrinal writing, it is a lavish display.

The Reformation savored too much of "the precepts of men." Human reason, separated from its divine source, is subject to all kinds of distortion. "All evil comes from within," just as all goodness does, and mere human precepts, limited by attachment to selfhood, cannot plumb the spiritual depths. Only God, working within the soul of man, can destroy the roots of evil.

Something, Penn believed, had gone radically wrong with the historical Reformation. Extraordinary cruelties and social chaos came in its wake, instigated by both Protestant and Catholic establishments. When those all too human institutions, the major churches, joined hands with the State, the original Reformation aims were warped and debased by the propagation of faith by force, just as, in an earlier time, the purity of the Church was destroyed by its marriage with the Empire.

Penn viewed the historical process as a series of God-given "dispensations" showing progress from one psychological level to another. "The World," Penn wrote, "began with innocency." When that childlike innocency was modified by the expansion of man's intellectual pretensions, his progress came to be guided by an "outward dispensation" through the secondary agency of the angels, suited to a people in "a low and servile state." Then followed the dispensation of the Law (the Mosaic Code), with an effect much like that of a "schoolmaster." Between the outward Mosaical dispensation and the heightened prophetic consciousness culminating in John the Baptist, man came closer and closer to the spiritual reality of things. The leap to a higher consciousness came with the ministry of Christ, when "the Spirit, that was more sparingly communicated in former dispensations, began to be poured forth upon all flesh." As time passed and the new Church joined forces with the State, however, "the true Church fled into the Wilderness."

Quakerism, Penn honestly believed, was a modern breaking forth of that true Church, for it refused on principle to ally itself with political coercion. The reformation of man's unregenerate spirit was the only reformation worth the name of religion, and such was the reformation sought by all the persistent minorities who, through the generations of Europe, aimed to recover and preserve the meaning of Christ.

Two powerful tendencies of Western culture—toward intellectual and political liberty and toward the still higher reformation of man's moral and spiritual nature—thus converged in the personality of William Penn. And, in essence, the history of modern man has been but a testing and an elaboration of those great impulses in the human heart.

Editors' Note

The editors have worked closely together in planning the general scope and character of this volume and in choosing the passages to be reprinted. The general introduction was primarily the work of E. Gordon Alderfer; the particular introductions and the editing and annotation of the texts were the primary responsibility of Frederick B. Tolles. But the editors have read and criticized each other's editorial contributions and they both gladly accept responsibility for the whole volume.

Each of the texts reprinted here is based (unless otherwise indicated in the introduction) on the first edition of the work in question, corrected in a few instances by later editions, when they were printed in Penn's lifetime and appear to reflect his own emendations. We have scrupulously respected Penn's language, but we have modernized the spelling, capitalization, and punctuation. In a book designed for the general reader there seemed no good reason for retaining his archaic orthography (for example, *stroak* for *stroke*, *publick* for *public*, *subtil* for *subtle*) or to follow his somewhat wayward practice of capitalizing the initial letters of some (but not all) nouns and adjectives. There seemed even less reason to perpetuate his punctuation. The seventeenth century's ideas on this subject are not ours, but Penn's were altogether his own and he was far from consistent in applying them. He had a special fondness, which the modern reader does not share, for the colon and the semicolon, and he used them in ways that often interrupt and impede rather than clarify the flow of his thought. His typical sentence structure being what it is—loose and straggling with clause piled on clause to the subversion of all syntax—the limited resources of modern punctuation, it must be confessed, are not always

equal to the task we have imposed upon them. Occasionally we have
made two or more units of his long, meandering sentences, and in a few
instances we have broken up his lengthy paragraphs. Wherever we
have omitted portions of the original, we have indicated the omission
with elision points (. . .), and in the few places where we have felt it
necessary to insert words to clarify Penn's meaning, we have enclosed
them in brackets ([ ]). In all this we do not feel that we have taken
undue liberties with Penn's text. The essentials—the words themselves—are still his; we have made adjustments only in the non-essen-
tials, and our sole purpose has been to enable his meaning to come
through to modern readers.

Footnotes have been kept to a minimum. They are provided only
where they appeared necessary in order to explain archaic or unfamiliar
terms or to elucidate historical references that might otherwise be
obscure.

1
The Apostolic Christian

God in History

When William Penn at fifty looked back over the era through which he had lived, he had a sense that it had been one of the great spiritual flowering times of history. He was not alone in this feeling. In the very year of his birth, another great Englishman had hailed the dawning of such a time in England: "I see a noble and puissant nation rousing herself like a strong man after a sleep and shaking her invincible locks," wrote John Milton. "Methinks I see her, as an eagle mewing her mighty youth and kindling her undazzled eyes at the full midday beam, purging and unsealing her long abused sight at the fountain itself of heavenly radiance. . . ." Naturally, for Penn the Quaker, the climax of this spiritual awakening had been the rise of the Society of Friends out of the creative exuberance, the religious profusion and confusion of the Commonwealth period. In *The Rise and Progress of the People Called Quakers*, written in 1694, he sought to give an account of the origin and character of this religious movement, to place it in its rightful setting in the progressive unfolding of God's Providence, and to pay tribute to its founder, George Fox.

He begins, in the manner of historians in his time, with Adam and Eve in Paradise. Starting from their primeval state of innocence, he swiftly traces the successive dispensations of God in human history as recorded in the Bible: the patriarchal, when God spoke to man through the ministry of angels; the Mosaic, when His law was graven on stone; the Christian, when God sent His own Son, the second Adam, to dwell among men. As the pristine Adamic dispensation had been ended by the catastrophe of the Fall, so the glory that was primitive Christianity was succeeded by a "long night of apostasy," when the Church gave way to the temptations of wealth and worldly dominion, married itself to the State, and lost its spiritual power.

So far Penn presents an orthodox, at least an orthodox Protestant, view of history. The originality, the distinctiveness of Penn's interpretation begins at this point. Others in his century, among the mystics and left-wing Puritans, had hinted at this kind of analysis, but few had had the boldness to carry it so far as he was prepared to take it.

3

Just as Abel and Seth and Enoch had been directly illuminated by God's spirit when the world was young, so even in the medieval darkness, Penn wrote, there had been a few chosen souls—perhaps he is thinking of the Waldensians in the twelfth century, the Brethren of the Free Spirit in the thirteenth, the Friends of God in the fourteenth—who had experienced some glimmerings of light direct from God Himself. The Protestant Reformation represented a further break in the clouds, but he did not see it as a sweeping revolution; to him it was no more than a feeble and abortive attempt at rolling away the spiritual darkness. The gradual dawning of the real, the spiritual reformation he traces through the emergence of the continental Anabaptists, the English Puritans, the Familists, and the mystical Seekers of the seventeenth century. Each successive group represents to him a measure of spiritual progress over the last, a further step toward the restoration of Adamic innocence and the purity of the primitive Church. But each is somehow flawed and imperfect; each comes short of the Truth, the full measure of Light. It remains for the Society of Friends through George Fox (here treated almost as a third Adam) to usher in the final dispensation—that of the Holy Spirit, the divine Light, inwardly known in the hearts of men.

A naïve view of history, surely, and a complacent one—as if the emergence of a tiny dissenting sect on an island off the coast of Europe were the final fulfillment of the divine plan, the culminating chapter in the human story. Yet there was about early Quakerism a pentecostal atmosphere and a promise of spiritual world conquest that made the fantastic claim seem credible—at least to Quakers like Penn. Penn's thumbnail sketch of human history may seem crude and simple to sophisticated twentieth century readers. Yet there is something suggestive in his perspective on the human story. A generation that has been captivated by the erudite simplicities of Arnold Toynbee may find some kernels of truth in Penn's less pretentious theory. And Penn's treatment of the mystical and sectarian traditions in Christianity bears a striking similarity to those of modern scholars like Ernst Troeltsch, Rufus M. Jones, and the English historian of the Holy Spirit, Geoffrey F. Nuttall.

Seventeenth century Quakerism to Penn was nothing less than "primitive Christianity revived." It is in this light that he presents his succinct and attractive sketch of the early Friends. Perhaps it is not quite history. Certainly it is no mere narrative of events: dates are scarce; important events like the schisms that threatened to disrupt the movement in the 1670's and 1680's are barely mentioned; and the tragic sufferings of these harmless zealots are only hinted at in passing. Penn is more concerned with the spiritual inwardness of the movement than with outward events. Moreover, there is none of the modern historian's cherished "objectivity" here, for obviously Penn's own emotions were deeply engaged in the movement he was describing. But granting that his approach was not that of the modern scholar, his picture of the "Children of the Light" has permanent value, not only as the record of an important historical experience by one who had known it at first hand but also as a suggestive commentary on the surprising power of radical Christianity to renew itself in history.

Radical Christianity does not pause long over theology, over abstract "notions of religion" (though the early Quakers, and Penn among them, could chop logic and quote texts with the best of their fellow Puritans when the occasion required). For the radical Christian, religion is experience, not an intellectual process. It expresses itself characteristically in daily living. It is a way of life, not a system of thought or a set of dogmas. So Penn touches quickly on the central tenet of Quakerism—"the light of Jesus Christ . . . a faithful and true witness and just monitor in every bosom." He mentions in a rather perfunctory manner the doctrines that "branched out" from this root—repentance, perfection, immortality. Then he rushes on to a schematic account of the Quaker "testimonies"—the practical outworkings of the Inward Light in the everyday "lives and examples" of the early Friends.

Penn enumerates eleven of these testimonies. Howard H. Brinton, a modern Quaker writer, has gathered them together under the four rubrics of Equality, Simplicity, Community, and Harmony or Peace. There was nothing essentially new about the religious insights that expressed themselves in the peculiar testimonies of the early Friends. What was remarkable was simply their undeviating consistency, their steadfast concern to make their religion irradiate every act of their lives, however mundane or trivial. No wonder less "concerned" people thought them "turners of the world upside down." So they were, says Penn; and so, he implies, would any group of people be who took their religion as seriously, who lived so close to the Spirit as the early Quakers did. To practice these Christian testimonies in the midst of a half-Christian world was simply "to bring things back into their primitive and right order again," to restore life to the level it had once attained in Eden and again in the early Christian Church.

Life before preaching, deeds before words, example before precept: this was the secret of the extraordinary success which attended the ministry of the early Friends as they traveled over the British Isles, up the valley of the Rhine, across the stormy Atlantic, up and down the raw, new North American colonies. Not that they were backward or timid about preaching, these Quaker "Publishers of Truth." But before they spoke a word, "their very lives did preach." This simple fact is the burden of Penn's discussion of their ministry, his elaboration of "eleven marks that it is Christian." The story of the early Quakers has been told many times since Penn wrote this lucid and winsome sketch. But modern scholarship has only filled out the outline that Penn laid down in this pioneering essay. The essence of the story remains the same. That is William Penn's achievement as a historian.

His achievement as a biographer is scarcely less. He could not describe the rise of Quakerism without placing in the foreground the commanding figure of George Fox. "An institution," wrote Emerson, "is the lengthened shadow of one man; as . . . Quakerism, of Fox." And so Penn concludes his account of this seventeenth century revival of apostolic Christianity with a pen portrait of its "instrumental author." George Fox, the founder of Quakerism, unquestionably belongs among the few authentic religious geniuses of the Western tradition. In all the history of the English people perhaps only John Wyclif and John Wesley stand with him as men who brought to their time a fresh new vision of the religious life and impressed it with irresistible force on their generation. An overwhelming personality, a powerful leader of men, a glowing prophet of righteousness in whom, as G. M. Trevelyan says, "ecstasy and common-sense, violence and peacefulness were strangely blended," Fox was much more than the founder of a small dissenting sect. He was one of the great figures of his century in England—a century which produced such towering personalities as John Milton, Oliver Cromwell, and Isaac Newton. Outside the revealing pages of his own *Journal* Fox is known to us chiefly through the sympathetic and perceptive sketch of his character which Penn wrote in 1694.

Penn had made the acquaintance of this strange, magnetic man soon after his own "convincement" as a Quaker. Thereafter until Fox's death, twenty years later, the two men were often in each other's company. Fox was a frequent visitor at Penn's country house; they saw each other regularly at Quaker business meetings in London; they traveled together to Holland in 1677. There are some hints in the records that they did not always see eye to eye in affairs of the church. It would have been remarkable if they had; after all, Fox was twenty years older than Penn, the son of a humble weaver with only the bare rudiments of formal schooling, whereas Penn was a well-educated gentleman, the son of an admiral, and a frequenter of the court. Moreover, both men were dominant personalities and both were acknowledged leaders among the Friends. Still, there was no jealousy or distrust, and Penn could write with perfect sincerity after Fox's death: "Many sons have done virtuously in this day, but, dear George, thou excellest them all."

In its literary form Penn's sketch of the founder of Quakerism is related to the tradition of the "character," a type of writing that goes back to Theophrastus in Greek literature and was much practiced in Penn's century by such authors as Sir Thomas Overbury, the Marquis of Halifax, and the French writer La Bruyère. With the writings of Izaak Walton and Thomas Fuller, Penn's portrait of Fox stands in the main stream of the emerging tradition of English biographical writing. It projects the clear image of a man who was indeed, as Penn insists, "an original, being no man's copy."

Written in the first instance as a preface for George Fox's *Journal* in 1694, Penn's essay was separately published as *A Brief Account of the Rise and Progress of the People Called Quakers* in the same year. We have omitted a section dealing with the corporate organization and discipline of the Society of Friends, as well as a few other passages not essential to the narrative, and have added subtitles.

The Rise and Progress of the People Called Quakers (1694)

THE DIVINE DISPENSATIONS

Divers have been the dispensations of God since the creation of the world unto the sons of men, but the great end of all of them has been the renown of His own excellent name in the creation and restoration of man—man, the emblem of Himself as a god on earth and the glory of all His works. The world began with innocency; all was then good that the good God had made. And as He blessed the works of His hands, so their natures and harmony magnified Him, their creator. Then the morning stars sang together for joy, and all parts of His works said Amen to His law. Not a jar in the whole frame, but man in Paradise, the beasts in the field, the fowl in the air, the fish in the sea, the lights in the heavens, the fruits of the earth, yea, the air, the earth, the water, and fire worshiped, praised, and exalted His power, wisdom, and goodness. O holy Sabbath, O holy day to the Lord!

But this happy state lasted not long, for man, the crown and glory of the whole, being tempted to aspire above his place, unhappily yielded against command and duty as well as interest and felicity, and so fell below it, lost the divine image, the wisdom, power, and purity he was made in. By which, being no longer fit for Paradise, he was expelled [from] that garden of God, his proper dwelling and residence, and was driven out as a poor vagabond from the presence of the Lord to wander in the earth, the habitation of beasts.

Yet God that made him had pity on him. For He, seeing man was deceived and that it was not of malice or an original presumption in him, but through the subtlety of the serpent (who had first fallen from his own state) and by the mediation of the woman, man's own nature and companion (whom the serpent had first deluded), in His infinite goodness and wisdom found out a way to repair the breach, recover the loss, and restore fallen man again by a nobler and more excellent Adam, promised to be born of a woman; that as by means of a woman the Evil One had prevailed upon man, by a woman also He should come into the world Who would prevail against him, and bruise his head, and deliver man from his power. And which in a signal manner, by the dispensation of the Son of God in the flesh, in the fullness of time was personally and fully accomplished by Him and in Him as man's Saviour and Redeemer.

But His power was not limited in the manifestation of it to that time, for both before and since His blessed manifestation in the flesh, He has been the light and life, the rock and strength of all that ever feared God; was present with them in their temptations, followed them in their travails and afflictions, and supported and carried them through and over the difficulties that have attended them in their earthly pilgrimage. By this Abel's heart excelled Cain's, and Seth obtained the pre-eminence, and Enoch walked with God. It was this that strove with the old world, and which they rebelled against, and which sanctified and instructed Noah to salvation.

But the outward dispensation that followed the benighted state of man after his fall, especially among the patriarchs, was generally that of angels, as the Scriptures of the Old Testament do in many places express, as to Abraham, Jacob, etc. The next was that of the law by Moses, which was also delivered by angels, as the Apostle tells us. This dispensation was much outward, and suited to a low and servile state, called therefore by the apostle Paul that of a schoolmaster, which was to point out and prepare that people to look and long for the Messiah, who would deliver them from servitude of a ceremonious and imperfect dispensation by knowing the realities of those mysterious representations in themselves. In this time the law was written on stone, the temple built with hands, attended with an outward priesthood and external rites and ceremonies that were shadows of the good things that were to come and were only to serve till the seed came or the more excellent and general manifestation of Christ, to Whom was the promise, and to all men only in Him in Whom it was yea and amen, even life from death, immortality, and eternal life.

This the prophets foresaw and comforted the believing Jews in the certainty of it, which was the top of the Mosaical dispensation and which ended in John's ministry, the forerunner of the Messiah, as John's was finished in Him, the fullness of all. And then God, that at sundry times and in divers manners had spoken to the fathers by His servants the prophets, spoke to men by His Son Christ Jesus, Who is heir of all things, being the gospel day, which is the dispensation of Sonship, bringing in thereby a nearer testament and a better hope, even the beginning of the glory of the latter days and of the restitution of all things, yea, the restoration of the Kingdom unto Israel.

Now the spirit that was more sparingly communicated in former dispensations began to be poured forth upon all flesh, according to the prophet Joel; and the light that shined in darkness or but dimly before, the most gracious God caused to shine out of darkness; and the daystar began to arise in the hearts of believers, giving unto them the knowledge of God in the face or appearance of His Son Christ Jesus.

Now the poor in spirit, the meek, the true mourners, the hungry and thirsty after righteousness, the peacemakers, the pure in heart, the merciful and persecuted came more especially in remembrance before the Lord, and were sought out and blessed by Israel's true shepherd. Old Jerusalem with her children grew out of date, and the New Jerusalem into request, the mother of the sons of the gospel day. Wherefore no more at Old Jerusalem nor at the mountain of Samaria will God be worshiped above other places; for behold, He is, by His own Son, declared and preached a spirit, and that He will be known as such and worshiped in the spirit and in the truth. He will now come nearer than of old time, and He will write His law in the heart and put His fear and spirit in the inward parts, according to His promise. Then signs, types, and shadows flew away, the day having discovered their insufficiency in not reaching to the inside of the cup to the cleansing of the conscience; and all elementary services were expired in and by Him that is the substance of all.

And to this great and blessed end of the dispensation of the Son of God did the apostles testify, whom He had chosen and anointed by His spirit to turn the Jews from their prejudice and superstition and the Gentiles from their vanity and idolatry to Christ's light and spirit that shined in them, that they might be quickened from the sins and trespasses in which they were dead to serve the living God in the newness of the spirit of life, and walk as children of the light and of the day, even the day of holiness. For such put on Christ, the Light of the World, and make no more provision for the flesh to fulfill the lusts thereof. So that the light, spirit, and grace that come by Christ and appear in man, were that divine principle the apostles ministered from and turned people's minds unto, and in which they gathered and built up the churches of Christ in their day. For which cause they advise them not to quench the spirit, but to wait for the spirit, and speak by the spirit, and pray by the spirit, and walk in the spirit too, as that which approved them the truly begotten children of God, born not of flesh and blood or of the will of man but of the will of God, by doing His will and denying their own, by drinking of Christ's cup and being baptized with His baptism of self-denial—the way and path that all the heirs of life have ever trod to blessedness.

But alas, even in the apostles' days, those bright stars of the first magnitude of the gospel light, some clouds foretelling an eclipse of this primitive glory began to appear, and several of them gave early caution of it to the Christians of their time, that even then there was, and yet would be more and more, a falling away from the power of godliness and the purity of that spiritual dispensation, by such as sought to make a fair show in the flesh, but with whom the offense of the Cross ceased, yet with this comfortable conclusion, that they saw beyond it a more glorious time than ever to the true church. Their sight was true and what they foretold to the churches gathered by them in the name and power of Jesus came to pass. For Christians degenerated apace into outsides, as days and meats and divers other ceremonies. And, which was worse, they fell into strife and contention about them, separating one from another, then envying and, as they had power, persecuting one another to the shame and scandal of their common Christianity, and grievous stumbling and offense of the heathen, among whom the Lord had so long and so marvelously preserved them. And having got at last the worldly power into their hands by kings and emperors embracing the Christian profession, they changed what they could, the Kingdom of Christ, which is not of this world, into a worldly kingdom; or at least styled the worldly kingdom that was in their hands the Kingdom of Christ, and so they became worldly, and not true Christians.

Then human inventions and novelties, both in doctrine and worship, crowded fast into the church, a door being opened thereunto by the grossness and carnality that appeared then among the generality of Christians, who had long since left the guidance of God's meek and heavenly spirit and given themselves up to superstition, will-worship, and voluntary humility. And as superstition is blind, so it is heady and furious, for all must stoop to its blind and boundless zeal or perish by it, in the name of the spirit persecuting the very appearance of the spirit of God in others, and opposing that in others which they resisted in themselves; viz., the light, grace, and spirit of the Lord Jesus Christ, but always under the notion of innovation, heresy, schism, or some such plausible name, though Christianity allows of no name or pretense whatever for persecuting of any man for matters of mere religion, being in its very nature meek, gentle, and forbearing, and consists of faith, hope, and charity, which no persecutor can have whilst he remains a persecutor (in that a man cannot believe well or hope well or have a charitable or tender regard to another whilst he would violate his mind or persecute his body for matters of faith or worship toward his God).

Thus the false church sprang up and mounted the chair. But though she lost her nature, she would needs keep her good name of the Lamb's bride, the true church, and mother of the faithful, constraining all to receive her mark either in their forehead or right hand, that is, publicly or privately. But indeed and in truth she was mystery Babylon, the mother of harlots, mother of those that, with all their show and outside of religion, were adulterated and gone from the spirit, nature, and life of Christ, and grown vain, worldly, ambitious, covetous, cruel, etc., which are the fruits of the flesh and not of the spirit.

Now it was that the true church fled into the wilderness, that is, from superstition and violence to a retired, solitary, and lonely state, hidden and, as it were, out of sight of men, though not out of the world; which shows that her wonted visibility was not essential to the being of a true church in the judgment of the Holy Ghost, she being as true a church in the wilderness, though not as visible and lustrous as when she was in her former splendor of profession. In this state many attempts she made to return, but the waters were yet too high and her way blocked up, and many of her excellent children in several nations and centuries fell by the cruelty of superstition because they would not fall from their faithfulness to the truth.

The last age did set some steps toward it, both as to doctrine, worship, and practice. But practice quickly failed, for wickedness flowed in a little time, as well among the professors of the Reformation[1] as those they reformed from, so that by the fruits of conversation they were not to be distinguished. And the children of the Reformers, if not

---

[1] By "professors of the Reformation" Penn means those who professed the doctrines of Luther, Calvin, and the other Reformers.

the Reformers themselves, betook themselves very early to earthly policy and power to uphold and carry on their Reformation that had been begun with spiritual weapons, which, I have often thought, has been one of the greatest reasons the Reformation made no better progress as to the life and soul of religion. For whilst the Reformers were lowly and spiritually minded, and trusted in God, and looked to Him, and lived in His fear, and consulted not with flesh and blood, nor sought deliverance in their own way, there were daily added to the church such as one might reasonably say should be saved. For they were not so careful to be safe from persecution as to be faithful and inoffensive under it, being more concerned to spread the truth by their faith and patience in tribulation than to get the worldly power out of their hands that inflicted those sufferings upon them. And it will be well if the Lord suffer them not to fall by the very same way they took to stand.

In doctrine they were in some things short; in other things to avoid one extreme they ran into another. And for worship, there was, for the generality, more of man in it than of God. They owned the Spirit, inspiration, and revelation indeed, and grounded their separation and reformation upon the sense and understanding they received from it in the reading of the Scriptures of truth. And this was their plea: the Scripture is the text, the Spirit the interpreter, and that to everyone for himself. But yet there was too much of human invention, tradition, and art that remained both in praying and preaching, and of worldly authority and worldly greatness in their ministers, especially in this kingdom, Sweden, Denmark, and some parts of Germany. God was therefore pleased in England to shift us from vessel to vessel. And the next remove humbled the ministry, so that they were more strict in preaching, devout in praying, and zealous for keeping the Lord's Day and catechizing of children and servants and repeating at home in their families what they had heard in public.[2] But even as these grew into power, they were not only for whipping some out but others into the temple. And they appeared rigid in their spirits rather than severe in

[2] Penn appears here to be speaking of the Puritan party as it first emerged in the Church of England.

their lives, and more for a party than for piety, which brought forth another people that were yet more retired and select.

They would not communicate at large or in common with others, but formed churches among themselves of such as could give some account of their conversion, at least of very promising experiences of the work of God's grace upon their hearts; and under mutual agreements and covenants of fellowship they kept together.[3] These people were somewhat of a softer temper, and seemed to recommend religion by the charms of its love, mercy, and goodness rather than by the terrors of its judgments and punishment, by which the former party would have awed people into religion. They also allowed greater liberty to prophecy than those before them, for they admitted any member to speak or pray as well as their pastor, whom they always chose, and not the civil magistrate. If such found anything pressing upon them to either duty, even without the distinction of clergy or laity, persons of any trade had their liberty, be it never so low and mechanical. But alas, even these people suffered great loss, for, tasting of worldly empire and the favor of princes and the gain that ensued, they degenerated but too much. For though they had cried down national churches and ministry and maintenance too, some of them, when it was their own turn to be tried, fell under the weight of worldly honor and advantage, got into profitable parsonages too much, and outlived and contradicted their own principles, and, which was yet worse, turned, some of them, absolute persecutors of other men for God's sake, that but so lately came themselves out of the furnace. Which drove many a step further, and that was into the water, another baptism, as believing they were not scripturally baptized, and hoping to find that presence and power of God in submitting to this watery ordinance, which they desired and wanted.

These people[4] made also profession of neglecting, if not renouncing

---

[3] Probably Penn is here referring to the Independents or Congregationalists.

[4] The Baptists, followers of John Smyth, the "Se-Baptist," who was the real founder of the movement in England. He was influenced by the Dutch Mennonites, heirs of the continental Anabaptist tradition, which dated from the earliest years of the Reformation.

and censuring, not only the necessity but use of all human learning as to the ministry, and all other qualifications to it, besides the helps and gifts of the spirit of God and those natural and common to men. And for a time they seemed, like John of old,[5] a burning and a shining light to other societies. They were very diligent, plain, and serious, strong in scripture, and bold in profession, bearing much reproach and contradiction. But that which others fell by proved their snare. For worldly power spoiled them too, who had enough of it to try them what they would do if they had more. And they rested also too much upon their watery dispensation, instead of passing on more fully to that of the fire and Holy Ghost, which was His baptism, Who came with a fan in His hand that He might thoroughly (and not in part only) purge His floor, and take away the dross and the tin of His people, and make a man finer than gold. Withal, they grew high, rough, and self-righteous, opposing further attainment, too much forgetting the day of their infancy and littleness, which gave them something of a real beauty; insomuch that many left them and all visible churches and societies, and wandered up and down as sheep without a shepherd and as doves without their mates, seeking their beloved but could not find Him (as their souls desired to know Him) Whom their souls loved above their chiefest joy.

These people were called Seekers by some and the Family of Love by others,[6] because as they came to the knowledge of one another they sometimes met together, not formally to pray or preach at appointed times or places in their own wills, as in times past they were accustomed

[5] John the Baptist.

[6] The Seekers and the Family of Love are usually regarded as separate groups, though Seekerism was more a pervasive movement or tendency in radical English religious thought than a distinct sect. The Seeker was characteristically a person of mystical temperament who felt that the outward church was in apostasy and who therefore joined with other like-minded persons in "seeking" or "waiting" for the manifestation of the true Church. Penn's is one of the best descriptions we have of these attractive but historically elusive groups of people. The Family of Love, an obscure sect founded by the Westphalian mystic Henry Nicholas in the sixteenth century, had attracted numerous adherents in England by the middle of the seventeenth century; they stood for holiness of life and for the perfection of human nature here on earth.

to do, but waited together in silence, and as anything rose in any one of their minds that they thought savored of a divine spring, they sometimes spoke. But so it was that some of them, not keeping in humility and in the fear of God after the abundance of revelation, were exalted above measure, and for want of staying their minds in a humble dependence upon Him that opened their understandings to see great things in His law, they ran out in their own imaginations and, mixing them with those divine openings, brought forth a monstrous birth to the scandal of those that feared God and waited daily in the temple not made with hands for the consolation of Israel, the Jew inward, and circumcision in spirit.

This people obtained the name of Ranters[7] from their extravagant discourses and practices. For they interpreted Christ's fulfilling of the law for us to be a discharging of us from any obligation and duty the law required of us, instead of the condemnation of the law for sins past upon faith and repentance; and that now it was no sin to do that which before it was a sin to commit, the slavish fear of the law being taken off by Christ; and all things good that man did, if he did but do them with the mind and persuasion that it was so—insomuch that divers fell into gross and enormous practices, pretending in excuse thereof that they could without evil commit the same act which was sin in another to do, thereby distinguishing between the action and the evil of it by the direction of the mind and intention in the doing of it. Which was to make sin superabound by the aboundings of grace and to turn from the grace of God into wantonness, a securer way of sinning than before, as if Christ came not to save us *from* our sins but *in* our sins, not to take away sin but that we might sin more freely at His cost and with less danger to ourselves. I say, this ensnared divers and brought them to an utter and lamentable loss as to their eternal state, and they grew very troublesome to the better sort of people, and furnished the looser with an occasion to profane.

---

[7] Ranterism or Antinomianism represented the "lunatic fringe" of spiritual religion in seventeenth century England. In the words of G. F. Nuttall, it was religious enthusiasm degenerated into "blasphemous identification of the soul with God and unethical claims to a freedom of spirit which was no more than license."

THE RESTORATION OF PRIMITIVE CHRISTIANITY

It was about that very time, as you may see in George Fox's annals,[8] that the eternal, wise, and good God was pleased, in His infinite love to honor and visit this benighted and bewildered nation with His glorious dayspring from on high, yea, with a most sure and certain sound of the word of light and life through the testimony of a chosen vessel[9] to an effectual and blessed purpose, can many thousands say, glory be to the name of the Lord forever. For as it reached the conscience and broke the heart and brought many to a sense and search, so that which people had been vainly seeking without with much pains and cost they by this ministry found within, where it was they wanted what they sought for, viz, the right way to peace with God. For they were directed to the light of Jesus Christ within them as the seed and leaven of the Kingdom of God, near all because in all, and God's talent to all: a faithful and true witness and just monitor in every bosom, the gift and grace of God to life and salvation, that appears to all, though few regard it. This the traditional Christian, conceited of himself and strong in his own will and righteousness, and overcome with blind zeal and passion, either despised as a low and common thing or opposed as a novelty under many hard names and opprobrious terms, denying, in his ignorant and angry mind, any fresh manifestation of God's power and spirit in man in these days, though never more needed to make true Christians. [They were] not unlike those Jews of old that rejected the Son of God at the very same time that they blindly professed to wait for the Messiah to come, because, alas, He appeared not among them according to their carnal mind and expectation.

This brought forth many abusive books, which filled the greater

---

[8] The *Journal* of George Fox, to the first edition of which (1694) Penn's essay served as a preface. The best and most recent edition is that of John L. Nickalls (Cambridge University Press, 1952).

[9] George Fox.

sort with envy and lesser with rage, and made the way and progress of this blessed testimony strait and narrow indeed to those that received it. However, God owned His own work, and this testimony did effectually reach, gather, comfort, and establish the weary and heavy-laden, the hungry and thirsty, the poor and needy, the mournful and sick of many maladies, that had spent all upon physicians of no value and waited for relief from heaven, help only from above; seeing, upon a serious trial of all things, nothing else would do but Christ Himself— the light of His countenance, a touch of His garment and help from His hand. . . . And as God had delivered their souls of the wearisome burdens of sin and vanity, and enriched their poverty of spirit, and satisfied their great hunger and thirst after eternal righteousness, and filled them with the good things of His own house, and made them stewards of His manifold gifts, so they went forth to all quarters of these nations, to declare to the inhabitants thereof what God had done for them, what they had found, and where and how they had found it, viz., the way to peace with God, inviting all to come and see and taste for themselves the truth of what they declared unto them.[10]

And as their testimony was to the principle of God in man, the precious pearl and leaven of the Kingdom, as the only blessed means appointed of God to quicken, convince, and sanctify man, so they opened to them what it was in itself, and what it was given to them for, how they might know it from their own spirit and that of the subtle appearance of the Evil One, and what it would do for all those whose minds should be turned off from the vanity of the world and its lifeless ways and teachers, and adhere to this blessed light in themselves, which discovers and condemns sin in all its appearances and shows how to overcome it, if minded and obeyed in its holy manifestations and convictions, giving power to such to avoid and resist those things that do not please God, and to grow strong in love, faith, and good works; that so man, whom sin hath made as a wilderness overrun

[10] Penn here refers to a group of ministers known in Quaker history as the "First Publishers of Truth," a band of sixty-odd men and women, mostly from humble walks of life in the Northwest of England, who carried the Quaker gospel of the Inward Light into every corner of the British Isles, across the Channel into western Europe, and over the Atlantic to the British colonies in America.

with briars and thorns, might become as the garden of God, cultivated by His divine power and replenished with the most virtuous and beautiful plants of God's own right hand planting to His eternal praise.

But these experimental preachers of glad tidings of God's truth and kingdom could not run when they list, or pray or preach when they pleased, but as Christ their Redeemer prepared and moved them by His own blessed spirit, for which they waited in their services and meetings, and spoke as that gave them utterance; and which was as those having authority, and not like the dreaming, dry, and formal Pharisees. And so it plainly appeared to the serious-minded, whose spiritual eye the Lord Jesus had in any measure opened, so that to one was given the word of exhortation, to another the word of reproof, to another the word of consolation, and all by the same spirit and in the good order thereof, to the convincing and edifying of many.

And truly they waxed strong and bold through faithfulness, and by the power and spirit of the Lord Jesus became very fruitful, thousands in a short time being turned to the Truth in the inward parts through their testimony in ministry and sufferings; insomuch as in most counties and many of the considerable towns of England meetings were settled, and daily there were added such as should be saved. For they were diligent to plant and to water, and the Lord blessed their labors with an exceeding great increase, notwithstanding all the opposition made to their blessed progress by false rumors, calumnies, and bitter persecutions, not only from the powers of the earth, but from everyone that listed to injure and abuse them, so that they seemed indeed to be as poor sheep appointed to the slaughter, and as a people killed all the day long. . . .

THE FAITH OF THE EARLY QUAKERS

Two things are to be considered: the doctrine they taught and the example they led among all people. I have already touched upon their fundamental principle, which is as the cornerstone of their fabric, and indeed, to speak eminently and properly, their characteristic or main distinguishing point or principle, viz., the light of Christ within, as

God's gift for man's salvation. This, I say, is as the root of the goodly tree of doctrines that grew and branched out from it, which I shall now mention in their natural and experimental order.

First, repentance from dead works to serve the living God. Which comprehends three operations: first, a sight of sin; secondly, a sense and godly sorrow for sin; thirdly, an amendment for the time to come. This was the repentance they preached and pressed and a natural result from the principle they turned all people unto. For of light came sight, and of sight came sense and sorrow, and of sense and sorrow came amendment of life. Which doctrine of repentance leads to justification; that is, forgiveness of the sins that are past through Christ, the alone propitiation, and the sanctification or purgation of the soul from the defiling nature and habits of sin present by the spirit of Christ in the soul, which is justification in the complete sense of that word, comprehending both justification from the guilt of the sins that are past, as if they had never been committed, through the love and mercy of God in Christ Jesus; and the creatures' being made inwardly just through the cleansing and sanctifying power and spirit of Christ revealed in the soul which is commonly called sanctification. But . . . none can come to know Christ to be their sacrifice that reject Him as their sanctifier, the end of His coming being to save His people from the nature and defilement as well as guilt of sin; and . . . therefore those that resist His light and spirit make His coming and offering of none effect to them.

From hence sprang a second doctrine they were led to declare as the mark of the price of the high calling to all true Christians, viz., perfection from sin, according to the Scriptures of truth, which testify it to be the end of Christ's coming and the nature of His Kingdom, and for which His spirit was and is given, viz., to be perfect as our Heavenly Father is perfect, and holy because God is holy. And this the apostles labored for, that the Christians should be sanctified throughout in body, soul, and spirit; but they never held a perfection in wisdom and glory in this life or from natural infirmities or death, as some have with a weak or ill mind imagined and insinuated against them. This they called a redeemed state, regeneration, or the new birth, teaching everywhere, according to their foundation, that without this work were known, there was no inheriting the Kingdom of God.

Thirdly, this leads to an acknowledgment of eternal rewards and punishments, as they have good reason; for else of all people certainly they must be the most miserable, who for above forty years have been exceeding great sufferers for their profession, and in some cases treated worse than the worst of men, yea, as the refuse and offscouring of all things.

This was the purport of their doctrine and ministry, which, for the most part, is what other professors of Christianity pretend to hold in words and forms, but not in the power of godliness, which, generally speaking, has been long lost by men's departing from that principle and seed of life that is in man, and which man has not regarded but lost the sense of, and in and by which he can only be quickened in his mind to serve the living God in newness of life. For as the life of religion was lost, and the generality lived and worshiped God after their own wills and not after the will of God, nor the mind of Christ, which stood in the works and fruits of the Holy Spirit, so that which they pressed was not notion but experience, not formality but godliness, as being sensible in themselves, through the work of God's righteous judgments, that without holiness no man shall ever see the Lord with comfort.

THE QUAKER TESTIMONIES

Besides these general doctrines, as the larger branches, there sprang forth several particular doctrines, that did exemplify and further explain the truth and efficacy of the general doctrine before observed in their lives and examples. As,

I. Communion and loving one another. This is a noted mark in the mouth of all sorts of people concerning them: they will meet, they will help and stick one to another; whence it is common to hear some say, "Look how the Quakers love and take care of one another." Others, less moderate, will say, "The Quakers love none but themselves." And if loving one another and having an intimate communion in religion and constant care to meet to worship God and help one another be any mark of primitive Christianity, they had it, blessed be the Lord, in an ample manner.

II. To love enemies. This they both taught and practiced. For they did not only refuse to be revenged for injuries done them, and condemned it as of an unchristian spirit, but they did freely forgive, yea, help and relieve those that had been cruel to them when it was in their power to have been even with them (of which many and singular instances might be given), endeavoring through faith and patience to overcome all injustice and oppression and preaching this doctrine as Christian for others to follow.

III. Another was the sufficiency of truth-speaking, according to Christ's own form of sound words of Yea, yea, and Nay, nay, among Christians without swearing, both from Christ's express prohibition to swear at all (Matthew v. 33–37) and for that they being under the tie and bond of truth in themselves, there was no necessity for an oath; and it would be a reproach to their Christian veracity to assure their truth by such an extraordinary way of speaking, simple and uncompounded answers, as yea and nay (without asseverations, attestations, or supernatural vouchers) being most suitable to evangelical righteousness. But offering at the same time to be punished to the full for false speaking, as others for perjury, if ever guilty of it. And hereby they exclude with all true, all false and profane swearing, for which the land did and doth mourn, and the great God was and is not a little offended with it.

IV. Not fighting, but suffering is another testimony peculiar to this people. They affirm that Christianity teacheth people to beat their swords into plowshares, and their spears into pruning hooks, and to learn war no more, that so the wolf may lie down with the lamb and the lion with the calf, and nothing that destroys be entertained in the hearts of people; exhorting them to employ their zeal against sin and turn their anger against Satan and no longer war one against another, because all wars and fightings come of men's own hearts' lusts, according to the apostle James, and not of the meek spirit of Christ Jesus, Who is captain of another warfare, . . . which is carried on with other weapons. Thus, as truth-speaking succeeded swearing, so faith and patience succeeded fighting in the doctrine and practice of this people. Nor ought they for this to be obnoxious to civil government, since if they cannot fight for it, neither can they fight against it, which is no mean security to any state. Nor is it reasonable that people should be blamed for not doing more for others than they can do for themselves. And, Christianity set aside, if the costs and fruits of war were well considered, peace with all its inconveniences is generally preferable. But though they were not for fighting, they were for submitting to government; and that not only for fear but for conscience' sake, where government doth not interfere with conscience, believing it to be an ordinance of God and, where it is justly administered, a great benefit to mankind, though it has been their lot, through blind zeal in some and interest in others, to have felt the strokes of it with greater weight and rigor than any other persuasion in this age, whilst they of all others, religion set aside, have given the civil magistrate the least occasion of trouble in the discharge of his office.

V. Another part of the character of this people was and is, they refuse to pay tithes or maintenance to a national ministry, and that for two reasons. The one is, they believe all compelled maintenance, even to gospel ministers, to be unlawful, because expressly contrary to Christ's command, Who said, "Freely you have received, freely give"; at least, that the maintenance of gospel ministers should be free and not forced. The other reason of their refusal is, because those ministers are not gospel ones in that the Holy Ghost is not their foundation, but human arts and parts. So that it is not matter of humor[11] or sullenness but pure conscience toward God that they cannot help to support national ministries where they dwell, which are but too much and too visibly become ways of worldly advantage and preferment.

VI. Not to respect persons was and is another of their doctrines and practices for which they were often buffeted and abused. They affirmed it to be sinful to give flattering titles or to use vain gestures and compliments of respect, though to virtue and authority they ever made a difference, but after their plain and homely manner, yet sincere and substantial way; well remembering the examples of Mordecai and

[11] Whim, caprice.

Elihu, but more especially the command of their Lord and Master
Jesus Christ, Who forbade His followers to call men Rabbi, which
implies Lord or Master; also the fashionable greetings and salutations
of those times, that so self-love and honor, to which the proud mind of
man is incident in his fallen estate, might not be indulged but rebuked.
And though this rendered their conversation disagreeable, yet they
that will remember what Christ said to the Jews—"How can you believe in me, who receive honor one of another?"—will abate of their
resentment if His doctrine has any credit with them.

VII. They also used the plain language of *thou* and *thee* to a single
person, whatever was his degree among men.[12] And indeed the wisdom
of God was much seen in bringing forth this people in so plain an appearance. For it was a close and distinguishing test upon the spirits of
those they came among, showing their insides and what predominated,
notwithstanding their high and great profession of religion. This
among the rest sounded so harsh to many of them, and they took it so
ill, that they would say, "Thou me, thou my dog! If thou thouest me,
I'll thou thy teeth down thy throat"; forgetting the language they use
to God in their own prayers, and the common style of the Scriptures,
and that it is an absolute and essential propriety of speech. And what
good, alas, had their religion done them, who were so sensibly touched
with indignation for the use of this plain, honest, and true speech?

VIII. They recommended silence by their example, having very few
words upon all occasions. They were at a word in dealing, nor could
their customers [with] many words tempt them from it, having more
regard to truth than custom, to example than gain. They sought solitude; but when in company they would neither use nor willingly hear
unnecessary as well as unlawful discourses, whereby they preserved
their minds pure and undisturbed from unprofitable thoughts and
diversions. Nor could they humor the custom of "Good night, good
morrow, Godspeed," for they knew the night was good and the day

[12] It was customary in seventeenth century England to use the pronoun you in
addressing a social superior and *thou* in speaking to an inferior. As a testimony of
their belief in the equality of all men before God (and also because it was gram-
matically more correct), the early Quakers insisted upon using *thou*, *thy*, and *thee*
in addressing an individual, whatever his social status.

was good without wishing of either, and that in the other expression the holy name of God was too lightly and unthinkingly used and therefore taken in vain. Besides, they were words and wishes of course,[13] and are usually as little meant as are love and service in the custom of cap and knee;[14] and superfluity in those, as well as in other things, was burdensome to them, and therefore they did not only decline to use them, but found themselves often pressed to reprove the practice.

IX. For the same reason they forbore drinking to people or pledging of them, as the manner of the world is: a practice that is not only unnecessary but, they thought, evil in the tendencies of it, being a provocation to drink more than did people good, as well as that it was in itself vain and heathenish.

X. Their way of marriage is peculiar to them, and shows a distinguishing care above other societies professing Christianity. They say that marriage is an ordinance of God, and that God only can rightly join man and woman in marriage. Therefore they use neither priest nor magistrate, but the man or woman concerned take each other as husband and wife in the presence of divers credible witnesses, promising unto each other, with God's assistance, to be loving and faithful in that relation till death shall separate them. But antecedent to all this, they first present themselves to the Monthly Meeting for the affairs of the church where they reside, there declaring their intentions to take one another as husband and wife if the said meeting have nothing material to object against it. They are constantly asked the necessary questions, as, in case of parents or guardians, if they have acquainted them with their intention and have their consent, etc. The method of the meeting is to take a minute thereof, and to appoint proper persons to inquire of their conversation[15] and clearness from all others, and whether they have discharged their duty to their parents or guardians, and [to] make report thereof to the next Monthly Meeting, where the same parties are desired to give their attendance. In case it appears

[13] Belonging to the ordinary custom or way of the world.
[14] By "the custom of cap and knee" Penn means the conventional courtesies of doffing the hat and making low, sweeping bows.
[15] Behavior, mode of life.

they have proceeded orderly, the meeting passes their proposal and so records it in their meeting book. And in case the woman be a widow and hath children, due care is there taken that provision also be made by her for the orphans before the meeting pass the proposal of marriage. [The meeting then advises] the parties concerned to appoint a convenient time and place and to give fitting notice to their relations and such friends and neighbors as they desire should be the witnesses of their marriage, where they take one another by the hand and by name promise reciprocally love and fidelity after the manner before expressed. Of all which proceedings a narrative in a way of certificate is made, to which the said parties first set their hands, thereby making it their act and deed, and then divers of the relations, spectators, and auditors set their names as witnesses of what they said and signed. And this certificate is afterward registered in the record belonging to the meeting where the marriage is solemnized. Which regular method has been, as it deserves, adjudged in courts of law a good marriage, where it has been by cross and ill people disputed and contested for want of the accustomed formality of priest and ring, etc. Ceremonies they have refused, not out of humor, but conscience reasonably grounded, inasmuch as no Scripture example tells us that the priest had any other part, of old time, than that of a witness among the rest before whom the Jews used to take one another; and therefore this people look upon it as an imposition to advance the power and profits of the clergy. And for the use of the ring, it is enough to say that it was a heathenish and vain custom, and never in practice among the people of God, Jews or primitive Christians. The words of the usual form, as "with my body I thee worship," etc., are hardly defensible. In short, they are more careful, exact, and regular than any form now used, and it is free of the inconveniences with which other methods are attended, their care and checks being so many and such as that no clandestine marriages can be performed among them.

XI. It may not be unfit to say something here of their births and burials, which make up so much of the pomp and solemnity of too many called Christians. For births, the parents name their own children, which is usually some days after they are born, in the presence of the midwife if she can be there, and those that were at the birth, who afterward sign a certificate, for that purpose prepared, of the birth and name of the child or children, which is recorded in a proper book in the Monthly Meeting to which the parents belong, avoiding the accustomed ceremonies and festivals.

XII. Their burials are performed with the same simplicity. If the body of the deceased be near any public meeting place, it is usually carried thither for the more convenient reception of those that accompany it to the burying ground. And it so falls out sometimes that while the meeting is gathering for the burial some or other has a word of exhortation for the sake of the people there met together. After which the body is born away by the young men or those that are of their neighborhood or that were most of the intimacy of the deceased party, the corpse being in a plain coffin without any covering or furniture upon it. At the ground they pause some time before they put the body into its grave, that if anyone there should have anything upon them to exhort the people, they may not be disappointed, and that the relations may the more retiredly and solemnly take their last leave of the body of their departed kindred, and the spectators have a sense of mortality by the occasion then given them to reflect upon their own latter end. Otherwise, they have no set rites or ceremonies on those occasions. Neither do the kindred of the deceased ever wear mourning, they looking upon it as a worldly ceremony and piece of pomp; and that what mourning is fit for a Christian to have at the departure of a beloved relation or friend should be worn in the mind, which is only sensible of the loss; and the love they had to them and remembrance of them to be outwardly expressed by a respect to their advice and care of those they have left behind them, and their love of that they loved. Which conduct of theirs, though unmodish or unfashionable, leaves nothing of the substance of things neglected or undone; and as they aim at no more, so that simplicity of life is what they observe with great satisfaction, though it sometimes happens not to be without the mockeries of the vain world they live in.

These things, to be sure, gave them a rough and disagreeable appearance with the generality, who thought them turners of the world upside down, as indeed in some sense they were, but in no other than that wherein Paul was so charged, viz., to bring things back into their primitive and right order again. For these and such-like practices of theirs were not the result of humor or for civil distinction, as some have fancied, but a fruit of inward sense, which God through His holy fear had begotten in them. They did not consider how to contradict the world or distinguish themselves as a party from others, it being none of their business, as it was not their interest. No, it was not the result of consultation or a framed design, by which to declare or recommend schism or novelty. But God having given them a sight of themselves, they saw the whole world in the same glass of Truth, and sensibly discerned the affections and passions of men and the rise and tendency of things—what it was that gratified the lust of the flesh, the lust of the eye, and the pride of life, which are not of the Father but of the world; and that from thence sprang, in the night of darkness and apostasy which hath been over people through their degeneration from the light and spirit of God, these and many other vain customs, which are seen by the heavenly day of Christ that dawns in the soul to be either wrong in their original or, by time and abuse, hurtful in their practice. And though these things seemed trivial to some and rendered these people stingy and conceited in such persons' opinion, there was and is more in them than they were or are aware of.

It was not very easy to our primitive Friends to make themselves sights and spectacles and the scorn and derision of the world, which they easily foresaw must be the consequence of so unfashionable a conversation in it. But herein was the wisdom of God seen in the foolishness of these things. First, that they discovered the satisfaction and concern that people had in and for the fashions of this world, notwithstanding their high pretenses to another, in that any disappointment about them came so very near them as that the greatest honesty, virtue, wisdom, and ability were unwelcome without them. Secondly, it seasonably and profitably divided conversation; for this making their society uneasy to their relations and acquaintance, it gave them the opportunity of more retirement and solitude, wherein they met with better company, even the Lord God their Redeemer, and grew strong in His love, power, and wisdom, and were thereby better qualified for His service. And the success abundantly showed it. Blessed be the name of the Lord.

And though they were not great and learned in the esteem of this world (for then they had not wanted followers upon their own credit and authority), yet they were generally of the most sober of the several persuasions they were in and of the most repute for religion, and many of them of good capacity, substance, and account among men. And also some among them wanted not for parts, learning, or estate, though then, as of old, not many wise or noble, etc., were called or at least received the heavenly call, because of the cross that attended the profession of it in sincerity. But neither do parts or learning make men the better Christians, though the better orators and disputants; and it is the ignorance of people about the divine gift that causes that vulgar and mischievous mistake. Theory and practice, speculation and enjoyment, words and life, are two things. . . .

THE QUAKER MINISTRY

I. They were changed men themselves before they went about to change others. Their hearts were rent as well as their garments, and they knew the power and work of God upon them. And this was seen by the great alteration it made and their stricter course of life and more godly conversation that immediately followed upon it.

II. They went not forth or preached in their own time or will but in the will of God, and spoke not their own studied matter, but as they were opened and moved of His spirit, with which they were well acquainted in their own conversion, which cannot be expressed to carnal men so as to give them any intelligible account, for to such it is, as Christ said, like the blowing of the wind, which no man knows whence it cometh or whither it goeth. Yet this proof and seal went along with their ministry, that many were turned from their lifeless professions and the evil of their ways to an inward and experimental knowledge of God and a holy life, as thousands can witness. And as they freely received what they had to say from the Lord, so they freely administered it to others.

III. The bent and stress of their ministry was conversion to God, regeneration, and holiness, not schemes of doctrines and verbal creeds or new forms of worship, but a leaving off in religion [of] the superfluous, and reducing the ceremonious and formal part, and pressing earnestly the substantial, the necessary and profitable part to the soul, as all, upon a serious reflection, must and do acknowledge.

IV. They directed people to a principle in themselves, though not of themselves, by which all that they asserted, preached, and exhorted others to might be wrought in them and known to them through experience to be true, which is a high and distinguishing mark of the truth of their ministry, both that they knew what they said and were not afraid of coming to the test. For as they were bold from certainty, so they required conformity upon no human authority, but upon conviction and the conviction of this principle, which they asserted was in them that they preached unto, and unto that they directed them, that they might examine and prove the reality of those things which they had affirmed of it as to its manifestation and work in man. And this is more than the many ministries in the world pretended to. They declare of religion, say many things true in words of God, Christ, and the Spirit, of holiness and heaven, that all men should repent and amend their lives or they will go to Hell, etc. But which of them all pretend to speak of their own knowledge and experience? Or ever directed men to a divine principle or agent placed of God in man to help him; and how to know it, and wait to feel its power to work that good and acceptable will of God in them?

Some of them indeed have spoke[n] of the Spirit and the operations of it to sanctification and performance of worship to God; but where and how to find it and wait in it, to perform our duty to God, was yet as a mystery to be declared by this further degree of reformation. So that this people did not only in words more than equally press repentance, conversion, and holiness, but did it knowingly and experimentally, and directed those to whom they preached to a sufficient principle, and told them where it was and by what tokens they might know it, and which way they might experience the power and efficacy of it to their souls' happiness. Which is more than theory and specula-

tion, upon which most other ministries depend; for here is certainty,
a bottom upon which man may boldly appear before God in the great
day of account.

V. They reached to the inward state and condition of people, which
is an evidence of the virtue of their principle and of their ministering
from it, and not from their own imaginations, glosses, or comments
upon Scripture. For nothing reaches the heart but what is from the
heart, or pierces the conscience but what comes from a living conscience. Insomuch as it hath often happened, where people have under
secrecy revealed their state or condition to some choice Friends for
advice or ease, they have been so particularly directed in the ministry
of this people that they have challenged their friends with discovering
their secrets and telling the preachers their cases, to whom a word had
not been spoken. Yea, the very thoughts and purposes of the hearts of
many have been so plainly detected that they have, like Nathaniel,
cried out of this inward appearance of Christ, "Thou art the Son of
God, Thou art the King of Israel." And those that have embraced
this divine principle have found this mark of its truth and divinity
(that the woman of Samaria did of Christ when in the flesh, to be the
Messiah); viz., it had told them all that ever they had done, shown
them their insides, the most inward secrets of their hearts, and laid
judgment to the line and righteousness to the plummet, of which
thousands can at this day give in their witness. So that nothing has
been affirmed by this people of the power and virtue of this heavenly
principle that such as have turned to it have not found true, and more,
and that one-half had not been told to them of what they have seen
of the power, purity, wisdom, and goodness of God therein.

VI. The accomplishments with which this principle fitted even
some of the meanest of this people for their work and service, furnish-
ing some of them with an extraordinary understanding in divine
things and an admirable fluency and taking way of expression, which
gave occasion to some to wonder, saying of them, as of their Master,
"Is not this such a mechanic's son? How came he by this learning?"
As from thence others took occasion to suspect and insinuate they were
Jesuits in disguise (who have had the reputation of learned men for

an age past), though there was not the least ground of truth for any such reflection, in that their ministers are known, the places of their abode, their kindred, and education.

VII. That they came forth low and despised and hated, as the primitive Christians did, and not by the help of worldly wisdom or power, as former reformations in part have done; but in all things it may be said: this people were brought forth in the cross, in a contradiction to the ways, worship, fashions, and customs of this world, yea, against wind and tide, that so no flesh might glory before God.

VIII. They could have no design to themselves in this work thus to expose themselves to scorn and abuse, to spend and be spent, leaving wife and children, house and land, and all that can be accounted dear to men, with their lives in their hands, being daily in jeopardy, to declare this primitive message, revived in their spirits by the good spirit and power of God; viz., that God is light, and in Him is no darkness at all; and that He has sent His Son, a light into the world to enlighten all men in order to salvation; and that they that say they have fellowship with God and are His children and people and yet walk in darkness—viz., in disobedience to the light in their consciences and after the vanity of this world—they lie and do not the truth. But that all such as love the light and bring their deeds to it and walk in the light, as God is light, the blood of Jesus Christ His Son, should cleanse them from all sin. Thus John i. 4. 9; iii. 20, 21; I John i. 5, 6, 7.

IX. Their known great constancy and patience in suffering for their testimony in all the branches of it, and that sometimes unto death by beatings, bruisings, long and crowded imprisonments, and noisome dungeons (four of them in New England dying by the hands of the executioner purely for preaching amongst that people),[16] besides banishments and excessive plunders and sequestrations of their goods and estates, almost in all parts, not easily to be expressed, and less to have been endured but by those that have the support of a good and glorious cause, refusing deliverance by any indirect ways or means, as often as it was offered to them.

---

[16] Four Quakers, Marmaduke Stephenson, William Robinson, Mary Dyer, and William Leddra, were hanged on Boston Common between 1659 and 1661.

X. That they did not only not show any disposition to revenge when it was at any time in their power, but forgave their cruel enemies, showing mercy to those that had none for them.

XI. Their plainness with those in authority, like the ancient prophets, not fearing to tell them to their faces of their private and public sins, and their prophecies to them of their afflictions and downfall, when in the top of their glory. Also of some national judgments, as of the plague and fire of London, in express terms;[17] and likewise particular ones to divers persecutors, which accordingly overtook them, and were very remarkable in the places where they dwelt, which in time may be made public for the glory of God.

Thus, reader, thou seest this people in their rise, principles, ministry, and progress, both their general and particular testimony, by which thou mayest be informed how and upon what foot they sprang and became so considerable a people. . . .

PORTRAIT OF A PROPHET

. . . George Fox was born in Leicestershire[18] about the year 1624. He descended of honest and sufficient parents, who endeavored to bring him up, as they did the rest of their children, in the way and worship of the nation,[19] especially his mother, who was a woman accomplished above most of her degree in the place where she lived.[20] But from a child he appeared of another frame of mind than the rest of his brethren, being more religious, inward, still, solid, and observing

---

[17] George Fox, in prison in Lancaster in 1665, had a premonition of the Great Plague and the Fire of London which followed: "I saw the angel of the Lord with a glittering drawn sword southward, and as though the Court had been all of a fire; and not long after . . . the sickness began, and the Lord's sword was drawn." Several years earlier, Thomas Briggs had preached repentance through the streets of the capital, crying out that "unless London repented, as Nineveh did, God would destroy it." And only a few days before the conflagration, according to the Quaker historian Willem Sewel, Thomas Ibbott went about the city "pronouncing a judgment by fire."

[18] At Drayton-in-the-Clay, now Fenny Drayton.

[19] I.e., in the Church of England.

[20] Fox tells us in his *Journal* that her name was Mary Lago and that she came of "the stock of the martyrs."

beyond his years, as the answers he would give and the questions he would put upon occasion manifested, to the astonishment of those that heard him, especially in divine things.

His mother taking notice of his singular temper, and the gravity, wisdom, and piety that very early shined through him, refusing childish and vain sports and company when very young, she was tender and indulgent over him, so that from her he met with little difficulty. As to his employment, he was brought up in country business, and as he took most delight in sheep, so he was very skillful in them, an employment that very well suited his mind in several respects, both for its innocency and solitude, and was a just emblem of his after ministry and service.

. . . when he was somewhat above twenty, he left his friends, and visited the most retired and religious people in those parts; and some there were . . . in this nation, who waited for the consolation of Israel night and day, as Zacharias, Anna, and good old Simeon did of old time. To these he was sent, and these he sought out in the neighboring counties, and among them he sojourned till his more ample ministry came upon him. At this time he taught and was an example of silence, endeavoring to bring them from self-performances, testifying of, and turning them to, the light of Christ within them, and encouraging them to wait in patience to feel the power of it to stir in their hearts, that their knowledge and worship of God might stand in the power of an endless life, which was to be found in the Light, as it was obeyed in the manifestation of it in man. . . . Accordingly, several meetings were gathered in those parts, and thus his time was employed for some years.

In 1652, he being in his usual retirement, his mind exercised toward the Lord, upon a very high mountain in some of the hither parts of Yorkshire,[21] as I take it, he had a vision of the great work of God in the earth and of the way that he was to go forth in a public ministry to begin it. He saw people as thick as motes in the sun, that should in time be brought home to the Lord, that there might be but one

[21] According to Fox's *Journal*, the vision here described came to him on Pendle Hill in Lancashire.

shepherd and one sheepfold in all the earth. There his eye was directed northward, beholding a great people that should receive him and his message in those parts. Upon this mountain he was moved of the Lord to sound out His great and notable day, as if he had been in a great auditory, and from thence went north, as the Lord had shown him. And in every place where he came, if not before he came to it, he had his particular exercise and service shown to him, so that the Lord was his leader indeed. For it was not in vain that he travailed, God in most places sealing his commission with the convincement of some of all sorts, as well publicans as sober professors of religion.[22]

Some of the first and most eminent of those that came forth in a public ministry, and which are now at rest, were Richard Farnsworth, James Nayler, William Dewsbury, Thomas Aldam, Francis Howgill, Edward Burrough, John Camm, John Audland, Richard Hubberthorn, Thomas Taylor, Thomas Holme, Alexander Parker, William Simpson, William Caton, John Stubbs, Robert Widders, Thomas Loe, Josiah Coale, John Burnyeat, Robert Lodge, Thomas Salthouse, and many more worthies[23] that cannot be well here named, together with divers yet living of the first and great convincement, who after the knowledge of God's purging judgment in themselves, and some time of waiting in silence upon Him to feel and receive power from on high to speak in His name (which none else rightly can, though they may use the same words), they felt its divine motions, and were frequently drawn forth, especially to visit the public assemblies to reprove, inform, and exhort them, sometimes in markets, fairs, streets, and by the highway-side, calling people to repentance, and to turn to the Lord with their hearts as well as their mouths, directing them to the light of Christ within them to see, examine, and consider their ways by, and to eschew the evil, and do the good and acceptable will

[22] There were many communities of Seekers in the parts of Westmorland and Yorkshire where Fox preached in 1652. Many were "convinced" and became Friends.

[23] Except for Thomas Loe and Josiah Coale these ministers all came from the Northwest of England. Thomas Loe, later the instrument of Penn's own "convincement," came from Oxford; Josiah Coale, who was to travel extensively in the American colonies, lived in Bristol.

of God. And they suffered great hardships for this their love and good will, being often stocked, stoned, beaten, whipped, and imprisoned, though honest men and of good report where they lived, that had left wives, children, and houses and lands to visit them with a living call to repentance. And though the priests[24] generally set themselves to oppose them and write against them, and insinuated most false and scandalous stories to defame them, stirring up the magistrates to suppress them, especially in those northern parts, yet God was pleased so to fill them with His living power and give them such an open door of utterance in His service that there was a mighty convincement over those parts.

And through the tender and singular indulgence of Judge Bradshaw and Judge Fell and Colonel West[25] in the infancy of things, the priests were never able to gain the point they labored for, which was to have proceeded to blood and, if possible, Herod-like, by a cruel exercise of the civil power, to have cut them off and rooted them out of the country, but especially Judge Fell, who was not only a check to their rage in the course of legal proceedings, but otherwise upon occasion, and finally countenanced this people. For his wife receiving the Truth with the first, it had that influence upon his spirit, being a just and wise man, and seeing in his own wife and family a full confutation of all the popular clamors against the way of Truth, that he covered them what he could, and freely opened his doors, and gave up his house to his wife and her friends; not valuing the reproach of ignorant or of evil-minded people, which I here mention to his and her honor, and which will be, I believe, an honor and a blessing to such of their name and family as shall be found in that tenderness, humility, love, and zeal for the Truth and people of the Lord.

That house[26] was for some years, at first especially, till the Truth

24 Clergymen of the Church of England.

25 Judge John Bradshaw had presided over the court that condemned Charles I to death. Judge Thomas Fell of Swarthmoor Hall was especially lenient toward the Quakers who came before him in the courtroom; his widow, Margaret Fell, later became George Fox's wife. Colonel William West, the Clerk of the Lancaster Assize, refused to make out a warrant for Fox's arrest.

26 Swarthmoor Hall, near Ulverston, in western Lancashire.

had opened its way into the southern parts of this island, an eminent receptacle of this people. Others of good note and substance in those northern countries had also opened their houses, with their hearts, to the many publishers that in a short time the Lord had raised to declare His salvation to the people . . . where meetings of the Lord's messengers were frequently held to communicate their services and exercises and comfort and edify one another in their blessed ministry.

But lest this may be thought a digression, having touched upon this before, I return to this excellent man, and for his personal qualities, both natural, moral, and divine, as they appeared in his converse with brethren and in the church of God, take as follows:

I. He was a man that God endued with a clear and wonderful depth, a discerner of others' spirits and very much a master of his own. And though that side of his understanding which lay next to the world, and especially the expression of it, might sound uncouth and unfashionable to nice ears, his matter was nevertheless very profound, and would not only bear to be often considered but the more it was so, the more weighty and instructing it appeared. And as abruptly and brokenly as sometimes his sentences would seem to fall from him about divine things, it is well known they were often as texts to many fairer declarations. And indeed it showed beyond all contradiction that God sent him, in that no arts or parts had any share in the matter or manner of his ministry, and that so many great, excellent, and necessary truths as he came forth to preach to mankind had therefore nothing of man's wit or wisdom to recommend them. So that as to man he was an original, being no man's copy. And his ministry and writings show they are from one that was not taught of man, nor had learned what he said by study. Nor were they notional or speculative, but sensible and practical truths, tending to conversion and regeneration and the setting up of the Kingdom of God in the hearts of men; and the way of it was his work, so that I have many times been overcome in myself and been made to say with my Lord and Master upon the like occasion, "I thank Thee, O Father, Lord of heaven and earth, that Thou hast hid these things from the wise and prudent of this world, and revealed them to babes." For many times hath my soul bowed in a humble thankfulness to the Lord that He did not choose any of the wise and learned of this world to be the first messenger in our age of His blessed Truth to men, but that He took one that was not of high degree or elegant speech or learned after the way of this world, that His message and work He sent him to do might come with less suspicion or jealousy of human wisdom and interest, and with more force and clearness upon the consciences of those that sincerely sought the way of Truth in the love of it. I say, beholding with the eye of my mind, which the God of heaven had opened in me, the marks of God's finger and hand visibly in this testimony from the clearness of the principle, the power and efficacy of it, in the exemplary sobriety, plainness, zeal, steadiness, humility, gravity, punctuality, charity, and circumspect care in the government of church affairs which shined in his and their life and testimony that God employed in this work, it greatly confirmed me that it was of God, and engaged my soul in a deep love, fear, reverence, and thankfulness for His love and mercy therein to mankind, in which mind I remain and shall, I hope, through the Lord's strength, to the end of my days.

II. In his testimony or ministry, he much labored to open Truth to the people's understandings and to bottom them upon the principle and principal, Christ Jesus, the Light of the World, that by bringing them to something that was from God in themselves, they might the better know and judge of Him and themselves.

III. He had an extraordinary gift in opening the Scriptures. He would go to the marrow of things, and show the mind, harmony, and fulfilling of them with much plainness and to great comfort and edification.

IV. The mystery of the first and second Adam, of the fall and restoration, of the law and gospel, of shadows and substance, of the servant's and son's state, and the fulfilling of the Scriptures in Christ and by Christ, the true Light, in all that are His through the obedience of faith, were much of the substance and drift of his testimonies. In all which he was witnessed to be of God, being sensibly felt to speak that which he had received of Christ and was his own experience, in that which never errs or fails.

V. But above all he excelled in prayer. The inwardness and weight of his spirit, the reverence and solemnity of his address and behavior, and the fewness and fullness of his words, have often struck even strangers with admiration, as they used to reach others with consolation. The most awful,[27] living, reverent frame I ever felt or beheld, I must say, was his in prayer. And truly it was a testimony he knew and lived nearer to the Lord than other men, for they that know Him most will see most reason to approach Him with reverence and fear.

VI. He was of an innocent life, no busybody nor self-seeker, neither touchy nor critical. What fell from him was very inoffensive, if not very edifying. [He was] so meek, contented, modest, easy, steady, tender, it was a pleasure to be in his company. He exercised no authority but over evil, and that everywhere and in all, but with love, compassion, and long-suffering. A most merciful man, as ready to forgive as unapt to take or give an offense. Thousands can truly say he was of an excellent spirit and savor among them, and because thereof the most excellent spirits loved him with an unfeigned and unfading love.

VII. He was an incessant laborer, for in his younger time, before his many great and deep sufferings and travails had enfeebled his body for itinerant services, he labored much in the word and doctrine and discipline in England, Scotland, and Ireland, turning many to God and confirming those that were convinced of the Truth, and settling good order as to church affairs among them. And toward the conclusion of his traveling services, between the years '71 and '77, he visited the churches of Christ in the plantations in America and in the United Provinces and Germany,[28] as his journal relates, to the convincement and consolation of many. After that time, he chiefly resided in and about the city of London, and besides his labor in the ministry, which was frequent and serviceable, he wrote much, both to them that are within and those that are without the communion.

[27] Awe-inspiring.
[28] Fox and twelve companions journeyed through the American colonies between 1671 and 1673, visiting Barbados, Jamaica, and all the North American provinces from North Carolina to Rhode Island. In 1677 he traveled through Holland and northern Germany with a number of Friends, including William Penn himself, who wrote an account of the trip. Fox visited Holland again in 1684.

But the care he took of the affairs of the church in general was very great.

VIII. He was often where the records of the business of the church are kept, and where the letters from the many meetings of God's people over all the world use to come, which letters he had read to him and communicated them to the meeting that is weekly held there for such services;[29] and he would be sure to stir them up to answer them, especially in suffering cases, showing great sympathy and compassion upon all such occasions, carefully looking into the respective cases and endeavoring speedy relief, according to the nature of them. So that the churches, or any of the suffering members thereof, were sure not to be forgotten or delayed in their desires, if he were there.

IX. As he was unwearied, so he was undaunted in his services for God and His people; he was no more to be moved to fear than to wrath. His behavior at Derby, Lichfield, Appleby, before Oliver Cromwell, at Launceston, Scarborough, Worcester, and Westminster Hall,[30] with many other places and exercises, did abundantly evidence it to his enemies as well as his friends.

But as in the primitive times, some rose up against the blessed apostles of our Lord Jesus Christ, even from among those that they had turned to the hope of the gospel, and they became their greatest trouble; so this man of God had his share of suffering from some that were convinced by him, who through prejudice or mistake ran against him as one that sought dominion over conscience because he pressed, by his presence or epistles, a ready and zealous compliance with such good and wholesome things as tended to an orderly conversation about

[29] The Meeting for Sufferings, which still meets, though now on a monthly basis, and serves as the executive body of the Society of Friends in Great Britain.

[30] Fox suffered imprisonments at Derby, at Launceston, at Scarborough, and at Worcester. He was tried twice before the King's Bench at Westminster Hall. In 1651, under the influence of strong religious emotion, he strode barefoot through the cathedral town of Lichfield, crying, "Woe to the bloody city of Lichfield!" He had several interviews with Oliver Cromwell, in which he addressed the Lord Protector in his usual forthright manner; after one such interview Cromwell said: "Come again to my house, for if thou and I were but an hour in a day together, we should be nearer one to the other." It is not clear what incident Penn has in mind at Appleby, but a number of Friends were tried and imprisoned there in 1652. All the incidents in which Fox was involved are described in his *Journal*.

the affairs of the church and in their walking before men. That which contributed much to this ill work was in some a begrudging of this meek man the love and esteem he had and deserved in the hearts of the people, and weakness in others that were taken with their ground-less suggestions of imposition and blind obedience.

They would have had every man independent,[31] that as he had the principle in himself, he should only stand and fall to that and nobody else, not considering that the principle is one in all. And though the measure of light or grace might differ, yet the nature of it was the same, and being so, they struck at the spiritual unity which a people guided by the same principle are naturally led into. So that what is an evil to one is so to all, and what is virtuous, honest, and of good re-pute to one is so to all from the sense and savor of the one universal principle which is common to all, and which the disaffected also profess to be the root of all true Christian fellowship and that spirit into which the people of God drink and come to be spiritually minded and of one heart and one soul.

Some weakly mistook good order in the government of church affairs for discipline in worship, and that it was so pressed or recom-mended by him and other brethren.[32] And thereupon they were ready to reflect the same things that dissenters had very reasonably objected upon the national churches that have coercively pressed conformity to their respective creeds and worships, whereas these things related wholly to conversation and the outward (and as I may say) civil part of the church, that men should walk[33] up to the principles of their belief and not be wanting in care and charity. But though some have stumbled and fallen through mistakes and an unreasonable obstinacy,

[31] Penn is here referring to the followers of John Perrot, who took an extremely subjective view of the Inward Light. They objected, among other things, to the custom of removing the hat in meeting when someone offered vocal prayer; hence this dispute, which occurred in the years 1661–1664 was known as the "hat controversy."

[32] This controversy, which followed upon Fox's activity in setting up a system of Monthly Meetings for discipline, lasted throughout the decade of the 1670's. The leading opponents of Fox were John Wilkinson and John Story, two of the "First Publishers of Truth."

[33] Act.

even to a prejudice, yet, blessed be God, the generality have returned
to their first love and seen the work of the enemy, that loses no opportunity or advantage by which he may check or hinder the work of
God and disquiet the peace of His church and chill the love of His
people to the Truth and one to another, and there is hope of divers
of the few that yet are at a distance.

In all these occasions, though there was no person the discontented
struck so sharply at as this good man, he bore all their weakness and
prejudice, and returned not reflection for reflection, but forgave them
their weak and bitter speeches, praying for them that they might have
a sense of their hurt, and see the subtlety of the enemy to rend and
divide, and return into their first love that thought no ill.

And truly I must say that though God had visibly clothed him with
a divine preference and authority, and indeed his very presence expressed a religious majesty, yet he never abused it, but held his place in
the church of God with great meekness and a most engaging humility
and moderation. For upon all occasions, like his blessed Master, he
was a servant to all, holding and exercising his eldership in the invisible
power that had gathered them with reverence to the Head and care
over the body, and was received only in that spirit and power of
Christ as the first and chief elder in this age who, as he was therefore
worthy of double honor, so for the same reason it was given by the
faithful of this day, because his authority was inward and not outward, and that he got it and kept it by the love of God and power of
an endless life. I write my knowledge, and not report; and my witness
is true, having been with him for weeks and months together on divers
occasions, and those of the nearest and most exercising nature, and
that by night and by day, by sea and by land, in this and in foreign
countries; and I can say I never saw him out of his place or not a match
for every service or occasion.

For in all things he acquitted himself like a man, yea, a strong man,
a new and heavenly-minded man, a divine and a naturalist, and all of
God Almighty's making. I have been surprised at his questions and
answers in natural things, that whilst he was ignorant of useless and
sophistical science, he had in him the grounds of useful and com-

mendable knowledge, and cherished it everywhere. [He was] civil beyond all forms of breeding in his behavior; very temperate, eating little and sleeping less, though a bulky person.

Thus he lived and sojourned among us; and as he lived, so he died, feeling the same eternal power that had raised and preserved him in his last moments. So full of assurance was he that he triumphed over death; and so even in his spirit to the last, as if death were hardly worth notice or a mention, recommending to some of us with him the dispatch and dispersion of an epistle just before given forth by him to the churches of Christ throughout the world, and his own books; but above all, Friends, and of all Friends, those in Ireland and America, twice over saying, "Mind poor Friends in Ireland and America." And to some that came in and inquired how he found himself, he answered, "Never heed; the Lord's power is over all weakness and death; the seed reigns, blessed be the Lord"; which was about four or five hours before his departure out of this world.

He was at the great meeting near Lombard Street on the First day of the week, and it was the Third following, about ten at night, when he left us, being at the house of Henry Gouldney in the same court.[34] In a good old age he went, after having lived to see his children's children to many generations in the Truth. He had the comfort of a short illness and the blessing of a clear sense to the last; and we may truly say, with a man of God of old, that being dead he yet speaketh, and though now absent in body he is present in spirit, neither time nor place being able to interrupt the communion of saints or dissolve the fellowships of the spirits of the just. His works praise him because they are to the praise of Him that worked by him, for which his memorial is and shall be blessed. I have done . . . when I have left this short epitaph to his name: "Many sons have done virtuously in this day, but, dear George, thou excellest them all."

[34] Fox died on January 13, 1691.

The Ethics of Radical Christianity

William Penn's most famous book, No Cross, No Crown, was conceived and written in its original form in the Tower of London, where he was a prisoner for conscience' sake in 1668 and 1669. It belongs to a long and honorable tradition of great books written behind bars—a tradition that includes Boethius' The Consolation of Philosophy, Sir Walter Raleigh's History of the World, Bunyan's The Pilgrim's Progress, and Nehru's Glimpses of World History. In substance it is a protracted sermon on the theme succinctly announced in its title: the necessity for the Christian to take up the Cross of Christ, to deny himself and the "world," if he would inherit the crown of eternal life.

This truth, indeed this very language, was Thomas Loe's legacy to him, the last message of the Quaker minister to whom he owed his "convincement" as a Friend, his conversion from the world of high fashion. Taking him by the hand, the dying minister had exhorted him: "Dear heart, bear thy cross; stand faithful for God and bear thy testimony in thy day and generation, and God will give thee an eternal crown of glory that none shall ever take from thee." Locked up in the Tower a few weeks later (for publishing The Sandy Foundation Shaken, which the government chose to consider a blasphemous attack on the Trinity), Penn bore his personal cross faithfully. "My prison shall be my grave," he informed the Bishop of London, "before I will budge a jot, for I owe my conscience to no mortal man." He used his enforced leisure to bear testimony in words to the Quaker way of life which he had adopted as his own.

It was inevitable that No Cross, No Crown should be deeply colored by the Puritan passion for moral righteousness. Quakerism, after all, had emerged out of the Puritan movement, and though the Puritan supremacy had passed, its characteristic austerity, its strenuous moral code, its rigorous nonconformity to the "world" remained central in the Quaker ethic. Penn's book was, first of all, a trenchant Puritan commentary on the follies, the immoralities, the unabashed worldliness of Restoration England. Pride, avarice, and luxury—these were the chief enemies of the soul in Charles II's kingdom, and the greatest of these, said Penn, was pride.

44

Whoso then would bear the Cross of Christ and win the eternal crown must wage ceaseless war on these besetting temptations.

Some of the specific manifestations of pride, avarice, and luxury against which Penn inveighs may seem out of date, and Penn's attitude may strike a modern as intolerably stuffy and strait-laced—especially his Quakerish fear of the imagination, which leads him to issue what amounts to a blanket proscription of all poetry, music, and drama. Yet one recalls that the moral tone of the Restoration theater was not exactly elevating. And if Penn in these pages strikes us as a humorless killjoy, let us do him the justice to admit that he was not satisfied to be vaguely "against" sin like the legendary preacher reported by a certain President of the United States; on the contrary, he was frank and courageous in cataloguing the vices and peccadilloes of an amoral society. (His book has incidental value as social history: it provides corroborative evidence, if any were needed, that Restoration comedy was an accurate mirror of certain aspects of English life; and its animadversions on snobbery or pride of ancestry cast an indirect light on an important social phenomenon of the time—the rise of "upstart gentlemen," men of no family, who, like Penn's own father, had made their way even into court circles on the basis of success in trade or the professions.) And let us bear in mind too that no modern theologian has been able to omit the sins of pride, greed, and sensuality from the catalogue of human weaknesses which it is the business of religion to diagnose and, if possible, to cure.

Penn insists that the spiritual warfare against sin cannot be carried on by retreating from the scene of battle. This is the point of his scornful remarks about the monastic life. Here Penn is utterly Protestant: one cannot ask for a clearer statement of that distinctively Protestant ethic to which Max Weber, the German sociologist, gave the clumsy name of "intramundane asceticism." The monkish life of retirement from the world, says Penn, is "a lazy, rusty, unprofitable self-denial." He who would carry the Cross of Christ must carry it in the midst of life; he must be in the world, though not of it. "True godliness," he proclaims in one of his most memorable sentences, "don't turn men out of the world, but enables them to live better in it, and excites their endeavors to mend it."

With this sentence Penn steps out of his Puritan framework and speaks in the distinctive accents of a Quaker. For Quakers, unlike most other Puritans, did not despair of the world; it was full of sin and suffering, to be sure, but it could be mended. Penn could not accept the Calvinist's easy rationalization that poverty and misery were but the visible signs of God's displeasure, the stigmata of damnation upon the lazy and indigent, and that there was no use therefore in trying to improve the lot of the unfortunate classes. He was a man of compassion; we should say he had a social conscience. He envisaged a time when there should be "no beggars in the land," when "the cry of the widow and the orphan would cease," and he linked his vision of justice for the poor to his condemnation of worldliness in the rich. His recommendations to the magistrates on this point are not too clear, but it appears that he had in mind some sort of levy on the wealthy—perhaps an excise tax—by which the money that would otherwise be wasted on expensive self-indulgence should be applied to the needs of the poor.

The first version of *No Cross, No Crown*—the one written in the Tower—was a slim volume barely a hundred pages long. The version the world remembers is the later revision and expansion—almost a new book—which fills nearly six hundred pages and was published in 1682, just as Penn was setting up his ideal commonwealth in America. This work contains some of Penn's most vigorous and colorful writing. It deserves a place, says Bonamy Dobrée, one of Penn's non-Quaker biographers, "not only in the literature of religion, but in literature without qualification." Charles Lamb, who was a good judge of prose style, liked it "immensely": it was "a capital book," he wrote to his friend Coleridge in 1797—"good thoughts in good language." We have drawn five little essays from five different parts of the book and given to each a descriptive title of our own.

From No Cross, No Crown (1669, 1682, 1694)

WORSHIP AND THE COMMON LIFE

That unlawful self in religion that ought to be mortified by the Cross of Christ is man's invention and performance of worship to God as divine which is not so either in its institution or performance. In this great error those people have the van of all that attribute to themselves the name of Christians that are most exterior, pompous, and superstitious in their worship; for they do not only miss exceedingly by a spiritual unpreparedness in the way of their performing worship to God Almighty, Who is an eternal spirit, but the worship itself is composed of what is utterly inconsistent with the very form and practice of Christ's doctrine and the apostolical example. For whereas that was plain and spiritual, this is gaudy and worldly; Christ's most inward and mental, theirs most outward and corporal; that suited to the nature of God, Who is a spirit, this accommodated to the most carnal part. So that instead of excluding flesh and blood, behold a worship calculated to gratify them, as if the business were not to present God with a worship to please Him but to make one to please themselves, a worship dressed with such stately buildings and imagery, rich furnitures and garments, rare voices and musics, costly lamps, wax candles, and perfumes, and all acted with that most pleasing variety to the external senses that art can invent or cost procure, as if the world were to turn Jew or Egyptian again or that God was an old man indeed and Christ a little boy to be treated with a kind of religious masque, for so they picture them in their temples and too many in their minds. And the truth is [that] such a worship may very well suit such an idea of God; for when men can think Him such a one as themselves, it is not to be wondered if they address to Him and entertain Him in a way that would be most pleasing from others to themselves. . . .

Nor is a recluse life (the boasted righteousness of some) much more commendable or one whit nearer to the nature of the true Cross; for if it be not unlawful as other things are, 'tis unnatural, which true religion teaches not. The Christian convent and monastery are within, where the soul is encloistered from sin; and this religious house the true followers of Christ carry about with them, who exempt not themselves from the conversation of the world, though they keep themselves from the evil of the world in their conversation. This is a lazy, rusty, unprofitable self-denial, burdensome to others to feed their idleness, religious bedlams[1] where people are kept up lest they should do mischief abroad: patience perforce, self-denial against their will, rather ignorant than virtuous, and out of the way of temptation than constant in it. No thanks if they commit not what they are not tempted to com-

[1] Madhouses—from the hospital of St. Mary of Bethlehem (Bedlam) in London.

mit. What the eye views not the heart craves not, as well as rues not.

The Cross of Christ is of another nature: it truly overcomes the world and leads a life of purity in the face of its allurements. They that bear it are not thus chained up for fear they should bite nor locked up lest they should be stole[n] away. No, they receive power from Christ, their captain, to resist the evil and do that which is good in the sight of God, to despise the world and love its reproach above its praise, and not only not to offend others but love those that offend them, though not for offending them. What a world should we have if everybody, for fear of transgressing, should mew himself up within four walls? No such matter; the perfection of Christian life extends to every honest labor or traffic used among men. This severity is not the effect of Christ's free spirit, but a voluntary, fleshly humility, mere trammels of their own making and putting on, without prescription or reason. In all which, 'tis plain, they are their own lawgivers and set their own rule, mulct, and ransom: a constrained harshness, out of joint to the rest of the creation, for society is one great end of it and [is] not to be destroyed for fear of evil, but sin [is to be] banished, that spoils it, by steady reproof and a conspicuous example of tried virtue. True godliness don't [sic] turn men out of the world, but enables them to live better in it and excites their endeavors to mend it: not hide their candle under a bushel but set it upon a table in a candlestick. Besides, 'tis a selfish invention; and that can never be the way of taking up the Cross which the true Cross is purely taken up to destroy. But again, this humor runs away by itself and leaves the world behind to be lost. Christians should keep the helm and guide the vessel to its port, not meanly steal out at the stern of the world and leave those that are in it without a pilot, to be driven by the fury of evil times upon the rock or sand of ruin. In fine, this sort of life, if taken up by young people, is to cover idleness or to pay portions, to save the lazy from the pain of punishment or quality from the disgrace of poverty; one won't work, and the other scorns it. If aged, a long life of guilt flies to superstition for a refuge, and after having had its own will in other things, would finish it in a willful religion to make God amends.

But taking up the Cross of Jesus is a more interior exercise—the circumspection and discipline of the soul in conformity to the divine mind there revealed. Does not the body follow the soul, and not the soul the body? Is it not preposterous, then, to think of limiting the soul by confining the body? Do not such consider that no outward cell can shut up the soul from lust, the mind from an infinity of unrighteous imaginations? The thoughts of man's heart are evil, and that continually. Evil comes from within and not from without; how then can an external application remove an internal cause, or a restraint upon the body work a confinement of the mind? Less much than without doors, for where there is least of action there is most time to think; and if those thoughts are not guided by a higher principle, convents are more mischievous to the world than exchanges. . . .

Not that I would be thought to slight a true retirement, for I do not only acknowledge but admire solitudes. Christ Himself was an example of it. He loved and chose to frequent mountains, gardens, seasides. They are requisite to the growth of piety, and I reverence the virtue that seeks and uses it, wishing there were more of it in the world. But then it should be free, not constrained. What benefit to the mind to have it for a punishment and not a pleasure? Nay, I have long thought it an error among all sorts that use not monastic lives that they have no retreats for the afflicted, the tempted, the solitary, and the devout, where they might undisturbedly wait upon God, pass through their religious exercises, and, being thereby strengthened, may with more power over their own spirits enter into the business of the world again, though the less the better, to be sure. For divine pleasures are found in a free solitude.[2]

PRIDE OF ANCESTRY

That people are generally proud of their persons is too visible and troublesome, especially if they have any pretense either to blood or beauty; the one has raised many quarrels among men, and the other among women, and men too often for their sakes and at their excite-

[2] The final paragraph, acknowledging the value of religious retreats, does not appear in the early editions of *No Cross, No Crown*; it was added by Penn in the edition of 1694.

ments. But to the first: what a pudder[3] has this noble blood made in the world: antiquity of name or family, whose father or mother, great-grandfather or great-grandmother was best descended or allied? What stock or what clan they came of? What coat of arms they gave? Which had of right the precedence? But methinks nothing of man's folly has less show of reason to palliate it.

For first, what matter is it of whom anyone is descended that is not of ill fame, since 'tis his own virtue that must raise or vice depress him? An ancestor's character is no excuse to a man's ill actions but an aggravation of his degeneracy. And since virtue comes not by generation, I neither am the better nor the worse for my forefather, to be sure, not in God's account nor should it be in man's. Nobody would endure injuries the easier or reject favors the more for coming by the hand of a man well or ill descended. I confess it were great honor to a house to have had no blots and with an hereditary estate to have had a lineal descent of worth; but that was never found, no, not in the most blessed of families upon earth, I mean Abraham's. To be descended of wealth and titles fills no man's head with brains nor heart with truth; those qualities come from a higher cause. 'Tis vanity, then, and most condemnable pride for a man of bulk and character to despise another of a less size in the world and of meaner alliance for want of them, because the latter may have the merit where the former has only the effects of it in an ancestor; and though the one be great by means of a forefather, the other is so too, but 'tis by his own. Then, pray, which is the bravest[4] man of the two?

Oh, says the person proud of blood, it was never good world since we have had so many upstart gentlemen. But what should those have said of that man's ancestor when he started first up into the knowledge of the world? For he, and all men and families, aye, and all states and kingdoms too have had their upstarts, that is, their beginnings. This is like being the true church because old, not because good, for families to be noble by being old and not by being virtuous. No such matter: it must be age in virtue or else virtue before age; for otherwise a

---

[3] Pother; i.e., commotion, uproar (originally, a cloud of dust).
[4] Worthiest.

man should be noble by the means of his predecessor and yet the predecessor less noble than he because he was the acquirer, which is a paradox that will puzzle all their heraldry to explain. Strange that they should be more noble than their ancestor that got their nobility for them! But if this be absurd, as it is, then the upstart is the nobleman, the man that got it by his virtue; and those are only entitled to his honor that are the imitators of his virtue; the rest may bear his name from his blood, but that is all. If virtue then give nobility (which heathens themselves agree), then families are no longer truly noble than they are virtuous. And if virtue go not by blood, but by the qualifications of the descendants, it follows [that] blood is excluded, else blood would bar virtue, and no man that wanted[5] one should be allowed the benefit of t'other, which were to stint and bound nobility for want of antiquity and make virtue useless. Such a nobility would be like our manors in England, which are held by custom, that is, ancient usage, which, because nothing so new as our own time can possibly be, no manor can be erected; that is, no nobility can be admitted, for old blood is wanting, though all blood be of an age. No, let blood and name go together, but pray let nobility and virtue keep company, for they are nearest of kin. 'Tis thus posited by God Himself, that best knows how to apportion things with an equal and just hand. He neither likes nor dislikes by descent, nor does He regard what people were, but [what they] are; He remembers not the righteousness of any man that leaves his righteousness, much less any unrighteous man for the righteousness of his ancestor.

THE ROOT OF ALL EVIL

And truly it is a reproach to a man, especially the religious man, that he knows not when he hath enough, when to leave off, when to be satisfied; that, notwithstanding God sends him one plenteous season of gain after another, is so far from making that the cause of withdrawing from the traffics of the world that he makes it a reason to launch further into it. The more he hath, the more he may. He therefore re-

[5] Lacked.

neweth his appetite, bestirs himself more than ever, that he may have his share in the scramble while anything is to be got. This is as if cumber, not retirement, and gain, not content were the duty and comfort of a Christian. Oh! that this thing were better considered! For by not being so observable nor obnoxious to the law as other vices are, there is the more danger for want of that check.

'Tis plain that most people strive not for subsistence but wealth. Some there be that love it strongly and spend it liberally when they have got it. Though this be sinful, yet more commendable than to love money for money's sake; that is one of the basest passions the mind of man can be captivated by, a perfect lust; and a greater and more soul-defiling one there is not in the catalogue of concupiscence, which considered, should quicken people into a serious examination how far this temptation of the love of money hath entered them; and the rather because the steps it maketh into the mind are almost insensible, which makes the danger greater. Thousands think themselves unconcerned in the caution that yet are perfectly guilty of the evil. How can it be otherwise when those that have from a low condition acquired thousands labor yet to advance those thousands and that with the same care and contrivance by which they got them? Is this to live comfortably or to be rich? Do we not see how early they rise, how late they go to bed? How full of the 'change, the shop, the warehouse, the customhouse, of bills, bonds, charter parties,[6] etc., they are running up and down as if it were to save the life of a condemned innocent? An insatiable lust and in that ungrateful to God (as well as hurtful to men), Who giveth it them to use and not to love; that's the abuse. And if this care, contrivance, and industry, and that continually, be not from the love of money in those that have ten times more than they began with (and much more than they spend or need), I know not what testimony man can give of his love to anything.

To conclude, it is an enemy to government in magistrates, for it tends to corruption, wherefore those that God ordained were such as feared Him and hated covetousness. Next, it hurts society, for old

---

[6] Contracts; specifically, agreements between shipowners and merchants for the hire of a ship and the safe delivery of a cargo.

traders keep the young ones poor, and the great reason why some have too little and so [are] forced to drudge like slaves to feed their families and keep their chin above water is because the rich hold hard to be richer and covet more, which dries up the little streams of profit from smaller folks. There should be a standard, both as to the quantity and time of traffic, and then the trade of the master to be shared amongst his servants that deserve it. This were both to help the young to get their livelihood and to give the old time to think of leaving this world well, in which they have been so busy, that they might obtain a share in the other, of which they have been so careless.

OF DRESS AND RECREATION

I am now come to the other extreme and that is luxury, which is an excessive indulgence of self in ease and pleasure. This is the last great impiety struck at in this discourse of the holy Cross of Christ, which indeed is much of the subject of its mortifying virtue and power; [it is] a disease as epidemical as killing. It creeps into all stations and ranks of men, the poorest often exceeding their ability to indulge their appetite and the rich frequently wallowing in those things that please the lusts of their eye and flesh, as regardless of the severe discipline of Jesus, whom they call Saviour, as if luxury, and not the Cross, were the ordained way to heaven. "What shall we eat?" "What shall we drink?" "And what shall we put on?"—once the care of luxurious heathens is now the practice and (which is worse) the study of pretended Christians. But let such be ashamed and repent, remembering that Jesus did not reproach the Gentiles for those things to indulge His followers in them. Sumptuous apparel, rich unguents, delicate washes, stately furniture, costly cookery, and such diversions as balls, masques, musics, plays, romances, etc., which are the delight and entertainment of the times, belong not to the holy path that Jesus and His true disciples and followers trod to glory....

Luxury has many parts, and the first that is forbidden by the self-denying Jesus is the belly. "Take no thought" (says He to His disciples) "saying 'What shall we eat, or what shall we drink?'—for after these things do the Gentiles seek"—that is, the uncircumcised, the heathen, such as live without the true God, and make a god of their belly, whose care is to please their appetite more than to seek God and His Kingdom. You must not do so, but "seek you first the Kingdom of God and His righteousness, and all other things shall be added." . . . This carries a serious reprehension to the luxurious eater and drinker who is taken up with an excessive care of his palate and belly, what he shall eat and what he shall drink, [is] often at a loss what to have next, and therefore has an officer to invent and a cook to dress, disguise, and drown the species that it may cheat the eye, look new and strange, and all to excite an appetite. To be sure, there is great variety, and that curious and costly, the sauce, it may be, dearer than the meat. And so full is he fed that without it he can scarce find out a stomach, which is to force a hunger rather than to satisfy it. And as he eats, he drinks; rarely for thirst, but [for] pleasure, to please his palate. For that purpose he will have divers sorts and he must taste them all: one, however good, is dull and tiresome. Variety is more delightful than the best, and therefore the whole world is little enough to fill his cellar. But were he temperate in his proportions, his variety might be imputed rather to curiosity than luxury. But what the temperate man uses as cordial, he drinks by full draughts till, inflamed by excess, he is fitted to be an instrument of mischief, if not to others, always to himself, whom perhaps at last he knows not. . . .

But there is another part of luxury which has great place with vain man and woman, and that is the gorgeousness of apparel, one of the foolishest (because most costly and unprofitable) excess[es] people can well be guilty of. We are taught by the Scriptures of Truth to believe that sin brought the first coat; and if consent of writers be of force, it was as well without as within. To those that so believe I direct my discourse, because they, I am sure, are the generality. I say, if sin brought the first coat, poor Adam's offspring have little reason to be proud or curious in their clothes, for it seems their original was base, and the finery of them will neither make them noble nor man innocent again. But doubtless blessed was that time when innocence, not ignorance, freed our first parents from such shifts; they were then naked and knew no shame, but sin made them ashamed to be longer naked. Since therefore guilt brought shame and shame an apron and a coat, how low are they fallen that glory in their shame, that are proud of their fall. For so they are that use care and cost to trim and set off the very badge and livery of that lamentable lapse.

It is all one as for a man that had lost his nose by a scandalous distemper to take pains to set out a false one in such shape and splendor as should give but the greater occasion for all to gaze upon him, as if he would tell them he had lost his nose for fear they should think he had not. But would a wise man be in love with such a false nose, however finely made? Surely no. And shall people that call themselves Christians show so much love for clothes as to neglect innocence, the first clothing? Doth it not show what cost of time and money people are at to set off their shame with the greatest show of folly? Is it not to delight in the effect of that cause for which they rather should lament?

If a thief were to wear chains all his life, would their being gold and well made abate his infamy? To be sure, his being choice of them would increase it. Why, this is the very case of the vain fashionmongers of this shameless age; yet will they be Christians, judges in religion, saints, what not? O miserable state indeed to be so blinded by the lust of the eye, the lust of the flesh, and pride of life, as to call shame decency and to be curious and expensive about that which should be their humiliation. And not only are they grown in love with these vanities and thereby express how wide they are from primitive innocence, but it's notorious how many fashions have been and are invented on purpose to excite to lust, which still puts them at greater distance from that harmless state and enslaves their minds to shameful concupiscence. . . .

That which further manifests the unlawfulness of these numerous fashions and recreations is that they are either the inventions of vain, idle, and wanton minds to gratify their own sensualities and raise the like wicked curiosity in others to imitate the same (by which nothing but lust and folly are promoted) or the contrivances of indigent and impoverished wits who make it the next way for their maintenance—

in both which respects and upon both which considerations they ought to be detested. For the first licenses express impiety and the latter countenances a wretched way of livelihood, and consequently diverts from more lawful, more serviceable, and more necessary employments.

That such persons are both the inventors and actors of all these follies cannot be difficult to demonstrate. For were it possible that anyone could bring us Father Adam's girdle and Mother Eve's apron, what laughing, what fleering, what mocking of their homely fashion would there be? Surely their tailor would find but little custom, although we hear 'twas God Himself that made them coats of skins. The like may be asked of all the other vanities concerning the holy men and women through all the generations of Holy Writ. How many pieces of ribbon, feathers, lace bands, and the like had Adam and Eve in Paradise or out of it? What rich embroideries, silks, points, etc., had Abel, Enoch, Noah, and good old Abraham? Did Eve, Sarah, Susanna, Elizabeth, and the Virgin Mary use to curl, powder, patch, paint, wear false locks of strange colors, rich points, trimmings, laced gowns, embroidered petticoats, shoes and slip-slaps[7] laced with silk or silver lace and ruffled like pigeons' feet, with several yards if not pieces of ribbons? How many plays did Jesus Christ and his apostles recreate themselves at? What poets, romances, comedies, and the like did the apostles and saints make or use to pass away their time withal? ...

But the best recreation is to do good. And all Christian customs tend to temperance and some good and beneficial end, which more or less may be in every action. For instance, if men and women would be diligent to follow their respective callings, frequent the assemblies of religious people, visit sober neighbors to be edified and wicked ones to reform them, be careful in the tuition of their children, exemplary to their servants, relieve the necessitous, see the sick, visit the imprisoned, administer to their infirmities and indispositions, endeavor peace amongst neighbors; also, study moderately such commendable and profitable arts as navigation, arithmetic, geometry, husbandry, handicraft, medicine; read the best reputed histories of ancient times;

[7] Slippers.

and that women spin, sew, knit, weave, garden, preserve, and the like housewife and honest employment (the practice of the greatest and noblest matrons and youth among the very heathens), helping others, who for want are unable to keep servants to ease them in their necessary affairs, often and private retirements from all worldly objects, to enjoy the Lord, secret and steady meditations on the divine life and heavenly inheritance—which to leave undone and prosecute other things under the notion of recreations is accursed lust and damnable impiety. It is most vain in any to object that they can't do these always, and therefore why mayn't they use these common diversions? For I ask what would such be at? What would they do? And what would they have? They that have trades have not time enough to do the half of what hath been recommended. And as for those who have nothing to do, and indeed do nothing (which is worse) but sin (which is worst of all), here is variety of pleasant, of profitable, nay, of very honorable employments and diversions for them. Such can with great delight sit at a play, a ball, a masque, at cards, dice, etc., drinking, reveling, feasting, and the like, an entire day; yes, turn night into day and invert the very order of the creation to humor their lusts. And were it not for eating and sleeping, it would be past a doubt whether they would ever find time to cease from those vain and sinful pastimes till the hasty calls of death should summon their appearance in another world. Yet do they think it intolerable and not possible for any to sit so long at a profitable or heavenly exercise?

RIGHTEOUSNESS AND SOCIAL POLICY

But the temperance I plead for is not only religiously but politically good; 'tis the interest of good government to curb and rebuke excesses. It prevents many mischiefs. Luxury brings effeminacy, laziness, poverty, and misery, but temperance preserves the land. It keeps out foreign vanities and improves our own commodities. Now we are their debtors; then they would be debtors to us for our native manufactures. By this means such persons who by their excess, not charity, have deeply engaged their estates may in short space be enabled to clear them from those encumbrances which otherwise, like moths, soon eat out very plentiful revenues. It helps persons of mean subsistence to improve their small stocks, that they may not expend their dear earnings and hard-got wages upon superfluous apparel, foolish May games, plays, dancing shows, taverns, alehouses, and the like folly and intemperance, of which this land is more infested and by which it's rendered more ridiculous than any kingdom in the world; for none I know of is so infested with cheating mountebanks, savage Morris dancers, pickpockets, and profane players and stagers to the slight of religion, the shame of government, and the great idleness, expense, and debauchery of the people. For which the spirit of the Lord is grieved and the judgments of the Almighty are at the door, and the sentence ready to be pronounced: Let him that is unjust, be unjust still. Wherefore it is that we cannot but loudly call upon the generality of the times and testify both by our life and doctrine against the like vanities and abuses if possibly any may be weaned from their folly and choose the good old path of temperance, wisdom, gravity, and holiness, the only way to inherit the blessings of peace and plenty here and eternal happiness hereafter.

Lastly, supposing we had none of these foregoing and important reasons to justify ourselves and justly to reprove the practice of the land in these particulars, however, let it be sufficient for us to say that when people have first learned to fear, worship, and obey their Creator, to pay their numerous vicious debts, to alleviate and abate their oppressed tenants, but above all outward regard, when the pale faces are more commiserated, the pinched bellies relieved and naked backs clothed, when the famished poor, the distressed widow, and helpless orphan (God's works and your fellow creatures) are provided for, then, I say (if then), it will be early enough for you to plead the indifferency of your pleasures. But that the sweat and tedious labor of the husbandman early and late, cold and hot, wet and dry, should be converted into the pleasure, ease, and pastime of a small number of men, that the cart, the plow, the thrash[8] should be in that continual severity laid upon nineteen parts of the land, to feed the inordinate lusts and de-

---

[8] Threshing implement, flail.

icious appetites of the twentieth, is so far from the appointment of
the great Governor of the World and God of the spirits of all flesh,
that to imagine such horrible injustice as the effect of His determinations and not the intemperance of men were wretched and blasphe-
nous. . . .

I therefore humbly offer an address to the serious consideration of
the civil magistrate, that if the money which is expended in every
parish in such vain fashions as wearing of laces, jewels, embroideries,
unnecessary ribbons, trimming, costly furniture and attendance, together with what is commonly consumed in taverns, feasts, gaming,
etc., could be collected in a public stock or something in lieu of this
extravagant and fruitless expense, there might be reparations to the
broken tenants, workhouses for the able, and almshouses for the aged
and impotent. Then should we have no beggars in the land, the cry
of the widow and the orphan would cease, and charitable reliefs might
easily be afforded toward the redemption of poor captives and refresh-
ment of such distressed Protestants as labor under the miseries of
persecution in other countries. Nay, the Exchequer's needs on just
emergencies might be supplied by such a bank. This sacrifice and
service would please the just and merciful God; it would be a noble
example of gravity and temperance to foreign states and an unspeak-
able benefit to ourselves at home.

Alas, why should men need persuasions to what their own felicity
so necessarily leads them to? Had these *Vitiosos*[9] of the times but a
sense of heathen Cato's generosity, they would rather deny their carnal
appetites than leave such noble enterprises unattempted. But that they
should eat, drink, play, game, and sport away their health, estates, and
above all their irrevocable precious time, which should be dedicated
to the Lord as a necessary introduction to a blessed eternity (and than
which, did they but know it, no worldly solace can come in competi-
tion), I say that they should be continually employed about these
poor, low things is to have the heathens judge them in God's day as
well as Christian precepts and examples condemn them. And their
final doom will prove the more astonishing in that this vanity and

[9] Vicious, depraved men.

excess are acted under a profession of the self-denying religion of
Jesus, Whose life and doctrine are a perpetual reproach to the most of
Christians. For He, blessed man, was humble, but they are proud; He
forgiving, they revengeful; He meek, they fierce; He plain, they gaudy;
He abstemious, they luxurious; He chaste, they lascivious; He a pilgrim
on earth, they citizens of the world. In fine, He was meanly born,
poorly attended, and obscurely brought up, lived despised, and died
hated of the men of His own nation. O you pretended followers of
this crucified Jesus, examine yourselves, try yourselves; know you not
your own selves, if He dwell not, if He rule not in you, that you are
reprobates? Be ye not deceived, for God will not be mocked at last with
forced repentances: such as you sow, such you shall, such you must
reap in God's day. . . .

But if you will daily bear the holy Cross of Christ and sow to the
Spirit; if you will listen to the light and grace that come by Jesus, and
which He has given to all people for salvation, and square your
thoughts, words, and deeds thereby, which leads and teaches the lover
of it to deny all ungodliness and the world's lusts and to live soberly,
righteously, and godly in this present evil world, then may you with
confidence look for the blessed hope and joyful coming and glorious
appearing of the great God and our Saviour Jesus Christ. . . . Remember that NO CROSS, NO CROWN.

2
The Christian Statesman

For Freedom of Religion

Admiral Penn's son became a Quaker when it cost most in terms of social ostracism, economic hardship, and personal suffering. Charles II's Cavalier Parliament had passed the harsh penal laws known collectively as the Clarendon Code—a whip with four cords designed to scourge every trace of Puritanism out of England. The avowed object of the Corporation Act (1661), the Act of Uniformity (1662), the Conventicle Act (1664), and the Five Mile Act (1665) was to outlaw all dissent from the Church of England, and impose a monolithic uniformity of religious belief (or at least of religious practice) upon the nation. Under this code the jails were crowded with pious men and women whose only crime was worshiping God as their consciences directed. The persecution of dissenters was general but the brunt of it fell on the Quakers; as one of them later put it: "We were the bulwark that received the shot." The Conventicle Act (forbidding nonconformist religious meetings of more than five persons) was the government's most effective weapon in its war against the Quakers. For the Friends, refusing to go underground, continued to hold their religious meetings openly. Consequently they were easy marks for the rancorous and vindictive magistrate abetted by his jackal crew of paid informers. "They go like lambs, without any resistance," wrote Samuel Pepys, who added compassionately, "I would to God they would either conform, or be more wise, and not be catched." During the quarter-century when Charles II was on the throne, no less than fifteen thousand Quakers were in prison. Four hundred and fifty died in jail.

Penn had his first taste of this treatment in Ireland only a few weeks after his "convincement" as a Quaker in 1667. Over the next two decades he was to become familiar with the inside of a number of English prisons. When he wrote against persecution, therefore, he knew whereof he spoke. But he was not concerned only for his own rights and those of his fellow Quakers. His commitment to freedom of conscience was absolute: he would extend it to all men without exception. To the literature of toleration he contributed nearly a dozen effective pamphlets, but the most systematic and compendious was his first, *The Great Case of Liberty of*

Conscience Once More Briefly Debated and Defended, which he com
posed in Ireland in 1670, the year when religious persecution in Restora
tion England reached its climax with the passage of the second Convent
cle Act—an act which the poet Andrew Marvell called "the quintessenc
of arbitrary malice." Under its terms a single justice, sitting without jury
could convict; fines could be recovered by distraint proceedings, an
one-third of the fine went to the informer. Though *The Great Case* wa
called forth by the desperate circumstances of 1670, its arguments fo
religious freedom are general and timeless. It has rightly been calle
(by A. A. Seaton) "the completest exposition of the theory of toleration
produced in Restoration England.

The most remarkable thing about this tract is the extraordinary rang
of Penn's arguments. He was not content to rest his case against perse
cution upon purely theological, religious, and Scriptural grounds, thoug
he did not neglect the well-worn arguments from these sources (we hav
omitted a collection of biblical quotations which make up Chapter III)
But he knew that the men in power whom he must persuade wer
worldly men, apt to be influenced chiefly by rational and pragmatic con
siderations. So he devoted a chapter to proving that persecution was con
trary to nature and reason, those twin deities which were beginning to ex
ercise a sway over the minds of men comparable to that once held b
dogma and Holy Writ. In this chapter Penn anticipates the spirit c
Thomas Jefferson's great Virginia statute of religious freedom, written mor
than a century later. In his next chapter, still arguing on the secular level, h
submits that religious persecution cannot be reconciled with good gover
ment because it is unjust, imprudent, and destructive of the people'
happiness. At the age of twenty-four, a full dozen years before he launche
his own political experiment in Pennsylvania, Penn was obviousl
thinking deeply about the nature, administration, and purposes of gover
ment.

His sixth chapter is omitted here, though it is highly characteristic c
his method of persuasion. It consists of "a brief collection of the sense an
practice of the greatest, wisest, and learned'st commonwealths, kingdom:
and particular persons of their times, concerning force upon conscience.
Here he refers briefly to the tolerant practices of the ancient Jews, Roman·
and Egyptians, as well as certain modern nations. He does not neglect t
point out how toleration promotes national prosperity. No country, h
submits, is "so improved in wealth, trade and power" as Holland. An
does she not owe it to "her indulgence in matters of faith and worship?
Even the infidels, he thinks, can teach the Christian nations something

Among the very Mahometans of Turkey and Persia, what variety of opinions, yet what unity and concord is there! We mean in matters of a civil
importance." He then summons a cloud of witnesses to testify on the wisdom and justice of toleration—classical writers like Cato and Tacitus,
church fathers like Justin Martyr and Tertullian, Reformers like Luther
and Calvin, monarchs like the kings of Poland and Bohemia, English
writers like Sir Walter Raleigh and Jeremy Taylor and even Geoffrey Chau-
cer ("whose matter," he adds, "and not his poetry heartily affects me").

Religious toleration, though not complete religious freedom—there is a
difference—finally came to England with the passage of the great Act of
Toleration in 1689. The theory behind that act received its definitive expression at the hands of John Locke in his *Letter Concerning Toleration*.
How much effect Penn's *The Great Case* may have had in preparing the
way for that victory cannot be measured. Neither can we tell how much
the world owes to the patience of those Quakers like William Penn who by
their willingness to suffer for their beliefs finally wearied out the malice of
the persecutors and brought the dawn of toleration closer. No doubt both
argument and example were important, and to a Quaker argument was of
little force unless supported by example. In reading Penn's cogent and
eloquent case against persecution one should remember that he made
his witness by suffering as well as by writing.

There were at least three printings of *The Great Case* in 1670. The
edition on which our text is based, is dated "Newgate, the 7th of the
12th month, called February, 1670."

The Great Case of Liberty of Conscience (1670)

THE PREFACE

Were some as Christian as they boast themselves to be, 'twould save
us all the labor we bestow in rendering persecution so unchristian as it
most truly is. Nay, were they those men of reason they character themselves, and what the civil law styles good citizens, it had been needless
for us to tell them that neither can any external coercive power con-

vince the understanding of the poorest idiot nor fines and prisons b
judged fit and adequate penalties for faults purely intellectual, as we
as that they are destructive of all civil government.

But we need not run so far as beyond the seas to fetch the sense c
the codes, institutes, and digests out of the *Corpus Civile*[1] to adjudg
such practices incongruous with the good of civil society, since our ow
good old admirable laws of England have made such excellent prov
sion for its inhabitants that if they were but thought as fit to be execute
by this present age as they were rightly judged necessary to be mad
by our careful ancestors, we know how great a stroke they would giv
such as venture to lead away our property in triumph as our just forfe
ture for only worshiping our God in a differing way from that which
more generally professed and established.

And indeed, it is most truly lamentable that above others who hav
been found in so unnatural and antichristian an employment thos
that by their own frequent practices and voluminous apologies hav
defended a separation from the Papacy should now become such earr
est persecuters for it, not considering that the enaction of such laws a
restrain persons from the free exercise of their consciences in matte
of religion is but a knotting whipcord to lash their own posterity, who
they can never promise to be conformed to a national religion. Na
since mankind is subject to such mutability, they can't ensure them
selves from being taken by some persuasions that are esteemed heter
dox, and consequently catch themselves in snares of their own provic
ing. And [for] men thus liable to change and no ways certain of the
own belief to be the most infallible (as by their multiplied concessior
may appear) to enact any religion or prohibit persons from the fre
exercise of theirs sounds harsh in the ears of all modest and unbiase
men. We are bold to say our Protestant ancestors thought of nothin
less than to be succeeded by persons vainglorious of their Reformatio
and yet adversaries to liberty of conscience, for to people in their wi
it seems a paradox.

[1] The Code, the Institutes, and the Digest are the three parts of the *Corp
Juris Civilis*, the great body of Roman law compiled 529–536 by order of t
Emperor Justinian, which still forms the basis of most European law codes.

Not that we are so ignorant as to think it is within the reach of human power to fetter conscience or to restrain its liberty strictly taken. But that plain English of liberty of conscience we would be understood to mean is this; namely, the free and uninterrupted exercise of our conscience in that way of worship we are most clearly persuaded God requires us to serve Him in (without endangering our undoubted birthright of English freedoms), which, being matter of faith, we sin if we omit, and they can't do less that shall endeavor it.

To tell us we are obstinate and enemies to government are but those groundless phrases the first Reformers were not a little pestered with; but as they said, so say we: the being called this or that does not conclude us so, and hitherto we have not been detected of that fact, which only justifies such criminations.

But however free we can approve ourselves of actions prejudicial of the civil government, 'tis most certain we have not suffered a little as criminals, and therefore have been far from being free from sufferings, indeed, in some respect, horrid plunders. Widows have lost their cows, orphans their beds, and laborers their tools—a tragedy so sad that methinks it should oblige them to do in England as they did at Athens when they had sacrificed their divine Socrates to the sottish fury of their lewd and comical multitude: they so regretted their hasty murder that not only the memorial of Socrates was most venerable with them but his enemies they esteemed so much theirs that none would trade or hold the least commerce with them, for which some turned their own executioners and, without any other warrant than their own guilt, hanged themselves. How near akin the wretched mercenary informers of our age are to those the great resemblance that is betwixt their actions manifestly shows.

And we are bold to say the grand fomenters of persecution are no better friends to the English state then were Anytus and Aristophanes[2] of old to that of Athens, the case being so nearly the same as that they did not more bitterly envy the reputation of Socrates amongst the Athenians for his grave and religious lectures, thereby giving the youth

---

[2] Anytus was one of Socrates' accusers. Aristophanes satirized Socrates in his comedy *The Clouds*.

a diversion from frequenting their plays, than some now emulate[3] the true dissenter for his pious life and great industry. And as that famous commonwealth was noted to decline and the most observing persons of it dated its decay from that illegal and ungrateful carriage toward Socrates—witness their dreadful plagues, with other multiplied disasters—so is it not less worthy [of] observation that Heaven hath not been wholly wanting to scourge this land for as well their cruelty to the conscientious as their other multiplied provocations.[4]

And when we seriously consider the dreadful judgments that now impend the nation by reason of the robbery, violence, and unwonted oppression that almost everywhere have not only been committed upon the poor, the widow, and the fatherless, but most tenaciously justified and the actors manifestly encouraged, in mere pity and concern for the everlasting welfare of such as have not quite sinned away their visitation—for some have—we once more bring to public view our reasons against persecution, backed with the plainest instances both of Scripture and antiquity, if but one may be persuaded to desist from making any further progress in such an anti-Protestant and truly anti-Christian path as that of persecuting honest and virtuous Englishmen for only worshiping the God that made them in the way they judge most acceptable with Him.

But if those who ought to think themselves obliged to weigh these affairs with the greatest deliberation will obstinately close their eyes to these last remonstrances and slightly[5] overlook the pinching case of so many thousand families that are by these severities exposed for prey to the insatiable appetites of a villainous crew of broken informers (daubing themselves with that deluding apprehension of pleasing God or at least of profiting the country whilst they greatly displease the one and evidently ruin the other), as certain as ever the Lord God Almighty destroyed Sodom and laid waste Gomorrah by the consuming flames

[3] Envy.
[4] Penn is no doubt referring here to the Plague of 1665 and the Great Fire of London which followed in 1666.
[5] Indifferently.

of His just indignation, will He hasten to make desolate this wanton land and not leave a hiding place for the oppressor.

Let no man therefore think himself too big to be admonished nor put too slight a value upon the lives, liberties, and properties of so many thousand freeborn English families embarked in that one concern of liberty of conscience. It will become him better to reflect upon his own mortality and not forget his breath is in his nostrils, and that every action of his life the everlasting God will bring to judgment and him for them.

CHAPTER I

. . . First, by liberty of conscience we understand not only a mere liberty of the mind in believing or disbelieving this or that principle or doctrine, but the exercise of ourselves in a visible way of worship upon our believing it to be indispensably required at our hands, that if we neglect it for fear or favor of any mortal man we sin and incur divine wrath. Yet we would be so understood to extend and justify the lawfulness of our so meeting to worship God as not to contrive or abet any contrivance destructive of the government and laws of the land tending to matters of an external nature, directly or indirectly, but so far only as it may refer to religious matters and a life to come and consequently wholly independent of the secular affairs of this wherein we are supposed to transgress.

Secondly, by imposition, restraint, and persecution we don't only mean the strict requiring of us to believe this to be true or that to be false, and, upon refusal, to incur the penalties enacted in such cases, but by those terms we mean thus much: any coercive let or hindrance to us from meeting together to perform those religious exercises which are according to our faith and persuasion.

For proof of the aforesaid terms thus given we singly state the question thus: whether imposition, restraint, and persecution upon persons for exercising such a liberty of conscience as is before expressed and so circumstantiated be not to impeach the honor of God, the meekness of the Christian religion, the authority of Scripture, the privilege of nature, the principles of common reason, the well-being of government, and apprehensions of the greatest personages of former and latter ages.

First, then, we say that imposition, restraint, and persecution for matters relating to conscience directly invade divine prerogative and divest the Almighty of a due, proper to none besides Himself. And this we prove by these five particulars:

First, if we do allow the honor of our creation due to God only and that no other besides Himself has endowed us with those excellent gifts of understanding, reason, judgment, and faith, and consequently that He only is the object as well as author both of our faith, worship, and service, then whoever shall interpose their authority to enact faith and worship in a way that seems not to us congruous with what He has discovered to us to be faith and worship (Whose alone property it is to do it) or to restrain us from what we are persuaded is our indispensable duty, they evidently usurp this authority and invade His incommunicable right of government over conscience. For the inspiration of the Almighty gives understanding, and faith is the gift of God, says the Divine Writ.[6]

Secondly, such magisterial determinations carry an evident claim to that infallibility which Protestants have been hitherto so jealous of owning that, to avoid the Papists, they have denied it to all but God Himself. Either they have forsook their old plea, or if not, we desire to know when and where they were invested with that divine excellency, and that imposition, restraint, and persecution were deemed by God ever the fruits of His spirit. However, that itself were not sufficient, for unless it appear as well to us that they have it as to them who have it, we cannot believe it upon any convincing evidence but by tradition only, an anti-Protestant way of believing.

Thirdly, it enthrones man as king over conscience, the alone just claim and privilege of his Creator, Whose thoughts are not as men's thoughts but [Who] has reserved to Himself that empire from all the Caesars on earth. For if men in reference to souls and bodies—things appertaining to this and t'other world—shall be subject to their fellow

[6] Job xxxii. 8; Ephesians ii. 8.

creatures, what follows but that Caesar, however he got it, has all God's share and his own too, and, being lord of both, both are Caesar's and nothing God's?

Fourthly, it defeats the work of His grace and the invisible operation of His eternal Spirit, which can alone beget faith and is only to be obeyed in and about religion and worship, and attributes men's conformity to outward force and corporal punishments—a faith subject to as many revolutions as the powers that enact it.

Fifthly and lastly, such persons assume the judgment of the great tribunal unto themselves; for to whomsoever men are imposedly or restrictively subject and accountable in matters of faith, worship, and conscience, in them alone must the power of judgment reside; but it is equally true that God shall judge all by Jesus Christ and that no man is so accountable to his fellow creatures as to be imposed upon, restrained, or persecuted for any matter of conscience whatever.

Thus and in many more particulars are men accustomed to entrench upon divine property to gratify particular interests in the world, and at best through a misguided apprehension to imagine they do God good service, that where they cannot give faith, they will use force, which kind of sacrifice is nothing less unreasonable than the other is abominable. God will not give His honor to another; and to Him only that searches the heart and tries the reins it is our duty to ascribe the gifts of understanding and faith without which none can please God.

CHAPTER II

The next great evil which attends external force in matters of faith and worship is no less than the overthrow of the whole Christian religion, and this we will briefly evidence in these four particulars: (first) that there can be nothing more remote from the nature, (secondly) the practice, (thirdly) the promotion, (fourthly) the rewards of it.

First, it is the privilege of the Christian faith above the dark suggestions of ancient and modern superstitious traditions to carry with it a most self-evidencing verity, which ever was sufficient to proselyte believers without the weak auxiliaries of external power. The Son of

God and great example of the world was so far from calling His Father's omnipotency in legions of angels to His defense that He at once repealed all acts of force and defined unto us the nature of His religion in this one great saying of His: "My kingdom is not of this world." It was spiritual, not carnal, accompanied with weapons as heavenly as its own nature, and designed for the good and salvation of the soul and not the injury and destruction of the body: no jails, fines, exiles, etc., but sound reason, clear truth, and a strict life. In short, the Christian religion entreats all but compels none.

Secondly, that restraint and persecution overturn the practice of it I need go no further than the allowed martyrologies of several ages, of which the Scriptures claim a share: begin with Abel, go down to Moses, so to the prophets, and then to the meek example of Jesus Christ Himself—how patiently devoted was He to undergo the contradictions of men and so far from persecuting any that He would not so much as revile His persecutors but prayed for them. Thus lived His apostles and the true Christians of the first three hundred years. Nor are the famous stories of our first Reformers silent in the matter; witness the Christian practices of the Waldenses, Lollards, Hussites,[7] Lutherans, and our noble martyrs who, as became the true followers of Jesus Christ, enacted and confirmed their religion with their own blood and not with the blood of their opposers.

Thirdly, restraint and persecution obstructs the promotion of the Christian religion, for if such as restrain confess themselves miserable sinners and altogether imperfect, it either follows that they never desire to be better or that they should encourage such as may be capable of further informing and reforming them. They condemn the Papists for encoffening[8] the Scriptures and their worship in an unknown tongue, and yet are guilty themselves of the same kind of fact.

[7] The Waldenses, Lollards, and Hussites were religious groups which developed quasi-Protestant ideas before the Protestant Reformation and suffered persecution for their beliefs. The Waldenses, disciples of Peter Waldo (d. 1217), arose in southern France and later spread to northern Italy, where they still exist as a church. The Lollards were English heretics, followers of John Wyclif (d. 1384). The Hussites accepted the teachings of the Bohemian reformer John Hus (d. 1415).

[8] Shutting up, hiding away (literally, putting into a coffin).

Fourthly, they prevent[9] many of eternal rewards, for where any are religious for fear, and that of men, 'tis slavish, and the recompense of such religion is condemnation, not peace. Besides, 'tis man that is served, who having no power but what is temporary, his reward must needs be so too; he that imposes a duty or restrains from one, must reward, but because no man can reward for such duties, no man can or ought to impose them or restrain from them. So that we conclude imposition, restraint, and persecution are destructive of the Christian religion in the nature, practice, promotion, and rewards of it, which are eternal.

CHAPTER IV

We further say that imposition, restraint, and persecution are also destructive of the great privilege of nature and principle of reason. Of nature in three instances:

1. If God Almighty has made of one blood all nations as Himself has declared, and that He has given them both senses corporal and intellectual to discern things and their differences, so as to assert or deny from evidences and reasons proper to each, then where any enacts the belief or disbelief of anything upon the rest or restrains any from the exercise of their faith to them indispensable, such exalts himself beyond his bounds, enslaves his fellow creatures, invades their right of liberty, and so perverts the whole order of nature.

2. Mankind is hereby robbed of the use and benefit of that instinct of a deity which is so natural to him that he can be no more without it and be than he can be without the most essential part of himself. For to what serves that divine principle in the universality of mankind if men be restricted by the prescriptions of some individuals? But if the excellent nature of it inclines men to God, not man; if the power of accusing and excusing be committed to it; if the troubled thought and sad reflections of forlorn and dying men make their tendency that way only, as being hopeless of all other relief and succor from any external power or command, what shall we say but that such as invalidate the authority of this heavenly instinct (as imposition and

[9] Deprive.

restraint evidently do) destroy nature or that privilege which men are born with and to?

All natural affection is destroyed, for those who have so little tenderness as to persecute men that cannot for conscience' sake yield them compliance manifestly act injuriously to their fellow creatures, and consequently are enemies to nature; for nature, being one in all, such as ruin those who are equally entitled with themselves to nature ruin it in them, as in liberty, property, etc., and so bring the state of nature to the state of war, [as] the great Leviathan of the times as ignorantly as boldly does assert.[10]

But secondly, we also prove them destructive of the noble principle of reason, and that in these eight particulars:

1. In that those who impose or restrain are uncertain of the truth and justifiableness of their actions in either of these, their own discourses and confessions are pregnant instances, where they tell us that they do not pretend to be infallible, only they humbly conceive 'tis thus, or it is not.

2. Since, then, they are uncertain and fallible, how can they impose upon or restrain others whom they are so far from assuring as they are not able to do so much for themselves? What is this but to impose an uncertain faith upon certain penalties?

3. As he that acts doubtfully is damned, so faith in all acts of religion is necessary. Now, in order to believe, we must first will; to will, we must first judge; to judge anything, we must first understand. If, then, we cannot be said to understand anything against our understanding, no more can we judge, will, and believe against our understanding. And if the doubter be damned, what must he be that conforms directly against his judgment and belief, and they, likewise, that require it from him? In short, that man cannot be said to have any religion that takes it by another man's choice, not his own.

4. Where men are limited in matters of religion, there the rewards which are entailed on the free acts of men are quite overthrown, and

[10] Penn is undoubtedly referring here to the ideas of Thomas Hobbes, who declared in his *Leviathan* (1651) that the state of nature was a state of constant and universal warfare.

such as supersede that grand charter of liberty of conscience frustrate all hopes of recompense by rendering the actions of men unavoidable. But those think perhaps they do not destroy all freedom because they use so much of their own.

5. They subvert all true religion, for where men believe, not because it is true but because they are required to do so, there they will unbelieve, not because 'tis false, but so commanded by their superiors, whose authority their interest and security oblige them rather to obey than dispute.

6. They delude, or rather compel, people out of their eternal rewards, for where men are commanded to act in reference to religion and can neither be secured of their rewards nor yet saved harmless from punishments, their so acting and believing disprivileges them forever of that recompense which is provided for the faithful.

7. Men have their liberty and choice in external matters; they are not compelled to marry this person, to converse with that, to buy here, to eat there, nor to sleep yonder. Yet if men had power to impose or restrain in anything, one would think it should be in such exterior matters; but that this liberty should be unquestioned and that of the mind destroyed issues here, that it does not unbrute us, but unman us, for take away understanding, reason, judgment, and faith, and, like Nebuchadnezzar, let us go graze with the beasts of the field.

8. That which most of all blackens the business is persecution, for though it is very unreasonable to require faith where men cannot choose but doubt, yet after all to punish them for disobedience, 'tis cruelty in the abstract, for, we demand, shall men suffer for not doing what they cannot do? Must they be persecuted here if they do not go against their consciences, and punished hereafter if they do? But neither is this all, for that part that is yet most unreasonable and that gives the clearest sight of persecution is still behind; namely, the monstrous arguments they have to convince a heretic with—not those of old, as spiritual as the Christian religion, which were to admonish, warn, and finally to reject, but such as were employed by the persecuting Jews and heathens against the great example of the world and such as followed Him, and by the inhuman Papists against our first Re-

formers, as clubs, staves, stocks, pillories, prisons, dungeons, exiles, etc.
—in a word, ruin to whole families, as if it were not so much their
design to convince the soul as to destroy the body.

To conclude, there ought to be an adequation and resemblance betwixt all ends and the means to them, but in this case there can be
none imaginable; the end is the conformity of our judgments and
understandings to the acts of such as require it; the means are fines
and imprisonments and bloody knocks to boot. Now, what proportion
or assimulation[11] these bear, let the sober judge. The understanding
can never be convinced nor properly submit but by such arguments as
are rational, persuasive, and suitable to its own nature, something that
can resolve its doubts, answer its objections, enervate its propositions;
but to imagine those barbarous Newgate[12] instruments of clubs, fines,
prisons, etc., with that whole troop of external and dumb materials of
force should be fit arguments to convince the understanding, scatter its
scruples, and finally convert it to their religion is altogether irrational,
cruel, and impossible. Force may make a hypocrite; 'tis faith grounded
upon knowledge and consent that makes a Christian. And to conclude,
as we can never betray the honor of our conformity (only due to
Truth) by a base and timorous hypocrisy to any external violence
under heaven, so must we needs say: unreasonable are those imposers
who secure not the imposed or restrained from what may occur to
them upon their account, and most inhuman are those persecutors
that punish men for not obeying them, though to their utter ruin.

CHAPTER V

We next urge that force in matters relating to conscience carries a
plain contradiction to government in the nature, execution, and end
of it. By government we understand an external order of justice or the
right and prudent disciplining of any society by just laws, either in the
relaxation or execution of them.

11 Resemblance.
12 The ancient jail in London, from which Penn, himself a prisoner for conscience' sake, issued the second edition of *The Great Case.*

First, it carries a contradiction to government in the nature of it, which is justice, and that in three respects:

1. It is the first lesson that great synteresis[13] so much renowned by philosophers and civilians learns mankind to do as he would be done to, since he that gives what he would not take or takes what he would not give only shows care for himself, but neither kindness nor justice for another.

2. The just nature of government lies in a fair and equal retribution, but what can be more unequal than that men should be rated more than their proportion to answer the necessities of government and yet that they should not only receive no protection from it but by it be disseized[14] of their dear liberty and properties? We say, to be compelled to pay that power that exerts itself to ruin those that pay it or that any should be required to enrich those that ruin them is hard and unequal, and therefore contrary to the just nature of government. If we must be contributaries to the maintenance of it, we are entitled to a protection from it.

3. It is the justice of government to proportion penalties to the crime committed. Now granting our dissent to be a fault, yet the infliction of a corporal or external punishment for a mere mental error (and that not voluntarily too) is unreasonable and inadequate as well as against particular directions of the Scriptures (Titus iii. 9, 10, 11).[15] For as corporal penalties cannot convince the understanding, so neither can they be commensurate punishments for faults purely intellectual. And for the government of this world to intermeddle with what belongs to the government of another and which can have no ill aspect or influence upon it shows more of invasion than right and justice.

Secondly, it carries a contradiction to government in the execution of it, which is prudence, and that in these instances:

[13] The function or department of conscience that serves as a guide to conduct.
[14] Dispossessed.
[15] "Avoid foolish questions, and genealogies, and contentions, and strivings about the law; for they are unprofitable and vain. . . ."

1. The state of the case is this, that there is no republic so great, no empire so vast, but the laws of them are resolvable into these two series or heads of laws fundamental, which are indispensable and immutable, and laws superficial, which are temporary and alterable. And as it is justice and prudence to be punctual in the execution of the former, so by circumstances it may be neither to execute the latter, they being suited to the present convenience and emergency of state, as the prohibiting of cattle out of Ireland was judged of advantage to the farmers of England, yet a murrain[16] would make it the good of the whole that the law should be broke[n] or at least the execution of it suspended. That the law of restraint in point of conscience is of this number we may further manifest and the imprudence of thinking otherwise: for, first, if the saying were as true as 'tis false, "No bishop, no king"[17] (which admits of various readings, as, No decimating clergy or no persecution, no king), we should be as silent as some would have us; but the confidence of their assertion and the impolicy of such as believe it makes us to say that a greater injury cannot be done to the present government. For if such laws and establishments are fundamental, they are as immutable as mankind itself; but that they are as alterable as the conjectures and opinions of governors have been is evident, since the same fundamental indispensable laws and policy of these kingdoms have still remained through all variety of opposite ruling opinions and judgments and disjoint[18] from them all. Therefore to admit such a fixation to temporary laws must needs be highly imprudent and destructive of the essential parts of the government of these countries.

2. That since there has been a time of connivance,[19] and that with no ill success to public affairs, it cannot be prudence to discontinue it

---

[16] A disease affecting domestic animals.

[17] This remark of James I at the Hampton Court conference of 1604 expressed his conviction that a uniform Church controlled by bishops and responsible to the Crown was necessary to the stability and security of the monarchy.

[18] Separate.

[19] An official shutting of the eyes to the non-execution of the laws. There was a brief lull in persecution in 1668 after the fall of the Earl of Clarendon, who had given his name to the harsh code of laws against dissenters.

unless it was imprudence before to give it, and such little deserve it that think so.

3. Dissenters not being conscious to themselves of any just forfeiture of that favor are as well grieved in their resentments of this alteration as the contrary did oblige them to very grateful acknowledgments.

4. This must be done to gratify all, or the greatest part, or but some few only. It is a demonstration all are not pleased with it; that the greatest number is not the empty public auditories will speak. In short, how should either be when six parties are sacrificed to the seventh? That this cannot be prudence common maxims and observations prove.

5. It strikes fatally at Protestant sincerity, for will the Papists say: Did Protestants exclaim against us for persecutors, and are they now the men themselves? Was it an instance of weakness in our religion, and is it become a demonstration in theirs? Have they transmuted it from anti-Christian in us to Christian in themselves? Let persecutors answer.

6. It is not only an example but an incentive to the Romanists to persecute the Reformed religion abroad, for when they see their actions (once void of all excuse) now defended by the example of Protestants that once accused them (but now themselves), doubtless they will revive their cruelty.

7. It overturns the very ground of the Protestants' retreat from Rome, for if men must be restrained upon pretended prudential considerations from the exercise of their conscience in England, why not the same in France, Holland, Germany, Constantinople, etc., where matters of state may equally be pleaded? This makes religion state policy, and faith and worship subservient to the humors and interests of superiors. Such doctrine would have prevented our ancestors' retreat, and we wish it be not the beginning of a back march, for some think it shrewdly to be suspected, where religion is suited to the government and conscience to its conveniency.

8. Vice is encouraged, for if licentious persons see men of virtue molested for assembling with a religious purpose to reverence and worship God and that are otherwise most serviceable to the commonwealth, they may and will infer it is better for them to be as they are,

since not to be demure,[20] as they call it, is halfway to that kind of accomplishment which procures preferment.

9. For such persons as are so poor-spirited as to truckle under such restraints, what conquest is there over them that before were conscientious men and now hypocrites? Who so forward to be avenged of them that brought this guilt upon them as they themselves? And how can the imposers be secure of their friendship whom they have taught to change with the times?

10. Such laws are so far from benefiting the country that the execution of them will be the assured ruin of it in the revenues and consequently in the power of it. For where there is a decay of families, there will be of trade, so of wealth, and, in the end, of strength and power; and if both kinds of relief fail—men, the prop of republics; money, the stay of monarchies (this[21] as requiring mercenaries, that[22] as needing freemen)—farewell the interest of England. 'Tis true the priests get (though that's but for a time), but the king and people lose, as the event will show.

11. It ever was the prudence of wise magistrates to oblige their people, but what comes shorter of it than persecution? What's dearer to them than the liberty of their conscience? What cannot they better spare than it? Their peace consists in the enjoyment of it, and he that by compliance has lost it carries his penalty with him and is his own prison. Surely such practices must render the government uneasy and beget a great disrespect to the governors in the hearts of the people.

12. But that which concludes our prudential part shall be this: that after all their pains and good will to stretch men to their measure, they never will be able to accomplish their end, and if he be an unwise man that provides means where he designs no end, how near is he kin to him that proposes an end unobtainable? Experience has told us how invective[23] it has made the imposed, what distractions have ensued such attempts, what reproach has followed to the Christian religion,

[20] Sober, staid.
[21] The latter; i.e., monarchies.
[22] The former; i.e., republics.
[23] Abusive, vituperative.

when the professors of it have used a coercive power upon conscience. And lastly, that force never yet made either a good Christian or a good subject.

Thirdly and lastly, since the proceedings we argue against are proved so destructive to the justice and prudence of government, we ought the less to wonder that they should hold the same malignity against the end of it, which is felicity, since the wonder would be to find it otherwise; and this is evident from these three brief considerations:

1. Peace (the end of war and government, and its great happiness too) has been, is, and yet will be broken by the frequent tumultuary disturbances that ensue the disquieting our meetings and the estreating[24] fines upon our goods and estates. And what these things may issue in concerneth the civil magistrate to consider.

2. Plenty (another great end of government) will be converted into poverty by the destruction of so many thousand families as refuse compliance and conformity, and that not only to the sufferers but influentially to all the rest—a demonstration of which we have in all those places where the late Act[25] has been anything considerably put in execution. Besides, how great provocation such incharity and cruel usage as stripping widows, fatherless, and poor of their very necessaries for human life merely upon an account of faith or worship must needs be to the just and righteous Lord of Heaven and earth, Scriptures and plenty of other stories plainly show us.

3. Unity (not the least but greatest end of government) is lost, for by seeking a unity of opinion by the ways intended, the unity requisite to uphold us as a civil society will be quite destroyed. And such as relinquish that to get the other, besides that they are unwise, will infallibly lose both in the end.

In short, we say that 'tis unreasonable we should not be entertained[26] as men because some think we are not as good Christians as they pretend to wish us, or that we should be deprived of our liberties and

[24] Levying.
[25] The second Conventicle Act.
[26] Treated.

properties who never broke the laws that gave them to us. What can be harder than to take that from us by a law which the great indulgence and solicitude of our ancestors took so much pains to entail upon us by law? [*Here Penn cites Magna Charta, the Petition of Right, and a number of English statutes safeguarding liberty and property.*]

And we are persuaded that no temporary subsequential law whatever to our fundamental rights (as this of force on conscience is) can invalidate so essential a part of the government as an English liberty and property. Nor that it's in the power of any on earth to deprive us of them till we have first done it ourselves by such enormous facts as those very laws prohibit and make our forfeiture of that benefit we should otherwise receive by them. For these being such cardinal and fundamental points of English law-doctrine, individually and by the collective body of the people agreed to, and on which, as the most solid basis, our secondary legislative power as well as executive is built, it seems most rational that the superstructure cannot quarrel or invalidate its own foundation without manifestly endangering its own security; the effect is ever less noble than the cause, the gift than the giver, and the superstructure than the foundation. The single question to be resolved in the case, briefly, will be this: whether any visible authority (being founded in its primitive institution upon those fundamental laws that inviolably preserve the people in all their just rights and privileges) may invalidate all or any of the said laws without an implicit shaking of its own foundation and a clear overthrow of its own constitution of government and so reduce them to their *statu quo prius* or first principles. The resolution is every man's at his own pleasure. . . .

Those who intend us no share or interest in the laws of England as they relate to civil matters unless we correspond with them in points of faith and worship must do two things: first, it will lie heavy on their parts to prove that the ancient compact and original of our laws carries that proviso with it, else we are manifestly disseized of our free customs.

Secondly, they are to prove the reasonableness of such proceedings to our understandings, that we may not be concluded[27] by a law we

[27] Restrained.

know not how to understand. For if I take the matter rightly (as I think I do), we must not buy or sell unless of this or that persuasion in religion, not considering civil society was in the world before the Protestant profession. Men as such and in affairs peculiarly relative of them in an external and civil capacity have subsisted many ages under great variety of religious apprehensions, and therefore [are] not so dependent on them as to receive any variation or revolution with them. What shall we say, then, but that some will not that we should live, breathe, and commerce as men because we are not such modeled Christians as they coercively would have us? They might with as much justice and reputation to themselves forbid us to look or see, unless our eyes were grey, black, brown, blue, or some one color best suiting theirs. For not to be able to give us faith or save our consciences harmless, and yet to persecute us for refusing conformity is intolerable hard measure.

In short, that coercive way of bringing all men to their height of persuasion must either arise from exorbitant zeal and superstition or from a consciousness of error and defect, which is unwilling anything more sincere and reformed should take place, being of that cardinal's mind who therefore would not hearken to a reformation at the sitting of the Council of Trent because he would not so far approve the reformers' judgment (for having once condescended to their apprehensions, he thought 'twould forever enslave them to their sense), though otherwise he saw as much as any man the grand necessity of a reformation both of the Roman doctrine and conversation. . . .

To conclude, liberty of conscience, as thus stated and defended, we ask as our undoubted right by the law of God, of nature, and of our own country. It has been often promised; we have long waited for it; we have writ much and suffered more in its defense, and have made many true complaints, but found little or no redress.

However, we take the righteous Holy God to record against all objections that are ignorantly or designedly raised against us, that

(1st) we hold no principle destructive of the English government;

(2nd) that we plead for no such dissenter (if such a one there be);

(3d) that we desire the temporal and eternal happiness of all persons (in submission to the divine will of God), heartily forgiving our cruel persecutors;

(4thly and lastly) we shall engage by God's assistance to lead peaceable, just, and industrious lives amongst men to the good and example of all. But if after all we have said, this short discourse should not be credited nor answered in any of its sober reasons and requests, but sufferings should be the present lot of our inheritance from this generation, be it known to them all that meet we must and meet we cannot but encourage all to do, whatever hardship we sustain in God's name and authority, Who is Lord of Hosts and King of Kings, at the revelation of Whose righteous judgments and glorious tribunal mortal men shall render an account of the deeds done in the body. And whatever the apprehensions of such may be concerning this discourse, 'twas writ in love and from a true sense of the present state of things, and time and the event will vindicate it from untruth. In the meanwhile, 'tis matter of great satisfaction to the author that he has so plainly cleared his conscience in pleading for the liberty of other mens' and publicly borne his honest testimony for God not out of season to his poor country.

Liberty on Trial

Experience taught William Penn, as it has taught other men before and since, that human liberty is indivisible, that when one freedom is under attack, all are in danger, that he who would defend it in one area must be watchful to prevent assaults at other points. Only a few months after he had finished the first version of *The Great Case of Liberty of Conscience*, he found himself in the Old Bailey in London, defending not so much himself as one of the fundamental rights of Englishmen—the right of a man to a free and uncoerced judgment by a jury of his peers. The trial of William Penn and William Mead in 1670 is a landmark in the history of English liberty.

The circumstances that led up to this famous trial can be briefly related. In the summer of 1670 the newly built Quaker meetinghouse at White Hart Court in Gracechurch Street, London, was seized, padlocked, and placed under guard. Undaunted, the Friends held their meetings for worship in the street outside the meetinghouse. On August 14, 1670, William Penn preached there to a concourse of several hundred persons, including many "rude people who came mostly to gaze." The presence of so many non-Quaker onlookers made the proceedings somewhat disorderly, and the soldiers who were stationed there tried unsuccessfully to reach Penn to arrest him as a fomenter of riot. At the end of the meeting Penn and William Mead, a recently convinced Quaker who had once been a captain in Cromwell's army, voluntarily put themselves in the soldiers' hands. They were taken before the Lord Mayor, who committed them to prison on charges of riot.

Their trial opened at the Old Bailey on September 1, 1670, and ran for four days. It was promptly reported in the pamphlet entitled *The People's Ancient and Just Liberties Asserted*, which is reprinted here. Based apparently on a stenographic report, the pamphlet presents an extraordinarily vivid and exciting courtroom drama. With very little rewriting or editing it has provided the script for several effective radio and television plays in recent years. In reproducing it here we have taken no liberties whatever with the text beyond modernizing the spelling and punctuation and omitting the word "Obser[vation]" which regularly prefaces the passages which serve as stage directions. What part Penn had in preparing and publishing the pamphlet is unknown. It has been suggested that it was largely the work of Thomas Rudyard, a Quaker lawyer. But Penn himself, who plays the leading role in the drama, was obviously well acquainted with the law—he had, after all, studied at Lincoln's Inn—and he undoubtedly had something to do with the production of the pamphlet.

The sequel of the dramatic Penn-Mead trial was of the utmost importance in the history of English liberty. The twelve jurymen, who had stoutly refused to violate their own consciences by rendering the verdict against Penn and Mead that the Court demanded, were sent to Newgate prison, from which they were presently released on a writ of *habeas corpus*. Thereupon they sued the Lord Mayor and the Recorder for illegal punishment. Their suit was tried before a full bench of twelve justices, who decided that a jury must have the right to hand in a verdict based on the facts as they saw them without coercion from the bench. A judge, the court said, "may try to open the eyes of the jurors, but not to lead them by the nose." Sir John Vaughan, the Lord Chief Justice, who delivered the decision, put the issue clearly: "If the judge from the evidence shall by his own judgment first resolve what the law is; and order the jury penally to find accordingly, what either necessary or convenient use can be fancied of juries, or to continue trials by them at all?"

"Bushel's case"—it takes its name from Edward Bushel, the stalwart juryman who nerved his fellow jurors to take their stand—established the independence of the jury beyond question in English (and American) courts. William Penn's courageous defiance of persecution in Gracechurch Street provided the occasion and his stirring defense of English rights in the courtroom the major inspiration for this notable triumph. For Penn the cause of liberty was a holy cause and any victory in its behalf was a victory for the spirit of man, which was the candle of the Lord.

The People's Ancient and Just Liberties Asserted (1670)

There being present on the bench as justices:

Samuel Starling, Mayor	John Robinson, Alderman
John Howell, Recorder	Joseph Shelden, Alderman
Thomas Bludworth, Alderman	Richard Brown, [Alderman]
William Peak, Alderman	John Smith ⎫
Richard Ford, Alderman	James Edwards ⎬ Sheriffs

The citizens of London that were summoned for jurors appearing were impaneled, viz:

CLERK. Call over the jury.

CRIER. Oyez. Thomas Veer, Edward Bushel, John Hammond, Charles Milson, Gregory Walklet, John Brightman, William Plumstead, Henry Henley, James Damask, Henry Michel, William Lever, John Baily.

The Form of the Oath

You shall well and truly try and true deliverance make betwixt our Sovereign Lord the King and the prisoners at the bar, according to your evidence, so help you God.

The Indictment

That William Penn, gentleman, and William Mead, late of London, linen draper, with divers other persons to the jurors unknown, to the number of three hundred, the 15th day of August, in the 22nd year of the King, about eleven of the clock in the forenoon the same day, with force and arms, etc., in the Parish of St. Bennet Gracechurch in Bridge Ward, London, in the street called Gracechurch Street, unlawfully and tumultuously did assemble and congregate themselves together to the disturbance of the peace of the said Lord the King. And the aforesaid William Penn and William Mead, together with other persons to the jurors aforesaid unknown, then and there so assembled and congregated together, the aforesaid William Penn by agreement between him and William Mead before made, and by abetment of the aforesaid William Mead, then and there in the open street did take upon himself to preach and speak and then and there did preach and speak unto the aforesaid William Mead and other persons there in the street aforesaid being assembled and congregated together, by reason whereof a great concourse and tumult of people in the street aforesaid then and there a long time did remain and continue in contempt of the said Lord the King and of his law to the great disturbance of his peace, to the great terror and disturbance of many of his liege people and subjects, to the ill example of all others in the like case offenders, and against the peace of the said Lord the King, his crown and dignity.

What say you, William Penn and William Mead, are you guilty as you stand indicted in manner and form as aforesaid, or not guilty?

PENN. It is impossible that we should be able to remember the indictment verbatim, and therefore we desire a copy of it, as is customary in the like occasions.

RECORDER. You must first plead to the indictment before you can have a copy of it.

PENN. I am unacquainted with the formality of the law and therefore before I shall answer directly I request two things of the Court. First, that no advantage may be taken against me nor I deprived of any benefit which I might otherwise have received. Secondly, that you will promise me a fair hearing and liberty of making my defense.

COURT. No advantage shall be taken against you. You shall have liberty; you shall be heard.

PENN. Then I plead not guilty in manner and form.

CLERK. What sayest thou, William Mead: art thou guilty in manner and form as thou standest indicted, or not guilty?

MEAD. I shall desire the same liberty as is promised to William Penn.

COURT. You shall have it.

MEAD. Then I plead not guilty in manner and form.

The Court adjourned until the afternoon.

CRIER. Oyez, etc.

CLERK. Bring William Penn and William Mead to the bar.

(The said prisoners were brought, but were set aside and other business prosecuted. Where we cannot choose but observe that it was the constant and unkind practice of the Court to the prisoners to make them wait upon the trials of felons and murderers, thereby designing in all probability both to affront and tire them.

(After five hours' attendance the Court broke up and adjourned to the third instant.)

The third of September, 1670, the Court sat.

CRIER. Oyez, etc.

MAYOR. Sirrah, who bid you put off their hats? Put on their hats again.

(Whereupon one of the officers, putting the prisoners' hats upon their heads, pursuant to the order of the Court, brought them to the bar.)

RECORDER. Do you know where you are?

PENN. Yes.

RECORDER. Do you know it is the King's Court?

PENN. I know it to be a Court, and I suppose it to be the King's Court.

RECORDER. Do you not know there is respect due to the Court?

PENN. Yes

RECORDER. Why do you not pay it then?

PENN. I do so.

RECORDER. Why do you not put off your hat then?

PENN. Because I do not believe that to be any respect.[1]

RECORDER. Well, the Court sets forty marks apiece upon your heads as a fine for your contempt of the Court.

PENN. I desire it might be observed that we came into the Court with our hats off (that is, taken off) and if they have been put on since, it was by order from the Bench, and therefore not we but the Bench should be fined.

MEAD. I have a question to ask the Recorder: Am I fined also?

RECORDER. Yes.

MEAD. I desire the jury and all people to take notice of this injustice of the Recorder, who spake not to me to pull off my hat, and yet hath he put a fine upon my head. O fear the Lord and dread His power, and yield to the guidance of His Holy Spirit, for He is not far from every one of you.

The Jury sworn again.

(*J. Robinson, Lieutenant of the Tower, disingenuously objected against Edward Bushel, as if he had not kissed the Book and therefore would have him sworn again, though indeed it was on purpose to have made use of his tenderness of conscience in avoiding reiterated oaths to have put him by his being a juryman, apprehending him to be a person not fit to answer their arbitrary ends.*)

(*The Clerk read the indictment as aforesaid.*)

CLERK. Crier, call James Cook into the Court; give him his oath.

CLERK. James Cook, lay your hand upon the Book: "The evidence you shall give to the Court, betwixt our Sovereign the King and the prisoners at the bar, shall be the truth, and the whole truth, and nothing but the truth, so help you God, etc."

COOK. I was sent for from the Exchange to go and disperse a meeting in Gracious Street, where I saw Mr. Penn speaking to the people, but I could not hear what he said because of the noise. I endeavored to

[1] The early Quakers bore a religious testimony against "hat-honor," i.e., against removing their hats as a mark of respect to social superiors or men in authority. This testimony reflected their belief in the equality of all men in the sight of God.

make way to take him, but I could not get to him for the crowd of people, upon which Captain Mead came to me about the kennel[2] of the street and desired me to let him go on, for when he had done he would bring Mr. Penn to me.

COURT. What number do you think might be there?

COOK. About three or four hundred people.

COURT. Call Richard Read; give him his oath.

(*Read, being sworn, was asked:* What do you know concerning the prisoners at the bar?)

READ. My Lord, I went to Gracious Street, where I found a great crowd of people, and I heard Mr. Penn preach to them, and I saw Captain Mead speaking to Lieutenant Cook, but what he said I could not tell.

MEAD. What did William Penn say?

READ. There was such a great noise that I could not tell what he said.

MEAD. Jury, observe this evidence; he saith he heard him preach, and yet saith he doth not know what he said.

Jury, take notice, he swears now a clean contrary thing to what he swore before the Mayor when we were committed; for now he swears that he saw me in Gracious Street, and yet swore before the Mayor when I was committed that he did not see me there. I appeal to the Mayor himself if this be not true (*but no answer was given.*)

COURT. What number do you think might be there?

READ. About four or five hundred.

PENN. I desire to know of him what day it was?

READ. The 14th day of August.

PENN. Did he speak to me, or let me know he was there, for I am very sure I never saw him.

CLERK. Crier, call ——— ——— into the Court.

COURT. Give him his oath.

——— ———. My Lord, I saw a great number of people, and Mr. Penn, I suppose, was speaking. I saw him make a motion with his hands

2 An open gutter which ran down the center or sides of the street.

and heard some noise but could not understand what he said; but for Captain Mead, I did not see him there.

RECORDER. What say you, Mr. Mead? Were you there?

MEAD. It is a maxim in your own law, *nemo tenetur accusare seipsum*,[3] which if it be not true Latin, I am sure that it is true English, that no man is bound to accuse himself. And why dost thou offer to ensnare me with such a question? Doth not this show thy malice? Is this like unto a judge that ought to be counsel for the prisoner at the bar?

RECORDER. Sir, hold your tongue; I did not go about to ensnare you.

PENN. I desire we may come more close to the point and that silence be commanded in the Court.

CRIER. Oyez, all manner of persons keep silence upon pain of imprisonment. Silence in the Court.

PENN. We confess ourselves to be so far from recanting or declining to vindicate the assembling of ourselves to preach, pray, or worship the eternal, holy, just God, that we declare to all the world that we do believe it to be our indispensable duty to meet incessantly upon so good an account. Nor shall all the powers upon earth be able to divert us from reverencing and adoring our God Who made us.

BROWN. You are not here for worshiping God, but for breaking the law. You do yourselves a great deal of wrong in going on in that discourse.

PENN. I affirm I have broken no law, nor am I guilty of the indictment that is laid to my charge. And to the end [that] the Bench, the jury, and myself, with these that hear us, may have a more direct understanding of this procedure, I desire you would let me know by what law it is you prosecute me and upon what law you ground my indictment.

RECORDER. Upon the common law.

---

[3] No man is required to incriminate himself. This ancient principle, which originated in the twelfth century, became established as part of the English common law in 1640 when "Freeborn John" Lilburne was vindicated by Parliament after refusing to incriminate himself on a charge of importing heretical and seditious books. This principle was written into the Fifth Amendment to the American Constitution in these words: "No person . . . shall be compelled in any criminal case to be a witness against himself."

PENN. Where is that common law?

RECORDER. You must not think that I am able to run up so many years and over so many adjudged cases which we call common law to answer your curiosity.

PENN. This answer, I am sure, is very short of my question, for if it be common, it should not be so hard to produce.

RECORDER. Sir, will you plead to your indictment?

PENN. Shall I plead to an indictment that hath no foundation in law? If it contain that law you say I have broken, why should you decline to produce that law, since it will be impossible for the jury to determine or agree to bring in their verdict who have not the law produced by which they should measure the truth of this indictment, and the guilt or contrary of my fact.

RECORDER. You are a saucy fellow. Speak to the indictment.

PENN. I say it is my place to speak to matter of law. I am arraigned a prisoner; my liberty, which is next to life itself, is now concerned; you are many mouths and ears against me, and if I must not be allowed to make the best of my case, it is hard. I say again, unless you show me and the people the law you ground your indictment upon, I shall take it for granted your proceedings are merely arbitrary.

(*At this time several upon the bench urged hard upon the prisoner to bear him down.*)

RECORDER. The question is whether you are guilty of this indictment.

PENN. The question is not whether I am guilty of this indictment, but whether this indictment be legal. It is too general and imperfect an answer to say it is the common law, unless we knew both where and what it is. For where there is no law there is no transgression, and that law which is not in being is so far from being common that it is no law at all.

RECORDER. You are an impertinent fellow. Will you teach the Court what law is? It's *lex non scripta*,[4] that which many have studied thirty or forty years to know, and would you have me tell you in a moment?

4 Unwritten law.

PENN. Certainly if the common law be so hard to be understood it's far from being very common; but if the Lord Coke[5] in his *Institutes* be of any consideration, he tells us that common law is common right, and that common right is the Great Charter privileges, confirmed 9 Hen. III, c.29; 25 Edw. I, c.1; 2 Edw. III, c.8; 2 Coke *Inst.* 56

RECORDER. Sir, you are a troublesome fellow, and it is not for the honor of the Court to suffer you to go on.

PENN. I have asked but one question, and you have not answered me, though the rights and privileges of every Englishman be concerned in it.

RECORDER. If I should suffer you to ask questions till tomorrow morning, you would be never the wiser.

PENN. That is according as the answers are.

RECORDER. Sir, we must not stand to hear you talk all night.

PENN. I design no affront to the Court, but to be heard in my just plea; and I must plainly tell you that if you will deny me oyer[6] of that law which you suggest I have broken, you do at once deny me an acknowledged right and evidence to the whole world your resolution to sacrifice the privileges of Englishmen to your sinister and arbitrary designs.

RECORDER. Take him away. My Lord, if you take not some course with this pestilent fellow to stop his mouth, we shall not be able to do anything tonight.

MAYOR. Take him away, take him away; turn him into the baildock.[7]

PENN. These are but so many vain exclamations. Is this justice or true judgment? Must I therefore be taken away because I plead for the fundamental laws of England? However, this I leave upon your consciences, who are of the jury and my sole judges, that if these

[5] Sir Edward Coke (1552–1634), Attorney General and later Chief Justice of England, was a vigorous upholder of the supremacy of the common law, and a zealous advocate of individual liberty. The *Institutes of the Laws of England* was his greatest work.

[6] The hearing of a document read in open court.

[7] A small closet in the corner of the courtroom, left open at the top.

ancient fundamental laws, which relate to liberty and property, and are not limited to particular persuasions in matters of religion, must not be indispensably maintained and observed, who can say he hath right to the coat upon his back? Certainly our liberties are openly to be invaded, our wives to be ravished, our children slaved, our families ruined, and our estates led away in triumph by every sturdy beggar and malicious informer as their trophies, but our pretended forfeits for conscience' sake. The Lord of heaven and earth will be judge between us in this matter.

RECORDER. Be silent there.

PENN. I am not to be silent in a case wherein I am so much concerned, and not only myself but many ten thousand families besides.

(They having rudely haled him into the bail-dock, William Mead they left in Court, who spake as followeth:)

MEAD. You men of the jury, here I do now stand to answer to an indictment against me which is a bundle of stuff, full of lies and falsehoods, for therein I am accused that I met vi et armis, illicite et tumultuose.[8] Time was when I had freedom to use a carnal weapon, and then I thought I feared no man; but now I fear the living God and dare not make use thereof, nor hurt any man, nor do I know I demeaned myself as a tumultuous person. I say I am a peaceable man; therefore it is a very proper question, what William Penn demanded in this case, an oyer of the law on which our indictment is grounded.

RECORDER. I have made answer to that already.

MEAD. (Turning his face to the jury, said:) You men of the jury, who are my judges, if the Recorder will not tell you what makes a riot, a rout, or an unlawful assembly, Coke, he that once they called the Lord Coke, tells us what makes a riot, a rout, and an unlawful assembly: a riot is when three or more are met together to beat a man, or to enter forcibly into another man's land to cut down his grass, his wood, or break down his pales.

(Here the Recorder interrupted him and said: I thank you sir, that you will tell me what the law is, scornfully pulling off his hat.)

[8] By force of arms, tumultuously and illegally.

MEAD. Thou mayest put on thy hat; I have never a fee for thee now.

BROWN. He talks at random, one while an Independent,[9] another while some other religion, and now a Quaker, and next a Papist.

MEAD. *Turpe est doctori cum culpa redarguit ipsum.*[10]

MAYOR. You deserve to have your tongue cut out.

RECORDER. If you discourse on this manner, I shall take occasion against you.

MEAD. Thou didst promise me I should have fair liberty to be heard. Why may I not have the privilege of an Englishman? I am an Englishman and you might be ashamed of this dealing.

RECORDER. I look upon you to be an enemy to the laws of England, which ought to be observed and kept, nor are you worthy of such privileges as others have.

MEAD. The Lord is judge between me and thee in this matter. (*Upon which they took him away into the bail-dock and the Recorder proceeded to give the jury their charge, as followeth:*)

RECORDER. You have heard what the indictment is. It is for preaching to the people and drawing a tumultuous company after them, and Mr. Penn was speaking. If they should not be disturbed, you see they will go on; there are three or four witnesses that have proved this, that he did preach there, that Mr. Mead did allow of it. After this you have heard by substantial witnesses what is said against them. Now we are upon the matter of fact, which you are to keep to and observe, as what hath been fully sworn, at your peril.

(*The prisoners were put out of the Court into the bail-dock, and the charge given to the jury in their absence, at which William Penn with a very raised voice, it being a considerable distance from the bench, spake:*)

PENN. I appeal to the jury, who are my judges, and this great assembly, whether the proceedings of the Court are not most arbitrary and void of all law in offering to give the jury their charge in the absence of the prisoners. I say it is directly opposite to and destructive of

[9] Congregationalist.
[10] It is a shameful thing for a learned man when his guilt refutes him.

the undoubted right of every English prisoner, as Coke in the 2 *Inst.*, 29. on the Chapter of Magna Charta speaks.

(*The Recorder being thus unexpectedly lashed for his extrajudicial procedure, said, with an enraged smile:*)

RECORDER. Why, ye are present; you do hear. Do you not?

PENN. No thanks to the Court that commanded me into the bail-dock; and you of the jury, take notice that I have not been heard, neither can you legally depart the Court before I have been fully heard, having at least ten or twelve material points to offer in order to invalidate their indictment.

RECORDER. Pull that fellow down, pull him down.

MEAD. Are these according to the rights and privileges of Englishmen, that we should not be heard, but turned into the bail-dock for making our defense, and the jury to have their charge given them in our absence? I say these are barbarous and unjust proceedings.

RECORDER. Take them away into the hole; to hear them talk all night as they would, that I think doth not become the honor of the Court, and I think you (*i.e.* the jury) yourselves would be tired out and not have patience to hear them.

(*The jury were commanded up to agree upon their verdict, the prisoners remaining in the stinking hole. After an hour and half's time, eight came down agreed, but four remained above. The Court sent an officer for them and they accordingly came down. The Bench used many unworthy threats to the four that dissented and the Recorder, addressing himself to Bushel, said: Sir, you are the cause of this disturbance, and manifestly show yourself an abettor of faction. I shall set a mark upon you, sir.*)

JOHN ROBINSON. Mr. Bushel, I have known you near this fourteen years. You have thrust yourself upon this jury because you think there is some service for you. I tell you you deserve to be indicted more than any man that hath been brought to the bar this day.

BUSHEL. No, Sir John, there were threescore before me, and I would willingly have got off, but could not.

BLUDWORTH. I said, when I saw Mr. Bushel, what I see is come to pass, for I knew he would never yield. Mr. Bushel, we know what you are.

MAYOR. Sirrah, you are an impudent fellow; I will put a mark upon you.

(*They used much menacing language and behaved themselves very imperiously to the jury, as persons not more void of justice than sober education. After this barbarous usage they sent them to consider of bringing in their verdict and after some considerable time they returned to the Court. Silence was called for and the jury called by their names.*)

CLERK. Are you agreed upon your verdict?

JURY. Yes.

CLERK. Who shall speak for you?

JURY. Our foreman.

CLERK. Look upon the prisoners at the bar. How say you? Is William Penn guilty of the matter whereof he stands indicted in manner and form, or not guilty?

FOREMAN. Guilty of speaking in Gracious Street.

COURT. Is that all?

FOREMAN. That is all I have in commission.

RECORDER. You had as good say nothing.

MAYOR. Was it not an unlawful assembly? You mean he was speaking to a tumult of people there?

FOREMAN. My Lord, this was all I had in commission.

(*Here some of the jury seemed to buckle to the questions of the Court, upon which Bushel, Hammond, and some others opposed themselves and said they allowed of no such word as an unlawful assembly in their verdict. At which the Recorder, Mayor, Robinson, and Bludworth took great occasion to vilify them with most opprobrious language, and this verdict not serving their turns, the Recorder expressed himself thus:*)

RECORDER. The law of England will not allow you to depart till you have given in your verdict.

JURY. We have given in our verdict and we can give in no other.

RECORDER. Gentlemen, you have not given in your verdict and you had as good say nothing. Therefore go and consider it once more that we may make an end of this troublesome business.

JURY. We desire we may have pen, ink, and paper.

(*The Court adjourns for half an hour, which being expired, the Court returns and the jury not long after. The prisoners were brought to the bar and the jury's names called over.*)

CLERK. Are you agreed of your verdict?

JURY. Yes.

CLERK. Who shall speak for you?

JURY. Our foreman.

CLERK. What say you? Look upon the prisoners. Is William Penn guilty in manner and form as he stands indicted, or not guilty?

FOREMAN. Here is our verdict (*holding forth a piece of paper to the clerk of the peace, which follows:*

We the jurors, hereafter named, do find William Penn to be guilty of speaking or preaching to an assembly met together in Gracious Street, the 14th of August last, 1670, and that William Mead is not guilty of the said indictment.

Foreman, Thomas Veer,	Henry Michel,	John Baily,
Edward Bushel,	John Brightman,	William Lever,
John Hammond,	Charles Milson,	James Damask,
Henry Henley,	Gregory Walklet,	William Plumstead.

(*This both Mayor and Recorder resented at so high a rate that they exceeded the bounds of all reason and civility.*)

MAYOR. What, will you be led by such a silly fellow as Bushel, an impudent, canting fellow? I warrant you, you shall come no more upon juries in haste. You are a foreman indeed (*addressing himself to the foreman*); I thought you had understand your place better.

RECORDER. Gentlemen, you shall not be dismissed till we have a verdict that the Court will accept, and you shall be locked up without meat, drink, fire, and tobacco. You shall not think thus to abuse the Court. We will have a verdict by the help of God, or you shall starve for it.

PENN. My jury, who are my judges, ought not to be thus menaced. Their verdict should be free and not compelled. The Bench ought to wait upon them, but not forestall them. I do desire that justice may be done me and that the arbitrary resolves of the Bench may not be made the measure of my jury's verdict.

RECORDER. Stop that prating fellow's mouth, or put him out of the Court.

MAYOR. You have heard that he preached, that he gathered a company of tumultuous people, and that they do not only disobey the martial power but the civil also.

PENN. It is a great mistake. We did not make the tumult, but they that interrupted us. The jury cannot be so ignorant as to think that we met there with a design to disturb the civil peace, since, first, we were by force of arms kept out of our lawful house, and met as near it in the street as their soldiers would give us leave; and, second, because it was no new thing nor with the circumstances expressed in the indictment, but what was usual and customary with us. 'Tis very well known that we are a peaceable people and cannot offer violence to any man.

(*The Court being ready to break up and willing to huddle the prisoners to their jail and the jury to their chamber, Penn spoke as follows:*)

PENN. The agreement of twelve men is a verdict in law, and such a one being given by the jury, I require the Clerk of the peace to record it, as he will answer it at his peril. And if the jury bring in another verdict contradictory to this, I affirm they are perjured men in law. (*And looking upon the jury, said:*) You are Englishmen; mind your privilege, give not away your right.

BUSHEL. etc. Nor will we ever do it.

(*One of the jurymen pleaded indisposition of body and therefore desired to be dismissed.*)

MAYOR. You are as strong as any of them. Starve then,[11] and hold your principles.

---

[11] All the early editions read *them*. We have accepted Joseph Besse's emendation of 1726.

RECORDER. Gentlemen, you must be content with your hard fate. Let your patience overcome it, for the Court is resolved to have a verdict and that before you can be dismissed.

JURY. We are agreed, we are agreed, we are agreed.

(*The Court swore several persons to keep the jury all night without meat, drink, fire, or any other accommodation. They had not so much as a chamber pot, though desired.*)

CRIER. Oyez, etc.

(*The Court adjourns till seven of the clock next morning [being the fourth instant, vulgarly called Sunday], at which time the prisoners were brought to the bar, the Court sat, and the jury called to bring in their verdict.*)

CRIER. Oyez, etc. Silence in the Court upon pain of imprisonment.

(*The jury's names called over.*)

CLERK. Are you agreed upon your verdict?

JURY. Yes.

CLERK. Who shall speak for you?

JURY. Our foreman.

CLERK. What say you? Look upon the prisoners at the bar. Is William Penn guilty of the matter whereof he stands indicted in manner and form as aforesaid, or not guilty?

FOREMAN. William Penn is guilty of speaking in Gracious Street.

MAYOR. To an unlawful assembly.

BUSHEL. No, my Lord, we give no other verdict than what we gave last night. We have no other verdict to give.

MAYOR. You are a factious fellow. I'll take a course with you.

BLUDWORTH. I knew Mr. Bushel would not yield.

BUSHEL. Sir Thomas, I have done according to my conscience.

MAYOR. That conscience of yours would cut my throat.

BUSHEL. No, my Lord, it never shall.

MAYOR. But I will cut yours so soon as I can.

RECORDER. He has inspired the jury. He has the spirit of divination;

methinks I feel him. I will have a positive verdict or you shall starve for it.

PENN. I desire to ask the Recorder one question: Do you allow of the verdict given of William Mead?

RECORDER. It cannot be a verdict because you are indicted for a conspiracy, and one being found not guilty and not the other, it could not be a verdict.

PENN. If not guilty be not a verdict, then you make of the jury and Magna Charta but a mere nose of wax.

MEAD. How! Is not guilty no verdict?

RECORDER. No, 'tis no verdict.

PENN. I affirm that the consent of a jury is a verdict in law, and if William Mead be not guilty, it consequently follows that I am clear, since you have indicted us of a conspiracy, and I could not possibly conspire alone.

(*There were many passages that could not be taken which passed between the jury and the Court. The jury went up again, having received a fresh charge from the bench, if possible to extort an unjust verdict.*)

CRIER. Oyez, etc. Silence in the Court.

COURT. Call over the jury (*which was done*).

CLERK. What say you? Is William Penn guilty of the matter whereof he stands indicted in manner and form aforesaid, or not guilty?

FOREMAN. Guilty of speaking in Gracious Street.

RECORDER. What is this to the purpose? I say I will have a verdict. (*And speaking to Edward Bushel, said:*) You are a factious fellow. I will set a mark upon you, and whilst I have any thing to do in the city, I will have an eye upon you.

MAYOR. Have you no more wit than to be led by such a pitiful fellow? I will cut his nose.

PENN. It is intolerable that my jury should be thus menaced. Is this according to the fundamental laws? Are not they my proper judges by the Great Charter of England? What hope is there of ever having justice done when juries are threatened and their verdicts rejected? I am concerned to speak and grieved to see such arbitrary proceedings. Did not the Lieutenant of the Tower render one of them worse than a felon? And do you not plainly seem to condemn such for factious fellows who answer not your ends? Unhappy are those juries who are threatened to be fined and starved and ruined if they give not in verdicts contrary to their consciences.

RECORDER. My Lord, you must take a course with that same fellow.

MAYOR. Stop his mouth, jailer; bring fetters and stake him to the ground.

PENN. Do your pleasure; I matter not your fetters.

RECORDER. Till now I never understood the reason of the policy and prudence of the Spaniards in suffering the Inquisition among them. And certainly it will never be well with us till something like the Spanish Inquisition be in England.

(*The jury being required to go together to find another verdict, and steadfastly refusing it [saying they could give no other verdict than what was already given], the Recorder in great passion was running off the bench with these words in his mouth, I protest I will sit here no longer to hear these things. At which the Mayor calling: stay, stay, he returned, and directed himself unto the jury and spake as followeth:*)

RECORDER. Gentlemen, we shall not be at this pass always with you; you will find, the next sessions of Parliament, there will be a law made that those that will not conform shall not have the protection of the law. Mr. Lee, draw up another verdict that they may bring it in special.

LEE. I cannot tell how to do it.

JURY. We ought not to be returned, having all agreed and set our hands to the verdict.

RECORDER. Your verdict is nothing; you play upon the Court. I say you shall go together and bring in another verdict or you shall starve; and I will have you carted about the city as in Edward the Third's time.

FOREMAN. We have given in our verdict and all agreed to it, and if we give in another, it will be a force upon us to save our lives.

MAYOR. Take them up.

OFFICER. My Lord, they will not go up.

(*The Mayor spoke to the Sheriff and he came off his seat and said:*)

SHERIFF. Come, gentlemen, you must go up; you see I am commanded to make you go.

(*Upon which the jury went up, and several [were] sworn to keep them without any accommodation, [as] aforesaid, till they brought in their verdict.*)

CRIER. Oyez, etc. The Court adjourns till tomorrow morning at seven of the clock.

(*The prisoners were remanded to Newgate, where they remained till next morning, and then were brought unto the Court, which being sat, they proceeded as followeth:*)

CRIER. Oyez, etc. Silence in the Court upon pain of imprisonment.

CLERK. Set William Penn and William Mead to the bar. Gentlemen of the jury, answer to your names: Thomas Veer, Edward Bushel, John Hammond, Henry Henley, Henry Michel, John Brightman, Charles Milson, Gregory Walklet, John Baily, William Lever, James Damask, William Plumstead. Are you all agreed of your verdict?

JURY. Yes.

CLERK. Who shall speak for you?

JURY. Our foreman.

CLERK. Look upon the prisoners. What say you? Is William Penn guilty of the matter whereof he stands indicted in manner and form, etc., or not guilty?

FOREMAN. You have there read in writing already our verdict and our hands subscribed.

(*The Clerk had the paper but was stopped by the Recorder from reading of it, and he [was] commanded to ask for a positive verdict.*)

FOREMAN. If you will not accept of it, I desire to have it back again.

COURT. That paper was no verdict, and there shall be no advantage taken against you by it.

CLERK. How say you? Is William Penn guilty, etc., or not guilty?

FOREMAN. Not guilty .

CLERK. How say you? Is William Mead guilty, etc., or not guilty?

FOREMAN. Not guilty.

CLERK. Then hearken to your verdict: you say that William Penn is not guilty in manner and form as he stands indicted; you say that William Mead is not guilty in manner and form as he stands indicted, and so you say all.

JURY. Yes, we do so.

(*The Bench, being unsatisfied with the verdict, commanded that every person should distinctly answer to their names and give in their verdict, which they unanimously did, in saying, not guilty, to the great satisfaction of the assembly.*)

RECORDER. I am sorry, gentlemen, you have followed your own judgments and opinions rather than the good and wholesome advice which was given you. God keep my life out of your hands, but for this the Court fines you forty marks a man and imprisonment till paid. (*At which Penn stepped up towards the bench and said:*)

PENN. I demand my liberty, being freed by the jury.

MAYOR. No, you are in for your fines.

PENN. Fines for what?

MAYOR. For contempt of the Court.

PENN. I ask if it be according to the fundamental laws of England that any Englishmen should be fined or amerced[12] but by the judgment of his peers or jury, since it expressly contradicts the Fourteenth and Twenty-ninth Chapters of the Great Charter of England, which say no freeman ought to be amerced but by the oath of good and lawful men of the vicinage?

RECORDER. Take him away, take him away, take him out of the Court.

PENN. I can never urge the fundamental laws of England but you cry, take him away, take him away. But 'tis no wonder, since the Spanish Inquisition hath so great a place in the Recorder's heart. God Almighty, who is just, will judge you all for these things.

(*They haled the prisoners into the bail-dock and from thence sent them to Newgate for non-payment of their fines, and so were their jury.*)

---

[12] Punished by a pecuniary penalty.

The Holy Experiment: Politics

Ten years after the Penn-Mead trial the jails of England were still crowded with dissenters. The Quakers continued to bear their testimony faithfully, showing the world how the Christian meekly accepts suffering and turns the other cheek. Yet it was discouraging after twenty years of patient endurance to see no improvement, no widening of the area of freedom for the religious conscience. Penn was close to despair in 1680. "There is no hope in England," he wrote; "the deaf adder cannot be charmed." The very circumstances of this relentless persecution prevented him and his fellow Quakers from bearing the comprehensive positive testimony they longed to make: to demonstrate to the world how a Christian society could be erected on the radical foundation of the Sermon on the Mount. Without relaxing in the struggle against persecution at home, Penn began looking abroad for an opportunity to realize his vision of a New Testament society of love and peace and freedom.

It was to America that he looked, to the Valley of the Delaware, an area still unoccupied except for a few Dutch and Swedish settlers. George Fox had traveled through the Delaware country in 1672. Penn presently became involved in the affairs of West New Jersey, the first Quaker colony in the New World. And by 1681 he found himself Lord Proprietor of a great province on the opposite side of the Delaware. It was his almost by accident, this vast domain across the sea: Charles II owed Penn's father, the Admiral, a large debt, which he chose to discharge by bestowing this princely fief on the Quaker son. But to William Penn it was no accident: it was a divine providence, a clear mandate from the Almighty to create in the wilderness an ideal Christian commonwealth in which religious men would be free to set a bright example before the nations. "There may be room there, though not here," he wrote to a friend in America, "for such a holy experiment."

His charter from the king gave him authority within wide limits to establish whatever kind of constitution he wished. Penn had reflected much on the problem of government. He knew what the greatest political thinkers, both ancient and modern, had to say about the three basic forms: monarchy, aristocracy, and democracy. He agreed with Polybius that elements of all three were necessary to a stable government, and with James Harrington that safety lay in the rule of law and not of men. Only recently he had been through the bitter experience of trying to elect Algernon Sidney, the radical republican, to Parliament. The attempt had failed, but Penn, though not quite a republican (for he still cherished the friendship of the royal Stuarts), was thoroughly committed to the platform of the radical Whigs; indeed his *England's Great Interest in the Choice of This New Parliament,* a campaign document of 1679, was one of the first and clearest statements of the Whig doctrines of liberty, property, and representative government. Even more recently he had seen his own king and friend, Charles II, the admirer and now the pensioner of the despotic Louis XIV, embark upon a career of arbitrary rule that threatened to wipe out every trace of English liberty.

All these things were in his mind as he sat down to frame a government for his colony. "As my understanding and inclination have been much directed to observe and reprove mischiefs in government," he wrote to some Friends in Ireland, "so it is now put into my power to settle one. For the matters of liberty and privilege I propose that which is extraordinary, and to leave myself and successors no power of doing mischief, that the will of one man may not hinder the good of a whole country." The English Whiggism of William Penn is one of the foundation stones of American democracy.

But the ultimate source of what is distinctive in Penn's political thought was his Quaker interpretation of Christianity. He set forth his theory of politics in the Preface to his first Frame of Government for Pennsylvania. That theory rested squarely on the biblical account of man —his primitive innocence and his disastrous fall. Government, Penn declared with St. Paul, is divinely ordained for the terrifying of evildoers. Sometimes Penn is taxed with being a Utopian, a starry-eyed idealist bemused and misled by an over-optimistic estimate of human nature. Yet he frankly acknowledges that men naturally tend to "side with their passions against their reason," that "their sinister interests" are all too apt to over-ride their attachment to the good. Hence the need for the coercive power of government.

But as a Quaker Penn also had a vision of what man could be under the quickening influence of the divine Spirit. He was, after all, framing a government for the "Children of Light," for a people who had accepted the guidance of the Inward Word written on their hearts. Such a people might be expected to live lives of primitive innocence like that of Adam before the fall. "Mine eye," he wrote, "is to a blessed government, and a virtuous, ingenious and industrious society." If Pennsylvania were to be another Garden of Eden, it did not follow that government would become unnecessary. The state had positive functions; it was "capable of kindness" as well as punishment; it was, as we might say, the teacher and the social worker as well as the policeman. Was Penn here adumbrating the welfare state?

He was, at any rate, not the prisoner of any doctrinaire theory of politics, not even that of the Whigs. He took a pragmatic, reformist position. Time, place, and circumstances were the proper determinants of governmental forms, and constitutions must not be so rigid that they could not be altered as occasion required—so he included in his Frame of Government the first amending clause in any written constitution. And he cut through the tedious theoretical debate over the ideal form of government with a single memorable "distinction": "any government is free to the people under it, whatever be the frame, where the laws rule, and the people are a party to those laws."

The Frame of Government itself (only its Preface is printed here) consisted of twenty-four sections in which Penn outlined the "liberties, franchises, and properties" which he thereby granted to the people of Pennsylvania: the twenty-fourth was a pledge on behalf of himself and his heirs never to infringe upon any of those liberties. In some respects the political machinery that Penn designed proved cumbersome and unworkable. But there were many features that showed Penn's good sense and his concern for democratic practice: staggered terms for the Councilors, as in the United States Senate; compulsory rotation of offices "that so all may be fitted for government and have experience in the care and burden of it"; a provision for the establishment of schools and the encouragement of "useful sciences and inventions"; the division of the executive Council into four working committees, one of which was to have responsibility for "manners, education, and arts"; all elections and all voting in the Assembly to be by ballot; and, most important of all, the amending clause.

In his insistence that constitutions should not be regarded as sacrosanct as in other respects, Penn anticipated Thomas Jefferson by a hundred years. And he showed that he meant what he said by agreeing to several successive overhaulings of the constitution of Pennsylvania. The last revision, called the Charter of Privileges, was signed by Penn in 1701, just before he left America for the last time. It proved so satisfactory to the people that it remained in force for seventy-five years. When the Charter of Privileges was half a century old, the Assembly ordered a bell installed in the tower of the State House (the building that would one day be called Independence Hall) in honor of its jubilee. The inscription on the bell, chosen from Leviticus by the Quaker Speaker of the Assembly, read: "Proclaim liberty throughout all the land unto all the inhabitants thereof." William Penn would have approved of that inscription.

Preface to the First Frame of Government for Pennsylvania (1682)

When the great and wise God had made the world of all of his creatures, it pleased Him to choose man His deputy to rule it, and to fit him for so great a charge and trust He did not only qualify him with skill and power but with integrity to use them justly. This native goodness was equally his honor and his happiness, and whilst he stood here, all went well; there was no need of coercive or compulsive means. The precept of divine love and truth in his own bosom was the guide and keeper of his innocency. But lust, prevailing against duty, made a lamentable breach upon it, and the law that before had no power over him took place upon him and his disobedient posterity, that such as would not live conformable to the holy law within should fall under the reproof and correction of the just law without in a judicial administration.

This the apostle teaches in divers of his epistles. "The law," says he, "was added because of transgression." In another place: "knowing that the law was not made for the righteous man but for the disobedient and ungodly, for sinners, for unholy and profane, for murderers, for whoremongers, for them that defile themselves with mankind, and for menstealers, for liars, for perjured persons," etc., but this is not all; he opens and carries the matter of government a little farther: "let every soul be subject to the higher powers, for there is no power but of God.

The powers that be are ordained of God; whosoever therefore resisteth the power resisteth the ordinance of God. For rulers are not a terror to good works, but to evil. Wilt thou then not be afraid of the power? Do that which is good, and thou shalt have praise of the same." "He is the minister of God to thee for good." "Wherefore ye must needs be subject not only for wrath but for conscience' sake."[1]

This settles the divine right of government beyond exception, and that for two ends: first, to terrify evildoers; secondly, to cherish those that do well; which gives government a life beyond corruption and makes it as durable in the world as good men shall be, so that government seems to me a part of religion itself, a thing sacred in its institution and end. For if it does not directly remove the cause, it crushes the effects of evil, and is as such, though a lower, yet an emanation of the same divine Power that is both author and object of pure religion, the difference lying here, that the one is more free and mental, the other more corporal and compulsive in its operations, but that is only to evildoers, government in itself being otherwise as capable of kindness, goodness, and charity, as a more private society. They weakly err that think there is no other use for government than correction, which is the coarsest part of it; daily experience tells us that the care and regulation of many other affairs more soft and daily necessary make up much the greatest part of government, and which must have followed the peopling of the world, had Adam never fell, and will continue among men on earth under the highest attainments they may arrive at by the coming of the blessed second Adam, the Lord from heaven. Thus much of government in general as to its rise and end.

For particular frames and models, it will become me to say little, and comparatively I will say nothing. My reasons are:

First. That the age is too nice[2] and difficult for it, there being nothing the wits of men are more busy and divided upon. 'Tis true, they seem to agree in the end, to wit, happiness; but in the means they differ, as to divine, so to this human felicity, and the cause is much the same, not always want of light and knowledge, but want of using them

---

[1] Galatians iii. 19; I Timothy 1.9–10; Romans xii. 1–5.
[2] Fastidious, hard to please.

rightly. Men side with their passions against their reason, and their sinister interests have so strong a bias upon their minds that they lean to them against the good of the things they know.

Secondly. I do not find a model in the world that time, place, and some singular emergencies have not necessarily altered, nor is it easy to frame a civil government that shall serve all places alike.

Thirdly. I know what is said by the several admirers of monarchy, aristocracy, and democracy, which are the rule of one, a few, and many, and are the three common ideas of government, when men discourse of that subject. But I choose to solve the controversy with this small distinction and it belongs to all three: any government is free to the people under it, whatever be the frame, where the laws rule and the people are a party to those laws, and more than this is tyranny, oligarchy, or confusion.

But lastly, when all is said, there is hardly one frame of government in the world so ill-designed by its first founders that in good hands, [it] would not do well enough, and story[3] tells us, the best in ill ones can do nothing that is great or good; witness the Jewish and Roman states. Governments, like clocks, go from the motion men give them, and as governments are made and moved by men, so by them they are ruined too. Wherefore governments rather depend upon men than men upon governments. Let men be good and the government cannot be bad: if it be ill, they will cure it. But if men be bad, let the government be never so good, they will endeavor to warp and spoil it to their turn.

I know some say, let us have good laws, and no matter for the men that execute them; but let them consider that though good laws do well, good men do better, for good laws want good men, and be abolished or evaded by ill men, but good men will never want good laws nor suffer ill ones. 'Tis true, good laws have some awe upon ill ministers, but that is where they have not power to escape or abolish them and the people are generally wise and good, but a loose and depraved people (which is the question) love laws and an administration like themselves. That, therefore, which makes a good constitution must keep it; viz., men of wisdom and virtue, qualities that, because

[3] History.

they descend not with worldly inheritances, must be carefully propagated by a virtuous education of youth, for which after-ages will owe more to the care and prudence of founders and the successive magistracy than to their parents for their private patrimonies.

These considerations of the weight of government and the nice and various opinions about it made it uneasy to me to think of publishing the ensuing frame and conditional laws, foreseeing both the censures they will meet with from men of differing humors and engagements and the occasion they may give of discourse beyond my design.

But, next to the power of necessity (which is a solicitor that will take no denial) this induced me to a compliance, that we have (with reverence to God and good conscience to men) to the best of our skill contrived and composed the frame and laws of this government to the great end of all government; viz., to support power in reverence with the people and to secure the people from the abuse of power, that they may be free by their just obedience and the magistrates honorable for their just administration; for liberty without obedience is confusion, and obedience without liberty is slavery. To carry this evenness is partly owing to the constitution and partly to the magistracy. Where either of these fail, government will be subject to convulsions, but where both are wanting, it must be totally subverted; then where both meet, the government is like to endure, which I humbly pray and hope God will please to make the lot of this of Pennsylvania. Amen.

WILLIAM PENN

The Holy Experiment: Economics

The founder of an overseas colony needed something more than lofty ideals and religious dedication. Plenty of high-minded attempts at colonization in the New World had come to grief because their sponsors, impractical visionaries expecting manna in the wilderness, had taken insufficient thought for the practical aspects of the venture—what the country afforded in the way of natural products, how the land was to be divided and settled, what kind of people would make the best colonists, how the settlers were to live through the first winter in the new environment. William Penn was a religious idealist, but he was also a man of affairs who had had valuable practical experience in managing his father's estates in Ireland. Moreover, his religious faith, though it was intensely spiritual, was never otherworldly. The Quaker ethic, which called for purposeful activity in the world, gave a practical cast to the Quaker temperament. Penn, after all, expected Pennsylvania not only to provide a haven for persecuted Friends and an example of liberty and democracy to the world but a comfortable living for himself and his family.

As soon as he had his charter from King Charles, he launched an advertising campaign by writing a promotional tract called *Some Account of the Province of Pennsylvania*. Copies were scattered broadcast over the British Isles and the Valley of the Rhine. Like any shrewd publicist, he knew that he must first overcome any lingering resistance to the idea he was promoting. Overseas expansion meant emigration, the drain of population away from England. Englishmen no longer believed, as they had earlier, when Massachusetts and Virginia had been founded, that their island was overpopulated, that Britain needed colonies as safety valves. On the contrary, prevailing opinion regarded people as wealth and feared that emigration would only weaken the metropolis. The time had not yet come when England would regard herself as the "mother of nations."

Against objections of this sort Penn marshaled all the arguments he could muster, Scriptural, historical, theoretical, and practical. His case for colonies ("plantations") as "the seeds of nations," as so many sources of strength to a mercantile empire, was a little masterpiece of "political arithmetic," as the emerging discipline of economics was called. Penn started with the basic assumption of contemporary mercantilist thought—that government policy should be consciously directed toward the strengthening and enriching of the national state—and went on to show how the encouragement of "plantations" overseas was the surest method of promoting both ends, how it would create new markets for Britain's goods, ensure a steady flow of essential raw materials, and build up the merchant marine.

Penn was prepared to admit that England had a population problem, but its nature and its cure, he thought, were quite different from what the opponents of colonization supposed. He found the root of the trouble in the decay of English country life, the decline of that simple, wholesome rural existence which was traditional in England and provided, so he believed, the only proper base for a virtuous society. The sharp contrast he drew between the idyllic life of the old countryside and the corruptions of Restoration London reflects in part the bewilderment of the moralist confronted by the ineluctable fact of social change. Penn's nostalgic appeal to a mythical Arcadian past foreshadows Thomas Jefferson's attachment to the myth of the sturdy, independent yeoman farmer as the only sound material for a healthy democratic society.

The difference lies in the fact that Penn was in a position to re-create in his virgin province the social conditions whose passing in England he so much lamented. For he could, and in this pamphlet did, issue an invitation to the dislocated and unfortunate classes of Restoration England to start life over again in his forested Arcadia across the sea—not only the poor industrious husbandmen and day laborers but the unemployed artisans, the impecunious intellectuals, the younger sons of country families who could not maintain their self-respect in old England. Penn did not overlook the need, even in a frontier society, for the type of exceptional men whom Jefferson was to call "natural aristocrats." He issued a special call for "men of universal spirits that have an eye to the good of posterity and that both understand and delight to promote good discipline and just government among a plain and well-intending people." The stones which the builders of Restoration society in England rejected, the same would become the head of the corner in the new society of Pennsylvania.

We have reprinted the portions of this pamphlet which deal on the theoretical and practical levels with the peopling of colonies. For the rest, Penn's tract is notable among promotional pamphlets of that day (or any other) for the remarkable modesty of its claims. To be sure, Penn had not yet seen his province himself and there were few sources of accurate information about its climate, topography, soil, and potential products; but in the long history of real-estate promotion ignorance of the facts has seldom restrained the imagination of the promoter. Penn not only observed Quaker moderation in describing the attractions of his province, but he was careful to remind the overoptimistic that "they must look for a winter before the summer comes." And he added a final caution to all intending emigrants that they should consider the step prayerfully and take it only after a careful inward search for divine guidance and full consultation with friends and relatives. In opening a "door of mercy" in Pennsylvania he was anxious that it not be simply an escape hatch for people looking to avoid persecution. He had, we recall, a positive purpose in view: to experiment with a new kind of society, a New Testament society, and for that experiment he needed dedicated people.

Some Account of the Province of Pennsylvania was the first of a series of promotional tracts. Two years later, from Philadelphia, Penn wrote *A Letter to the Free Society of Traders*, describing the province more fully on the basis of direct observation. In 1685, when he was back in England, he wrote the third and last, *A Further Account of the Province of Pennsylvania*, in which he was able to report that the population of the colony was already more than eight thousand. His "holy experiment" was well launched. Despite vicissitudes, it was destined to last for three-quarters of a century. But alongside that politico-religious experiment ran another one, whose long-term significance for America would be even greater—the experiment of creating in an atmosphere of freedom a new mixed nationality, a people composed of many peoples. For Penn's promotional tracts and their promise of liberty and prosperity stimulated an outpouring of people from many nations to live beside the Scandinavians and Dutchmen already settled by the Delaware. Let Penn (in *A Further Account*) describe the beginning of that experiment in a multinational society: "The people are a collection of divers nations in Europe, as French, Dutch, Germans, Swedes, Danes, Finns, Scotch, Irish, and English, and of the last equal to all the rest . . . but as they are of one kind and in one place and under one allegiance, so they live like people of one country, which civil union has had a considerable influence toward the prosperity of that place."

Some Account of the Province of Pennsylvania (1681)

Since by the good providence of God a country in America is fallen to my lot, I thought it not less my duty than my honest interest to give some public notice of it to the world, that those of our own or other nations that are inclined to transport themselves or families beyond the seas may find another country added to their choice, that if they shall happen to like the place, conditions, and constitutions (so far as the present infancy of things will allow us any prospect), they may, if they please, fix with me in the province hereafter described. But before I come to treat of my particular concernment, I shall take leave to say something of the benefit of plantations or colonies in general, to obviate a common objection.

Colonies, then, are the seeds of nations, begun and nourished by the care of wise and populous countries, as conceiving them best for the increase of human stock and beneficial for commerce.

Some of the wisest men in history have justly taken their fame from this design and service. We read of the reputation given on this account to Moses, Joshua, and Caleb in Scripture-records, and what renown the Greek story yields to Lycurgus, Theseus, and those Greeks that planted many parts of Asia. Nor is the Roman account wanting of instances to the credit of that people: they had a Romulus, a Numa Pompilius, and not only reduced but moralized the manners of the nations they subjected, so that they may have been rather said to conquer their barbarity than them.

Nor did any of these ever dream it was the way of decreasing their people or wealth. For the cause of the decay of any of those states or empires was not their plantations but their luxury and corruption of manners. For when they grew to neglect their ancient discipline, that maintained and rewarded virtue and industry, and addicted themselves to pleasure and effeminacy, they debased their spirits and debauched their morals, from whence ruin did never fail to follow to any people. With justice therefore I deny the vulgar opinion against plantations that they weaken England; they have manifestly enriched and so strengthened her, which I briefly evidence thus:

First, those that go into a foreign plantation, their industry there is worth more than if they stayed at home, the product of their labor being in commodities of a superior nature to those of this country. For instance, what is an improved acre in Jamaica or Barbados worth to an improved acre in England? We know 'tis three times the value, and the product of it comes for England, and is usually paid for in English growth and manufacture. Nay, Virginia shows that an ordinary industry in one man produces three thousand pound weight of tobacco and twenty barrels of corn yearly. He feeds himself and brings as much of commodity into England besides as, being returned in the growth and workmanship of this country, is much more than he could have spent here. Let it also be remembered that the three thousand weight of tobacco brings in three thousand twopences by way of custom to the King, which makes twenty-five pounds, an extraordinary profit.

Secondly, more being produced and imported than we can spend here, we export it to other countries in Europe, which brings in money or the growth of those countries, which is the same thing. And this is the advantage of the English merchants and seamen.

Thirdly, such as could not only not marry here, but hardly live and allow themselves clothes, do marry there and bestow thrice more in all necessaries and conveniencies (and not a little in ornamental things too) for themselves, their wives, and children, both as to apparel and household stuff, which coming out of England, I say 'tis impossible that England should not be a considerable gainer.

Fourthly, but let it be considered that the plantations employ many hundreds of shipping and many thousands of seamen, which must be in divers respects an advantage to England, being an island and by nature fitted for navigation above any country in Europe. This is followed by other depending trades, as shipwrights, carpenters, sawyers, hewers, trunnel-makers, joiners, slopsellers, drysalters, ironworkers, the Eastland merchants, timber-sellers, and victuallers, with many more trades which hang upon navigation.[1] So that we may easily see the objection that colonies or plantations hurt England is at least of no strength, especially if we consider how many thousand blacks and Indians are also accommodated with clothes and many sorts of tools and utensils from England, and that their labor is mostly brought hither, which adds wealth and people to the English dominions. But 'tis further said, they injure England in that they draw away too many of the people, for we are not so populous in the countries as formerly. I say there are other reasons for that.

First, country people are so extremely addicted to put their children into gentlemens' service or send them to towns to learn trades that husbandry is neglected. And after a soft and delicate usage there, they are forever unfitted for the labor of a farming life.

Secondly, the pride of the age in its attendance and retinue is so gross and universal that where a man of £1000 a year formerly kept but four or five servants, he now keeps more than twice the number. He must have a gentleman to wait upon him in his chambers, a coachman, a groom or two, a butler, a man cook, a gardener, two or three lackeys, it may be a huntsman and a falconer, the wife a gentlewoman and maids accordingly. This was not known by our ancestors of like quality. This hinders the plow and the dairy from whence they are taken, and instead of keeping people to manly labor, they are effeminated by a lazy and luxurious living. But which is worse, these people rarely marry, though many of them do worse, but if they do, it is when they are in age. And the reason is clear: because their usual keeping at their master's is too great and costly for them with a family at their own charge and they scarcely know how to live lower, so that too many of them choose rather to vend their lusts at an evil ordinary[2] than hon-

---

[1] Trunnel- or treenail-makers fashioned the wooden pegs used in shipbuilding. Slopsellers purveyed cheap, ready-made clothing, especially for sailors. Drysalters dealt in salted foods, dyes, and crude, dry chemicals. Eastland merchants were traders carrying on commerce with the Baltic countries.
[2] Tavern.

estly marry and work, the excess and sloth of the age not allowing of marriage and the charge that follows—all which hinders the increase of our people. If men, they often turn either soldiers or gamesters or highwaymen. If women, they too frequently dress themselves for a bad market rather than know the dairy again or honestly return to labor, whereby it happens that both the stock of the nation decays and the issue is corrupted.

Thirdly, of old time the nobility and gentry spent their estates in the country and that kept the people in it, and their servants married and sat at easy rents under their masters' favor, which peopled the place. Now the great men, too much loving the town and resorting to London, draw many people thither to attend them, who either don't marry or if they do, they pine away[3] their small gains in some petty shop, for there are so many they prey upon one another.

Fourthly, the country being thus neglected and no due balance kept between trade and husbandry, city and country, the poor countryman takes double toil and cannot, for want of hands, dress and manure his land to the advantage it formerly yielded him; yet must he pay the old rents, which occasions servants and such children as go not to trades to continue single at least all their youthful time, which also obstructs the increase of our people.

Fifthly, the decay of some country manufactures, where no provision is made to supply the people with a new way of living, causes the more industrious to go abroad to seek their bread in other countries and gives the lazy an occasion to loiter and beg or do worse, by which means the land swarms with beggars. Formerly 'twas rare to find any asking alms but the maimed or blind or very aged. Now thousands of both sexes run up and down both city and country, that are sound and youthful and able to work, with false pretenses and certificates, nor is there any care taken to employ or deter such vagrants, which weakens the country as to people and labor.

To which let me add that the great debauchery in this kingdom has not only rendered many unfruitful when married, but they live not out half their time through excesses, which might be prevented by a

[3] Spend.

vigorous execution of our good laws against corruption of manners. These and the like evils are the true grounds of the decay of our people in the country, to say nothing of plague and wars. Towns and cities cannot complain of the decay of people, being more replenished than ever, especially London, which with reason helps the countryman to this objection. And though some do go to the plantations, yet numbering the parishes in England and computing how many live more than die and are born than buried, there goes not over to all the plantations a fourth part of the yearly increase of the people. And when they are there, they are not (as I said before) lost to England, since they furnish them with much clothes, household stuff, tools, and the like necessaries, and that in greater quantities than here their condition could have needed or they could have bought, being there well to pass that were but low here, if not poor; and now masters of families too, when here they had none and could hardly keep themselves. And very often it happens that some of them, after their industry and success there have made them wealthy, they return and empty their riches into England, one in this capacity being able to buy out twenty of what he was when he went over. . . .

These persons that Providence seems to have most fitted for plantations are:

First, industrious husbandmen and day laborers, that are hardly able with extreme labor to maintain their families and portion their children.

Secondly, laborious handicrafts, especially carpenters, masons, smiths, weavers, tailors, tanners, shoemakers, shipwrights, etc., where they may be spared or are low in the world. And as they shall want no encouragement, so their labor is worth more there than here, and their provision cheaper.

Thirdly, a plantation seems a fit place for those ingenious spirits that, being low in the world, are much clogged and oppressed about a livelihood, for, the means of subsisting being easy there, they may have time and opportunity to gratify their inclinations and thereby improve science and help nurseries of people.

Fourthly, a fourth sort of men to whom a plantation would be proper takes in those that are younger brothers of small inheritances, yet because they would live in sight of their kindred in some proportion to their quality and can't do it without a labor that looks like farming, their condition is too strait for them, and if married, their children are often too numerous for the estate and are frequently bred up to no trades, but are a kind of hangers-on or retainers to the elder brother's table and charity, which is a mischief, as in itself to be lamented, so here to be remedied. For land they have for next to nothing, which with moderate labor produces plenty of all things necessary for life and such an increase as by traffic may supply them with all conveniencies.

Lastly, there are another sort of persons not only fit for but necessary in plantations, and that is, men of universal spirits that have an eye to the good of posterity and that both understand and delight to promote good discipline and just government among a plain and well-intending people. Such persons may find room in colonies for their good counsel and contrivance, who are shut out from being of much use or service to great nations under settled customs. These men deserve much esteem and would be harkened to. Doubtless 'twas this, as I observed before, that put some of the famous Greeks and Romans upon transplanting and regulating colonies of people in divers parts of the world, whose names for giving so great proof of their wisdom, virtue, labor, and constancy are with justice honorably delivered down by story[4] to the praise of our own times, though the world, after all its higher pretenses of religion, barbarously errs from their excellent example. . . .

To conclude, I desire all my dear countryfolks who may be inclined to go into those parts to consider seriously the premises, as well the present inconveniences as future ease and plenty, that so none may move rashly or from a fickle but solid mind, having above all things an eye to the Providence of God in the disposal of themselves. And I would further advise all such at least to have the permission, if not the good liking, of their near relations, for that is both natural and a duty incumbent upon all. And by this means will natural affection be pre-

---

[4] History.

served and a friendly and profitable correspondence be maintained between them. In all which I beseech Almighty God to direct us, that his blessing may attend our honest endeavor and then the consequence of all our undertaking will turn to the glory of His great name and the true happiness of us and our posterity. Amen.

The Natives of Pennsylvania

History, political science, economics, sociology—Penn's restless mind took him into nearly every one of the fields of thought which we sum up nowadays in the inclusive term "social science." In Pennsylvania in 1682 he made a foray into what we should call anthropology.

As Proprietor of "Penn's Woods" in America, he found himself in the role of protector of the aboriginal inhabitants of those woods. Everyone knows how consistently and how successfully Penn pursued his policy of fair and generous dealing with the indigenous people of Pennsylvania. That policy was foreshadowed in a remarkable letter which he addressed to "the Kings of the Indians in America" almost as soon as the province was his. Because its tender, loving spirit contrasts so strikingly with that of most of the documents we have on Anglo-Indian relations in early America, it deserves to be quoted in full:

"MY FRIENDS:

"There is one great God and power that hath made the world and all things therein, to whom you and I and all people owe their being and well-being, and to whom you and I must one day give an account for all that we do in this world. This great God hath written His law in our hearts, by which we are taught and commanded to love and help and do good to one another, and not to do harm or mischief one to another.

"Now this great God hath been pleased to make me concerned in your parts of the world, and the King of the country where I live hath given unto me a great province therein, but I desire to enjoy it with your love and consent, that we may always live together as neighbors and friends, else what would the great God say to us Who hath made us not to devour and destroy one another but [to] live soberly and kindly together in the world? Now I would have [you] well to observe that I am very sensible of the unkindness and injustice that hath been too much exercised toward you by the people of these parts of the world, who have sought themselves and to make great advantages by you rather than [to] be examples of justice and goodness unto you, which I hear hath been a

123

matter of trouble to you and caused great grudgings and animosities, some
times to the shedding of blood, which hath made the great God angry
But I am not such a man, as is well known in my own country. I have
great love and regard toward you, and I desire to win and gain your love
and friendship by a kind, just, and peaceable life, and the people I send
are of the same mind and shall in all things behave themselves accordingly
and if in anything any shall offend you or your people, you shall have a
full and speedy satisfaction for the same by an equal number of honest
men on both sides, that by no means you may have just occasion of being
offended against them.

"I shall shortly come to see you myself, at which time we may more
largely and freely confer and discourse of these matters. In the meantime
I have sent my commissioners to treat with you about land and a firm
league of peace. Let me desire you to be kind to them and to the people
and receive the presents and tokens which I have sent you as a testimony
of my good will to you and of my resolution to live justly, peaceably, and
friendly with you.

"I am your loving friend,

"WILLIAM PENN."

Though Penn the benevolent White Father is justly celebrated, Penn
the scientific observer of aboriginal culture is hardly known at all. Yet it
was natural that a Fellow of the Royal Society, imbued with the pervading
scientific curiosity of the age, should have studied the ways of the Indians
with close attention. We may be amused by his efforts to prove that they
were descended from the Ten Lost Tribes of Israel, though that hy
pothesis was perhaps no more implausible than many of the other theo
ries held by learned men in that dawning-time of modern science—the
theory that Noah's flood was responsible for the present state of the earth'.
surface, for instance, or that comets and earthquakes were warning sign
of God's displeasure with humanity. What is impressive about Penn'
field report on the Pennsylvania Indians is the same thing that was ex
ceptional about his practical relations with them—his freedom from the
prejudice against "savagism" that colored most seventeenth century ac
counts of the native Americans. Because he took them for what they
were—no less human, no less endowed with Inward Light than white
men—he was able to appreciate and understand their culture in some
thing of the spirit of the modern anthropologist.

The Indians he found in Pennsylvania and described in this report were

he people known to history as the Delawares and to themselves as the
Lenni Lenape. In 1682 they occupied the Valley of the Delaware on
both sides of the great river; their country extended north to Manhattan
Island, south to Cape Henlopen, east to the Atlantic, west to the edge of
he Susquehanna watershed. Part of the great Algonquian linguistic family,
hey numbered perhaps eight thousand in all. In the summer they lived
n communities of two or three hundred along the creeks and rivers; in
winter they traveled to their hunting grounds in the interior. Penn's brief
but perceptive account of their language (which he took the trouble to
earn), their matrilineal society (which he took the trouble to under-
tand), and their folkways (which he took the trouble to set down in some
detail) is still a primary document for the ethnologist studying the culture
of the Lenni Lenape.

When Penn observed this people in 1682, their culture was no longer
intact. Its character had already been affected, its integrity somewhat impaired, by two generations of contact with the Dutch traders of New
Amsterdam, the scattered white settlers of New Jersey, the Swedes and
Finns of the lower Delaware. Penn was aware of the disintegrative effects
of this experience. Unlike most contemporary observers, who took it for
granted that contact with the white man's "civilization" could only have
beneficent consequences for the "savage," and that any wayward or
treacherous behavior by the Indians must be a result of their corrupt
natures, he could write: "The worst is that they are the worse for the
Christians, who have propagated their vices and yielded them tradition
for ill and not for good things." He recognized that, left to himself, the
"savage" Delaware was blessed with a remarkably equable temperament
and enjoyed a simple way of life that left him relatively free from the
characteristic tensions and disquiets of "civilized" life. In a letter to his
friend Robert Boyle, the scientist, he remarked with acute psychological
insight that "if they have not had their passions raised to the same degree
after the luxury of Europe by like enjoyments, neither have they the
anxieties that follow those pleasures." Penn notes, as most observers did,
the Indians' addiction to the white man's liquor, but his comments suggest that he had some inkling of the reason for it—the Indian's need for
relief from the intolerable tensions created by the conflict of cultural
values in which he was caught. There is pathos and perceptiveness, not
scorn or pharisaic condemnation, in his observation that "if they are
heated with liquors, they are restless till they have enough to sleep—that
is their cry: 'Some more, and I will go to sleep.' "

And what is most remarkable of all, there is in Penn's account, a genuine

appreciation of the Indian's religious nature. Most seventeenth centur
Englishmen, from Captain John Smith of Virginia to the Reverend Joh
Eliot of Massachusetts, wrote Indian religion off as the worship of Satan
Even Roger Williams of Rhode Island, though he was scrupulously re
spectful of the Indians' rights, confessed himself appalled by their "hide
ous worships of creatures and devils." But Penn's Quakerism taught him
to look for signs of God's indwelling presence in every human soul. The
Indians might be "under a dark night" with respect to the Christian tra
dition, but it was enough for Penn that they believed in God and .
future life. Persuaded that the root of religion was in them, he coul
watch their strange ritual dances with equanimity and interest, and se
down for us one of the earliest and best brief descriptions of the centra
Delaware religious rite—the *Cantico* or "Big House Ceremony."

This account of the Delaware Indians was incorporated in A Lette
from William Penn, Proprietary and Governor of Pennsylvania in Americ
to the Committee of the Free Society of Traders . . . , the longest o
Penn's promotional tracts for his colony. First published in London i
1683 and thrice reprinted in the same year, it was promptly translate
into Dutch, German, and French and published the following year o
the continent of Europe. Our text has been corrected in a few passage
by comparison with Albert Cook Myers's transcript of the original manu
script in William Penn, His Own Account of the Lenni Lenape or Dela
ware Indians, 1683 (Moylan, Pennsylvania, 1937).

From A Letter to the Free Society of Traders (1683

The natives I shall consider in their persons, language, manners, rel
gion, and government, with my sense of their original. For their pe
sons, they are generally tall, straight, well-built, and of singular propo
tion; they tread strong and clever[1] and mostly walk with a lofty chi
[They are] of complexion black,[2] but by design, as the gypsies i

---

[1] Nimbly.
[2] Dark, swarthy.

England. They grease themselves with bears' fat clarified and, using no defense against sun or weather, their skins must needs be swarthy. Their eye is little and black, not unlike a straight-looked Jew. The thick lip and flat nose so frequent with the East Indians and blacks are not common to them, for I have seen as comely European-like faces among them of both as on your side the sea, and truly an Italian complexion hath not much more of the white and the noses of several of them have as much of the Roman.

Their language is lofty yet narrow, but, like the Hebrew, in signification full, like shorthand in writing: one word serveth in the place of three, and the rest are supplied by the understanding of the hearer; imperfect in their tenses, wanting in their moods, participles, adverbs, conjunctions, interjections. I have made it my business to understand it, that I might not want an interpreter on any occasion. And I must say that I know not a language spoken in Europe that hath words of more sweetness or greatness in accent and emphasis than theirs. For instance, *Octorockon, Rancocas, Oricton, Shakamaxon, Poquessin*,[3] all of which are names of places and have grandeur in them. Of words of sweetness, *anna* is mother; *issimus*, a brother; *netap*, friend; *usque oret*, very good; *pone*, bread; *metse*, eat; *matta*, no; *hatta*, to have; *payo*, to come; *Sepassen, Passion*,[4] the names of places; *Tamany, Siccane, Menanse, Secatareus*[5] are the names of persons. If one ask them for anything they have not, they will answer, *Mattá ne hattá*, which, to translate, is, "Not I have," instead of "I have not."

Of their customs and manners there is much to be said. I will begin with children. So soon as they are born, they wash them in water, and

[3] Octorara Creek flows into the Susquehanna River near the Maryland-Pennsylvania border. Rancocas Creek is an affluent of the Delaware River in Burlington County, New Jersey. Orecton Island (now Biles Island) is in the Delaware just below the Falls. Shackamaxon is now Kensington, a part of Philadelphia. Poquessing Creek flows into the Delaware north of Philadelphia.

[4] Sepassing Land was the name applied to that part of Bucks County north of Philadelphia, where Penn built his country seat of Pennsbury. Passyunk was an area on the east bank of the Schuylkill River, now part of Philadelphia.

[5] Tamany (sometimes spelled Tamanend, Taminent, etc.), Siccane, Menanse (Menangy), and Secatareus were all chiefs of the Delaware Indians. The first-named became the patron saint of numerous American societies, including the Tammany Society of New York.

while very young, and in cold weather to choose,[6] they plunge them in
the rivers to harden and embolden them. Having wrapped them in a
clout, they lay them on a straight, thin board a little more than the
length and breadth of the child and swaddle it fast upon the board to
make it straight (wherefore all Indians have flat heads), and thus they
carry them at their backs. The children will go[7] very young, at nine
months commonly. They wear only a small clout around their waist
until they are big. If boys, they go a-fishing until ripe for the woods,
which is about fifteen. Then they hunt, and after having given some
proofs of their manhood by a good return of skins, they may marry,
else it is a shame to think of a wife. The girls stay with their mothers
and help to hoe the ground, plant corn, and carry burdens. And they do
well to use[8] them to that young [which] they must do when they are
old. For the wives are the true servants of their husbands; otherwise the
men are very affectionate to them.

When the young women are fit for marriage, they wear something
upon their heads for an advertisement, but so as their faces are hardly
to be seen but when they please. The age they marry at, if women, is
about thirteen and fourteen; if men, seventeen and eighteen; they are
rarely older.

Their houses are mats or barks of trees set on poles in the fashion of
an English barn, but out of the power of the winds, for they are hardly
higher than a man; they lie on reeds or grass. In travel they lodge in the
woods about a great fire with the mantle of duffels[9] they wear by day
wrapped about them and a few boughs stuck around them.

Their diet is maize, or Indian corn, divers ways prepared: sometimes
roasted in the ashes, sometimes beaten and boiled with water, which
they call *hominy*; they also make cakes not unpleasant to eat. They
have likewise several sorts of beans and peas that are good nourish-
ment, and the woods and rivers are their larder.

[6] By choice.
[7] Walk.
[8] Accustom.
[9] Coarse woolen cloth.

If a European comes to see them or calls for lodging at their house
r wigwam, they give him the best place and first cut.[10] If they come to
isit us, they salute us with an *Itah*, which is as much as to say, "good
e to you," and set them down, which is mostly on the ground, close
) their heels, their legs upright. Maybe they speak not a word more,
ut observe all passages. If you give them anything to eat or drink,
ell, for they will not ask, and be it little or much, if it be with kind-
ess, they are well pleased, else they go away sullen but say nothing.

They are great concealers of their own resentments, brought to it I
elieve by the revenge that hath been practiced among them; in either
f these they are not exceeded by the Italians. A tragical instance fell
ut since I came into the country: a king's daughter, thinking herself
lighted by her husband in suffering another woman to lie down be-
veen them, rose up, went out, plucked a root out of the ground and
te it, upon which she immediately died; and for which last week he
iade an offering to her kindred for atonement and liberty of marriage,
s two others did to the kindred of their wives that died a natural
eath. For till widowers have done so they must not marry again. Some
f the young women are said to take undue liberty before marriage for
portion, but when married [they are] chaste. When with child they
now their husbands no more till delivered; and during their month
hey touch no meat, they eat but with a stick lest they should defile it,
or do their husbands frequent them till that time be expired.

But in liberality they excel; nothing is too good for their friend.
Give them a fine gun, coat, or other thing, it may pass twenty hands
efore it sticks. [They are] light of heart, [with] strong affections, but
oon spent; the most merry creatures that live, [they] feast and dance
erpetually. They never have much nor want much; wealth circulateth
ike the blood; all parts partake and though none shall want what an-
ther hath, yet [they are] exact observers of property. Some kings have
old, others presented me with several parcels of land. The pay or
resents I made them were not hoarded by the particular owners, but,
he neighboring kings and their clans being present when the goods

[10] I.e., of meat.

were brought out, the parties chiefly concerned consulted what and to whom they should give them. To every king then, by the hands of a person for that work appointed, is a proportion sent so sorted and folded and with that gravity that is admirable. Then that king subdivideth it in like manner among his dependents, they hardly leaving themselves an equal share with one of their subjects. And be it on such occasions, at festivals, or at their common meals, the kings distribute and to themselves last. They care for little because they want but little, and the reason is, a little contents them. In this they are sufficiently revenged on us: if they are ignorant of our pleasures, they are also free from our pains. They are not disquieted with bills of lading and exchange, nor perplexed with chancery suits and exchequer reckonings. We sweat and toil to live; their pleasure feeds them—I mean their hunting, fishing, and fowling—and this table is spread everywhere; they eat twice a day, morning and evening, their seats and table are the ground. Since the European came into these parts, they are grown great lovers of strong liquors, rum especially, and for it exchange the richest of their skins and furs. If they are heated with liquors, they are restless till they have enough to sleep—that is their cry: "Some more and I will go to sleep"—but when drunk, one of the most wretched spectacles in the world.

In sickness [they are] impatient to be cured, and for it give anything, especially for their children, to whom they are extremely natural.[11] They drink at those times a teran, or decoction of some roots in spring water, and if they eat any flesh it must be of the female of any creature. If they die they bury them with their apparel, be they men or women, and the nearest of kin fling in something precious with them as a token of their love. Their mourning is blacking of their faces, which they continue for a year. They are choice of the graves of their dead, for lest they should be lost by time and fall to common use, they pick off the grass that grows upon them and heap up the fallen earth with great care and exactness.

These poor people are under a dark night in things relating to rel

11 Kind, affectionate.

gion, to be sure, the tradition of it. Yet they believe [in] a God and immortality without the help of metaphysics. For they say there is a great king that made them, who dwells in a glorious country to the southward of them, and that the souls of the good shall go thither where they shall live again. Their worship consists of two parts, sacrifice and *cantico*. Their sacrifice is their first fruits: the first and fattest buck they kill goeth to the fire, where he is all burnt with a mournful ditty of him that performeth the ceremony, but with such marvelous fervency and labor of body that he will even sweat to a foam. The other part is their *cantico*, performed by round dances, sometimes words, sometimes songs, then shouts, two being in the middle that begin and, by singing and drumming on a board, direct the chorus. Their postures in the dance are very antic and differing, but all keep measure. This is done with equal earnestness and labor, but great appearance of joy. In the fall, when the corn cometh in, they begin to feast one another. There have been two great festivals already, to which all come that will. I was at one myself: their entertainment was a green seat by a spring under some shady trees and twenty bucks with hot cakes of new corn, both wheat and beans, which they make up in a square form in the leaves of the stem and bake them in the ashes. And after that they fell to dance, but they that go must carry a small present in their money, it may be sixpence, which is made of the bone of a fish; the black is with them as gold, the white, silver; they call it all *wampum*.

Their government is by kings which they call *sachema*, and those by succession, but always of the mother's side. For instance, the children of him that is now king will not succeed, but his brother by the mother, or the children of his sister, whose sons (and after them the children of her daughters) will reign, for no woman inherits. The reason they render for this way of descent is that their issue may not be spurious.

Every king hath his council, and that consists of all the old and wise men of his nation, which perhaps is two hundred people. Nothing of moment is undertaken, be it war, peace, selling of land, or traffic, without advising with them, and, which is more, with the young men too.

'Tis admirable to consider how powerful the kings are and yet how they move by the breath of their people.

I have had occasion to be in council with them upon treaties for land and to adjust the terms of trade. Their order is thus: the king sits in the middle of a half-moon and hath his council, the old and wise on each hand; behind them or at a little distance sit the younger fry in the same figure. Having consulted and resolved their business, the king ordered one of them to speak to me. He stood up, came to me, and in the name of his king saluted me; then took me by the hand and told me that he was ordered by his king to speak to me and that now it was not he but the king that spoke, because what he should say was the king's mind. He first prayed me to excuse them that they had not complied with me the last time. He feared there might be some fault in the interpreter, being neither Indian nor English. Besides, it was the Indian custom to deliberate and take up much time in council before they resolve, and that if the young people and owners of the land had been as ready as he, I had not met with so much delay. Having thus introduced his matter, he fell to the bounds of the land they had agreed to dispose of and the price (which now is little and dear, that which would have bought twenty miles not buying now two). During the time that this person spoke, not a man of them was observed to whisper or smile, the old grave, the young reverend in their deportment.

They do speak little, but fervently and with elegancy. I have never seen more natural sagacity, considering them without the help (I was a-going to say, the spoil) of tradition, and he will deserve the name of wise that outwits them in any treaty about a thing they understand. When the purchase was agreed, great promises passed between us of kindness and good neighborhood and that the Indians and English must live in love as long as the sun gave light; which done, another made a speech to the Indians in the name of all the *sachamakers*, or kings: first to tell them what was done, next to charge and command them to love the Christians and particularly live in peace with me and the people under my government; that many governors had been in the river[12] but no governor had come himself to live and stay here before, and having now such a one that had treated them well, they should never do him or his any wrong—at every sentence of which they shouted and said "Amen" in their way.

The justice they have is pecuniary. In case of any wrong or evil fact, be it murder itself, they atone by feasts and presents of their wampum, which is proportioned to the quality of the offense or person injured or of the sex they are of. For in case they kill a woman, they pay double, and the reason they render is, that she breedeth children, which men cannot do. 'Tis rare that they fall out if sober and, if drunk, they forgive it, saying it was the drink and not the man that abused them.

We have agreed that in all differences between us six of each side shall end the matter. Don't abuse them, but let them have justice and you win them. The worst is that they are the worse for the Christians, who have propagated their vices and yielded them tradition for ill and not for good things. But as low an ebb as they are at and as glorious as their condition looks, the Christians have not outlived their sight with all their pretensions to a higher manifestation. What good then might not a good people graft where there is so distinct a knowledge left between good and evil? I beseech God to incline the hearts of all that come into these parts to outlive the knowledge of the natives by a fixed obedience to their greater knowledge of the will of God, for it were miserable indeed for us to fall under the unjust censure of the poor Indians' conscience while we make profession of things so far transcending.

For their original, I am ready to believe them of the Jewish race, I mean of the stock of the Ten Tribes, and that for the following reasons: first, they were to go to a land not planted or known which, to be sure, Asia and Africa were, if not Europe; and He that intended that extraordinary judgment upon them might make the passage not uneasy to them, as it is not impossible in itself, from the easternmost parts of Asia to the westernmost of America. In the next place, I find them of

---

[12] The speaker is referring to the governors of the earlier Swedish and Dutch colonies in the Delaware Valley.

like countenance and their children of so lively resemblance that a man would think himself in Duke's Place or Berry Street in London[13] when he seeth them. But this is not all: they agree in rites, they reckon by moons, they offer their first fruits, they have a kind of feast of tabernacles, they are said to lay their altar upon twelve stones, their mourning a year, customs of women, with many things that do not now occur.

[13] Duke's Place and Berry Street were in the heart of the Jewish quarter of London. The German-Jewish synagogue was located in Duke's Place, and the Portuguese Jews had a place of worship in Berry Street, near Bevis Marks (originally Buries Marks, whence Berry Street).

The First Plan of Union for America

Penn's interest in America was not limited to his own province on the Delaware. A far-seeing intercolonial statesman, he appreciated, as no other colonist before Benjamin Franklin did, the necessity of finding a solution to the baffling problem of imperial order. It was given to him to catch a distant glimpse of the federal solution that would finally be worked out for the United States in the Constitution of 1787 and for the British Empire in the Statute of Westminster of 1931.

In the year 1696 England was at war with France. The Board of Trade, newly created to superintend all colonial affairs, was discussing ways and means to establish a unified command in America and secure military contingents for the defense of New York's exposed frontier. Penn appeared before the Board with a plea that if quotas were to be demanded of the colonies, it was only just that they should be fixed by the colonies themselves through representatives meeting "in one common assembly." When the Lords of Trade invited him to present "a scheme more fully in writing," he drew up the brief sketch reprinted here. He proposed a continental Congress in which each colony should be represented, and carefully defined the areas of its competence. Though he had been led to propose his plan by the exigencies of war, he made it clear to the Board that "his meaning in it was principally for adjusting the differences that might arise between any of those colonies in civil matters, not military." In other words, he went beyond the Board's request and submitted a blueprint for a permanent union, whose object would be "better understanding" among the colonies and "the public tranquillity and safety."

The Board took no action. Nor can it be proved that any of those statesmen who later wrestled with the problem—Franklin, who drafted the Albany Plan of Union; Joseph Galloway, who proposed a kind of dominion status for North America in 1774; the authors of the Articles of Confederation, the Fathers of the Federal Constitution—ever heard of Penn's "scheme." Its importance lies chiefly in the fact that as early as 1696 William Penn's mind grasped the nature of the problem and hinted at the solution—the distribution of powers between central and local governments.

Penn's plan of union was first published in 1698 by Charles Davenant in his *Discourses on the Publick Revenues and on the Trade of England.* Our text is based on the copy printed in the *Memoirs of the Historical Society of Pennsylvania,* VI (1858), Part ii, 264–265.

A Plan of Union for the American Colonies (1696)

A BRIEF AND PLAIN SCHEME HOW THE ENGLISH COLONIES IN THE NORTH PARTS OF AMERICA (VIZ., BOSTON, CONNECTICUT, RHODE IS-LAND, NEW YORK, NEW JERSEYS, PENNSYLVANIA, MARYLAND, VIRGINIA, AND CAROLINA) MAY BE MADE MORE USEFUL TO THE CROWN AND ONE ANOTHER'S PEACE AND SAFETY WITH A UNIVERSAL CONCURRENCE.

1. That the several colonies before mentioned do meet once a year, and oftener if need be, during the war, and at least once in two years in times of peace by their stated and appointed deputies to debate and resolve of such measures as are most advisable for their better under-standing and the public tranquillity and safety.

2. That in order to it two persons well qualified for sense, sobriety, and substance be appointed by each province as their representatives or deputies, which in the whole make the Congress to consist of twenty persons.

3. That the King's Commissioner for that purpose specially ap-pointed shall have the chair and preside in the said Congress.

4. That they shall meet as near as conveniently may be to the most central colony for ease of the deputies.

5. Since that may in all probability be New York, both because it is near the center of the colonies and for that it is a frontier[1] and in the

---

[1] A border colony, having a common boundary with enemy territory—in this case, French Canada.

King's nomination,[2] the Governor of that colony may therefore also be the King's High Commissioner during the session, after the manner of Scotland.

6. That their business shall be to hear and adjust all matters of complaint or difference between province and province, as (first) where persons quit their own province and go to another that they may avoid their just debts, though they be able to pay them; (second) where offenders fly justice or justice cannot well be had upon such offenders in the provinces that entertain them; (third) to prevent or cure injuries in point of commerce; (fourth) to consider of ways and means to support the union and safety of these provinces against the public enemies. In which Congress the quotas of men and charges will be much easier and more equally set than it is possible for any establishment made here[3] to do, for the provinces, knowing their own condition and one another's, can debate that matter with more freedom and satisfaction and better adjust and balance their affairs in all respects for their common safety.

7. That in times of war the King's High Commissioner shall be general or chief commander of the several quotas upon service against the common enemy, as he shall be advised, for the good and benefit of the whole.

[2] New York was a royal colony: its governor was appointed directly by the Crown, as in Massachusetts, Virginia, the Carolinas, and (temporarily) Maryland. Connecticut and Rhode Island elected their own governors. In Pennsylvania, the Jerseys, and (normally) Maryland the governors were appointed by the proprietors.
[3] In England.

Towards a Peaceful World

If William Penn's plan for a union of the American colonies was the first faint adumbration of our Constitution, his *Essay Towards the Present and Future Peace of Europe* was certainly one of the most remarkable early blueprints for the Charter of the United Nations. Penn was not the first European to dream of a world united for peace; Dante, Erasmus, Henry IV of France, Hugo Grotius, a handful of other farsighted men, had caught a glimpse of that bright vision and had drawn up schemes to give it reality. Penn's *Essay* is notable among these early peace plans for its combination of idealism and realism, for the noble and disinterested nature of its ends and the practical character of its proposed means.

The essay was first published in 1693. Penn was living in retirement, harried and kept under close surveillance by William III, whose ministers suspected him of treason because of his unconcealed and unrepentant friendship for the deposed James II. England was embroiled with France in the War of the League of Augsburg, a war in which most of the countries of Europe—Sweden, Spain, Savoy, Holland, and several of the German states—were involved. All his humane Quaker feelings were stirred by the continued senseless bloodshed and suffering on the Continent, but he did not write primarily as a religious pacifist. The *Essay* is a treatise in practical statecraft. Penn stresses above all the economic advantages of peace. He considers the origin and purpose of government in a purely secular framework, rather than the theological context in which he had treated it in the Preface to his first Frame of Government. In projecting his plan for a parliament of nations he accepts the existing state system of Europe, and suggests that representation be proportioned to economic power. He proposes realistic solutions to the practical difficulties that might be expected to arise in such an international assembly (see, for instance, his ingenious answer to the vexing question of precedence, his proposal for the use of the secret ballot, his provision that all complaints be submitted in writing and be accessible to all members).

Though Penn frankly confesses his debt to the famous "Grand Design" attributed to Henry IV (but probably conceived by his chief minister, the Duc de Sully), he improves upon his model in several important respects. The "Grand Design" was basically a scheme to achieve the prime goal of French policy by destroying the power of Austria, and it was predicated upon a radical and highhanded rearrangement of the map of Europe. Penn's plan, on the contrary, was directed against no nation or group of nations; indeed, he was willing that his own country should have relatively few votes in the assembly in comparison with France, Spain, and the Empire. Moreover, he anticipated the principle of universal membership by envisaging the adherence of Russia and, even more surprisingly, Turkey, the infidel nation which all Europe feared and hated. (In this last provision, however, he was not unique: Émeric Crucé had suggested admitting nonchristian princes to the council of sovereigns proposed in his remarkable book *Le Nouveau Cynée* in 1623, though there is no evidence that Penn knew this book.) And finally, Penn's plan, unlike its predecessors, looked forward to disarmament as the only ultimate guaranty of international peace.

There are naïvetés and ambiguities, to be sure, in Penn's project. His statement that national sovereignty would not be lessened under his scheme because princes would still be "as sovereign at home as ever" underestimates the stubborn attachment of nations then as now to the "rights" of sovereignty in international affairs; Penn's argument would scarcely recommend his plan to a Louis XIV in the 1690's or to the isolationist detractors of the United Nations in the 1950's. And on the crucial question of sanctions he is—perhaps deliberately—vague. He provides that if one member nation violates its undertakings or commits aggression upon another, "all the other sovereignties, united as one strength, shall compel the submission and performance of the sentence"; but whether the compulsion should be by force or by other kinds of pressure he does not make clear.

Still, this essay is a document of extraordinary interest in the history of man's efforts to find a way out of the dead end of war by means of international organization; and Penn's conception of a world community under law is one that can yet excite our admiration and raise our hopes. First published anonymously in two editions in 1693, this little book, unlike most of Penn's other writings, has been reprinted more often in our own time than in his, a fact which bears witness to its remarkable contemporaneity.

An Essay Towards the Present and Future Peace of Europe (1693)

TO THE READER:

I have undertaken a subject that, I am very sensible, requires one of
more sufficiency than I am master of to treat it as in truth it deserves
and the groaning state of Europe calls for; but since bunglers may
stumble upon the game as well as masters, though it belongs to the skillful to hunt and catch it, I hope this essay will not be charged upon me
for a fault, if it appear to be neither chimerical nor injurious, and may
provoke abler pens to improve and perform the design with better
judgment and success. I will say no more in excuse of myself for this
undertaking but that it is the fruit of many solicitous thoughts for the
peace of Europe, and they must want charity as much as the world
needs quiet to be offended with me for so pacific a proposal. Let them
censure my management, so they prosecute the advantage of the design; for till the millenary doctrine[1] be accomplished, there is nothing
appears to me so beneficial an expedient to the peace and happiness of
this quarter of the world.

SECTION I.   OF PEACE AND ITS ADVANTAGES

He must not be a man but a statue of brass or stone, whose bowels
do not melt when he beholds the bloody tragedies of this war in Hungary, Germany, Flanders, Ireland, and at sea; the mortality of sickly
and languishing camps and navies; and the mighty prey the devouring
winds and waves have made upon ships and men since '88.[2] And as

---

[1] The doctrine of the millennium—the thousand-year reign of Christ prophesied
in the book of Revelation.
[2] The War of the League of Augsburg began in 1688.

this with reason ought to affect human nature, and deeply kindred, so there is something very moving that becomes prudent men to consider, and that is the vast charge that has accompanied that blood, and which makes no mean part of these tragedies; especially if they deliberate upon the uncertainty of the war, that they know not when nor how it will end, and that the expense cannot be less and the hazard is as great as before. So that in the contraries of peace we see the beauties and benefits of it, which under it—such is the unhappiness of mankind— we are too apt to nauseate, as the full stomach loathes the honeycomb, and like that unfortunate gentleman that, having a fine and a good woman to his wife and searching his pleasure in forbidden and less agreeable company, said, when reproached with his neglect of better enjoyments, that he could love his wife of all women if she were not his wife, though that increased his obligation to prefer her. It is a great mark of the corruption of our natures, and what ought to humble us extremely and excite the exercise of our reason to a nobler and juster sense, that we cannot see the use and pleasure of our comforts but by the want of them. As if we could not taste the benefit of health but by the help of sickness, nor understand the satisfaction of fullness without the instruction of want, nor, finally, know the comfort of peace but by the smart and penance of the vices of war—and without dispute that is not the least reason that God is pleased to chastise us so frequently with it.

What can we desire better than peace but the grace to use it? Peace preserves our possessions: we are in no danger of invasions, our trade is free and safe, and we rise and lie down without anxiety. The rich bring out their hoards and employ the poor manufactors.[3] Buildings and divers projections[4] for profit and pleasure go on. It excites industry, which brings wealth, as that gives the means of charity and hospitality, not the lowest ornaments of a kingdom or commonwealth. But war, like the frost of '83, seizes all these comforts at once, and stops the civil channel of society. The rich draw in their stock, the poor turn soldiers or thieves, or starve: no industry, no building, no manufactury,

---

[3] Artisans.
[4] Projects.

little hospitality or charity; but what the peace gave the war devours. I need say no more upon this head, when the advantages of peace and mischiefs of war are so many and sensible to every capacity under all governments, as either of them prevails. I shall proceed to the next point: what is the best means of peace? which will conduce much to open my way to what I have to propose.

SECTION II.   OF THE MEANS OF PEACE, WHICH IS JUSTICE RATHER THAN WAR

As justice is a preserver, so it is a better procurer of peace than war. Though *pax quaeritur bello* (peace is the end of war) be a usual saying, and as such it was taken up by O[liver] C[romwell] for his motto, yet the use generally made of that expression shows us that, properly and truly speaking, men seek their wills by war rather than peace, and that, as they will violate it to obtain them, so they will hardly be brought to think of peace unless their appetites be some way gratified. If we look over the stories of all times, we shall find the aggressors generally moved by ambition, [by] the pride of conquest and greatness of dominion more than right. But as those Leviathans appear rarely in the world, so I shall anon endeavor to make it evident they had never been able to devour the peace of the world and engross whole countries as they have done, if the proposal I have to make for the benefit of our present age had been then in practice. The advantage that justice has upon war is seen by the success of embassies, that so often prevent war by hearing the pleas and memorials of justice in the hands and mouths of the wronged party. Perhaps it may be in a good degree owing to reputation or poverty or some particular interest or conveniency of princes and states as much as justice, but it is certain that, as war cannot in any sense be justified but upon wrongs received and right, upon complaint, refused, so the generality of wars have their rise from some such pretension.

This is better seen and understood at home, for that which prevents a civil war in a nation is that which may prevent it abroad, viz., justice; and we see where that is notably obstructed, war is kindled between the magistrates and people in particular kingdoms and states, which, however it may be unlawful on the side of the people, we see never fails to follow, and ought to give the same caution to princes as if it were the right of the people to do it (though I must needs say the remedy is almost ever worse than the disease—the aggressors seldom getting what they seek, or performing, if they prevail, what they promised— and the blood and poverty that usually attend the enterprise weigh more on earth, as well as in heaven, than what they lost or suffered, or what they get by endeavoring to mend their condition comes to, which disappointment seems to be the voice of heaven and judgment of God against those violent attempts). But to return, I say justice is the means of peace betwixt the government and the people, and [between] one man and company and another. It prevents strife and at last ends it, for besides shame or fear to contend longer, he or they, being under government, are constrained to bound their desires and resentment with the satisfaction the law gives. Thus peace is maintained by justice, which is a fruit of government, as government of laws [is] from society, and society from consent.

SECTION III. GOVERNMENT, ITS RISE AND END UNDER ALL MODELS

Government is an expedient against confusion, a restraint upon all disorder: just weights and an even balance, that one man may not injure another nor himself by intemperance.

This was at first, without controversy, patrimonial; and upon the death of the father or head of the family, the eldest son or male of kin succeeded. But time breaking in upon this way of governing as the world multiplied, it fell under other claims and forms, and is as hard to trace to its original as are the copies we have of the first writings of sacred or civil matters. It is certain the most natural and human is that of consent, for that binds freely, as I may say, when men hold their liberty by their true obedience to rules of their own making. No man is judge in his own cause, which ends the confusion and blood of so many judges and executioners. For out of society every man is his own king, does what he lists at his own peril. But when he comes to incorporate himself, he submits that royalty to the conveniency of the whole, from whom he receives the returns of protection, so that he is not now his own judge nor avenger, neither is his antagonist; but the law, in indifferent[5] hands between both. And if he be a servant to others that before was free, he is also served of others that formerly owed him no obligation. Thus while we are not our own, everybody is ours, and we get more than we lose, the safety of the society being the safety of the particulars that constitute it. So that while we seem to submit to and hold all we have from society, it is by society that we keep what we have.

Government, then, is the prevention or cure of disorder and the means of justice, as that[6] is of peace. For this cause we have our sessions, terms, assizes, and parliaments to overrule men's passions and resentments, that they may not be judges in their own cause nor punishers of their own wrongs, which, as it is very incident to men in their corrupt state, so, for that reason, they would observe no measure, nor on the other hand would any be easily reduced to their duty. Not that men know not what is right, their excesses, and wherein they are to blame, by no means; nothing is plainer to them. But so depraved is human nature that, without compulsion some way or other, too many would not readily be brought to do what they know is right and fit, or avoid what they are satisfied they should not do. Which brings me near to the point I have undertaken, and for the better understanding of which I have thus briefly treated of peace, justice, and government as a necessary introduction, because the ways and methods by which peace is preserved in particular governments will help those readers most concerned in my proposal to conceive with what ease as well as advantage the peace of Europe might be procured and kept, which is the end designed by me with all submission to those interested in this little treatise.

5 Impartial.
6 I.e., justice.

SECTION IV. OF A GENERAL PEACE, OR THE PEACE OF EUROPE, AND THE MEANS OF IT

In my first section I showed the desirableness of peace; in my next, the truest means of it, to wit, justice not war. And in my last, that this justice was the fruit of government, as government itself was the result of society, which first came from a reasonable design in men of peace. Now if the sovereign princes of Europe, that represent that sovereign or independent state of men that was previous to the obligations of society would, for the same reason that engaged men first into society, viz., love of peace and order, agree to meet by their stated deputies in a general diet, estates, or parliament, and there establish rules of justice for sovereign princes to observe one to another; and this to meet yearly or once in two or three years at farthest, or as they shall see cause, and to be styled the sovereign or imperial diet, parliament, or states of Europe, before which sovereign assembly should be brought all difference depending between one sovereign and another that cannot be made up by private embassies before the sessions begin; and that if any of the sovereignties that constitute these imperial states shall refuse to submit their claim or pretensions to them or to abide and perform the judgment thereof, and seek their remedy by arms or delay their compliance beyond the time prefixed in their resolutions, all the other sovereignties, united as one strength, shall compel the submission and performance of the sentence with damages to the suffering party and charges to the sovereignties that obliged their submission; to be sure, Europe would quietly obtain the so much desired and needed peace to her harassed inhabitants, no sovereignty in Europe having the power, and therefore cannot show the will, to dispute the conclusion; and consequently peace would be procured and continued in Europe.

SECTION V. OF THE CAUSES OF DIFFERENCE AND MOTIVES TO VIOLATE PEACE

There appears to me but three things upon which peace is broken; viz., to keep, to recover, to add. First, to keep what is one's right from the invasion of an enemy, in which I am purely defensive. Secondly, to recover, when I think myself strong enough, that which by violence I or my ancestors have lost to the arms of a stronger power, in which I am offensive. Or lastly, to increase my dominion by the acquisition of my neighbor's countries, as I find them weak and myself strong, to gratify which passion there will never want some accident or other for a pretense, and, knowing my own strength, I will be my own judge and carver. This last will find no room in the imperial states: they are an unpassable limit to that ambition. But the other two may come as soon as they please and find the justice of that sovereign court. And considering how few there are of those sons of prey and how early they show themselves—maybe not once in an age or two—this expedient being established, the balance cannot well be broken.

SECTION VI.   OF TITLES, UPON WHICH THOSE DIFFERENCES MAY ARISE

But I easily foresee a question that must be answered in our way, and that is this: what is right? or else we can never know what is wrong; it is very fit that this should be established. But that is fitter for the sovereign states to resolve than me. And yet that I may lead a way to the matter, I say that title is either by a long and undoubted succession, as the crowns of Spain, France, and England; or by election, as the crown of Poland and the Empire;[7] or by marriage, as the family of the Stuarts came by England, the elector of Brandenburg to the duchy of Cleves, and we, in ancient time, to divers places abroad; or by purchase, as hath been frequently done in Italy and Germany; or by conquest, as the Turk in Christendom, the Spaniards in Flanders, formerly mostly in the French hands, and the French in Burgundy, Normandy, Lorraine, French-County,[8] etc. This last title is, morally speaking, only questionable. It has indeed obtained a place among the rolls of titles, but it was engrossed and recorded by the point of the sword and in bloody characters. What cannot be controlled or resisted must be submitted to; but all the world knows the date of the lease of such empires and that

---

[7] The Holy Roman Empire.
[8] Franche-Comté, the Free County of Burgundy.

they expire with the power of the possessor to defend them. And yet there is a little allowed to conquest too, when it has had the sanction of articles of peace to confirm it, though that doth not always extinguish the fire, but it lies, like embers under ashes, ready to kindle so soon as there is a fit matter prepared for it. Nevertheless, when conquest has been confirmed by a treaty and conclusion of peace, I must confess it is an adopted title; and if not so genuine and natural, yet, being engrafted, it is fed by that which is the security of better titles, consent. There is but one thing more to be mentioned in this section, and that is from what time titles shall take their beginning, or how far back we may look to confirm or dispute them. It would be very bold and inexcusable in me to determine so tender a point, but be it more or less time, as to the last general peace at Nimeguen,[9] or to the commencing of this war, or to the time of the beginning of the treaty of peace, I must submit it to the great pretenders and masters in that affair. But something everybody must be willing to give or quit that he may keep the rest and by this establishment be forever freed of the necessity of losing more.

SECTION VII. OF THE COMPOSITION OF THESE IMPERIAL STATES

The composition and proportion of this sovereign part or imperial state does, at the first look, seem to carry with it no small difficulty what votes to allow for the inequality of the princes and states. But with submission to better judgments, I cannot think it invincible, for if it be possible to have an estimate of the yearly value of the several sovereign countries whose delegates are to make up this august assembly, the determination of the number of persons or votes in the states for every sovereignty will not be impracticable. Now that England, France, Spain, the Empire, etc., may be pretty exactly estimated is so plain a case, by considering the revenue of lands, the exports and entries at the Custom Houses, the books of rates and surveys that are in all governments to proportion taxes for the support of them, that the least incli-

[9] The treaties of Nimeguen (Nijmeegen, Nimwegen) in 1678–1679 ended the war of Louis XIV of France (with Sweden) against Holland, Spain, the Holy Roman Empire, and Denmark.

nation to the peace of Europe will not stand or halt at this objection.

I will, with pardon on all sides, give an instance far from exact, nor do I pretend to it or offer it for an estimate, for I do it at random; only this, as wide as it is from the just proportion, will give some aim to my judicious reader what I would be at, remembering I design not by any computation an estimate from the revenue of the prince, but the value of the territory, the whole being concerned as well as the prince. And a juster measure it is to go by, since one prince may have more revenue than another, that has much a richer country, though in the instance I am now about to make the caution is not so necessary, because, as I said before, I pretend to no manner of exactness, but go wholly by guess, being but for example's sake. I suppose the Empire of Germany to send twelve; France, ten; Spain, ten; Italy, which comes to France, eight; England, six; Portugal, three; Sweden, four; Denmark, three; Poland, four; Venice, three; the seven provinces,[10] four; [the] thirteen cantons[11] and little neighboring sovereignties, two; [the] duke of Holstein and Courland, one; and if the Turks and Muscovites are taken in, as seems but fit and just, they will make ten apiece more. The whole makes ninety—a great presence when they represent the fourth, and now the best and wealthiest, part of the known world, where religion and learning, civility and arts have their seat and empire. But it is not absolutely necessary there should be always so many persons to represent the larger sovereignties, for the votes may be given by one man of any sovereignty as well as by ten or twelve; though the fuller the assembly of states is, the more solemn, effectual, and free the debates will be, and the resolutions must needs come with greater authority. The place of their [first] session should be central, as much as is possible; afterward as they agree.

SECTION VIII. OF THE REGULATION OF THE IMPERIAL STATES IN SESSION

To avoid quarrel for precedency the room may be round, and have divers doors to come in and out at to prevent exceptions. If the whole

---

[10] The United Provinces of the Netherlands.
[11] Switzerland.

number be cast into tens, each choosing one, they may preside by turns, to whom all speeches should be addressed, and who should collect the sense of the debates and state the question for a vote, which in my opinion, should be by the ballot after the prudent and commendable method of the Venetians, which in a great degree prevents the ill effects of corruption, because if any of the delegates of that high and mighty estates could be so vile, false, and dishonorable as to be influenced by money, they have the advantage of taking their money that will give it them and of voting undiscovered to the interest of their principals and their own inclination, as they that understand the balloting box do very well know: a shrewd stratagem and an experimented remedy against corruption, at least against corrupting, for who will give their money where they may so easily be cozened, and where it is two to one they will be so; for they that will take money in such cases will not stick to lie heartily to them that give it rather than wrong their country, when they know their lie cannot be detected.

It seems to me that nothing in this imperial parliament should pass but by three-quarters of the whole, at least seven above the balance. I am sure it helps to prevent treachery, because if money could ever be a temptation in such a court, it would cost a great deal of money to weigh down the wrong scale. All complaints should be delivered in writing in the nature of memorials, and journals kept by a proper person in a trunk or chest, which hath as many differing locks as there are tens in the states. And if there were a clerk for each ten, and a pew or table for those clerks in the assembly, and at the end of every session one out of each ten were appointed to examine and compare the journals of those clerks and then lock them up, as I have before expressed, it would be clear and satisfactory. And each sovereignty, if they please, as is but very fit, may have an exemplification or copy of the said memorials and the journals of proceedings upon them.

The liberty and rules of speech, to be sure, they cannot fail in, who will be the wisest and noblest of each sovereignty, for its own honor and safety. If any difference can arise between those that come from the same sovereignty, that one of the major number do give the balls[12] of

[12] Ballots.

that sovereignty. I should think it extremely necessary that every sovereignty should be present under great penalties, and that none leave the session without leave till all be finished, and that neutralities in debates should by no means be endured, for any such latitude will quickly open a way to unfair proceeding and be followed by a train both of seen and unseen inconveniences. I will say little of the language in which the session of the sovereign estates should be held but, to be sure, it must be in Latin or French: the first would be very well for civilians,[13] but the last most easy for men of quality.

SECTION IX. OF THE OBJECTIONS THAT MAY BE ADVANCED AGAINST THE DESIGN

I will first give an answer to the objections that may be offered against my proposal, and in my next and last section I shall endeavor to show some of the manifold conveniences that would follow this European league or confederacy.

The first of them is this, that the strongest and richest sovereignty will never agree to it, and if it should, there would be danger of corruption more than of force at one time or other. I answer to the first part, he is not stronger than all the rest, and for that reason you should promote this and compel him into it, especially before he be so, for then it will be too late to deal with such a one. To the last part of the objection I say the way is as open now as then and it may be the number fewer and as easily come at. However, if men of sense and honor and substance are chosen, they will either scorn the baseness or have wherewith to pay for the knavery; at least they may be watched so, that one may be a check upon the other, and all prudently limited by the sovereignty they represent. In all great points, especially before a final resolve, they may be obliged to transmit to their principals the merits of such important cases depending, and receive their last instruction, which may be done in four and twenty days at the most, as the place of their session may be appointed.

The second is, that it will endanger an effeminacy by such a disuse of the trade of soldiery, that if there should be any need for it upon any

---

13 Experts in the civil or Roman law.

occasion, we should be at a loss, as they were in Holland in '72.[14] There can be no danger of effeminacy, because each sovereignty may introduce as temperate or severe a discipline in the education of youth as they please by low living[15] and due labor. Instruct them in mechanical knowledge and in natural philosophy by operation, which is the honor of the German nobility. This would make them men, neither women nor lions, for soldiers are t'other extreme to effeminacy. But the knowledge of nature and the useful as well as agreeable operations of art give men an understanding of themselves, of the world they are born into, how to be useful and serviceable, both to themselves and others, and how to save and help, not injure or destroy. The knowledge of government in general, the particular constitutions of Europe, and, above all, of his own country are very recommending accomplishments. This fits him for the parliament and council at home and the courts of princes and services in the imperial states abroad. At least, he is a good commonwealths-man and can be useful to the public or retire, as there may be occasion.

To the other part of the objection, of being at a loss for soldiery as they were in Holland in '72, the proposal answers for itself. One has war no more than the other, and will be as much to seek upon occasion. Nor is it to be thought that anyone will keep up such an army after such an umpire is on foot, which may hazard the safety of the rest. However, if it be seen requisite, the question may be asked by order of the sovereign states, why such a one either raises or keeps up a formidable body of troops, and to oblige him forthwith to reform or reduce them, lest anyone, by keeping up a great body of troops, should surprise a neighbor. But a small force in every other sovereignty, to what it is capable or accustomed to maintain, will certainly prevent that danger and vanquish any such fear.

The third objection is that there will be great want of employment for younger brothers of families, and that the poor must either turn soldiers or thieves. I have answered that in my return to the second

[14] Louis XIV caught the Dutch entirely unprepared for a land war when he invaded their borders in 1672.
[15] Moderation, austerity.

objection. We shall have the more merchants and husbandmen or ingenious naturalists if the government be but anything solicitous of
the education of their youth, which, next to the present and immediate happiness of any country, ought of all things to be the care and
skill of the government. For such as the youth of any country is bred,
such is the next generation, and the government in good or bad hands.

I am come now to the last objection, that sovereign princes and states
will hereby become not sovereign, a thing they will never be brought
to. But this also, under correction, is a mistake, for they remain as
sovereign at home as ever they were. Neither their power over their
people nor the usual revenue they pay them is diminished; it may be
the war establishment may be reduced, which will indeed of course
follow, or be better employed to the advantage of the public. So that
the sovereignties are as they were, for none of them have now any sovereignty over one another; and if this be called a lessening of their power,
it must be only because the great fish can no longer eat up the little
ones and that each sovereignty is equally defended from injuries and
disabled from committing them. *Cedant arma togae*[16] is a glorious
sentence; the voice of the dove, the olive branch of peace, a blessing
so great that when it pleases God to chastise us severely for our sins, it
is with the rod of war that, for the most part, He whips us, and experience tells us none leaves deeper marks behind it.

SECTION X.   OF THE REAL BENEFITS THAT FLOW
FROM THIS PROPOSAL ABOUT PEACE

I am come to my last section, in which I shall enumerate some of
those many real benefits that flow from this proposal for the present
and future peace of Europe.

Let it not, I pray, be the least that it prevents the spilling of so much
human and Christian blood, for a thing so offensive to God and ter-
rible and afflicting to men as that has ever been must recommend our
expedient beyond all objections. For what can a man give in exchange
for his life as well as his soul? And though the chiefest in government
are seldom personally exposed, yet it is a duty incumbent upon them to

16 Let wars yield to peace (Cicero, *De officiis*).

be tender of the lives of their people, since without all doubt they are accountable to God for the blood that is spilt in their service. So that besides the loss of so many lives, of importance to any government both for labor and propagation, the cries of so many widows, parents, and fatherless are prevented, that cannot be very pleasant in the ears of any government, and is the natural consequence of war in all governments.

There is another manifest benefit which redounds to Christendom by this peaceable expedient: the reputation of Christianity will in some degree be recovered in the sight of infidels, which, by the many bloody and unjust wars of Christians, not only with them, but one with another, hath been greatly impaired. For, to the scandal of that holy profession, Christians that glory in their Saviour's name have long devoted the credit and dignity of it to their worldly passions as often as they have been excited by the impulses of ambition or revenge. They have not always been in the right, nor has right been for a reason of war; and not only Christians against Christians, but the same sort of Christians have imbrued their hands in one another's blood, invoking and interesting, all they could, the good and merciful God to prosper their arms to their brethren's destruction; yet their Saviour has told them that He came to save and not to destroy the lives of men, to give and plant peace among men, and if in any sense He may be said to send war, it is the holy war indeed, for it is against the Devil and not the persons of men. Of all His titles this seems the most glorious as well as comfortable for us, that He is the Prince of Peace: it is His nature, His office, His work, and the end and excelling blessing of His coming, Who is both the maker and preserver of our peace with God. And it is very remarkable that in all the New Testament He is but once called lion, but frequently the lamb of God, to denote to us His gentle, meek, and harmless nature, and that those that desire to be the disciples of His Cross and Kingdom (for they are inseparable) must be like Him, as St. Paul, St. Peter, and St. John tell us. Nor is it said the lamb shall lie down with the lion, but the lion shall lie down with the lamb; that is, war shall yield to peace, and the soldier turn hermit. To be sure, Christians should not be apt to strive, nor swift to anger against anybody, and less with one another, and least of all for the uncertain and fading enjoyments of this lower world; and no quality is exempted from this doctrine. Here is a wide field for the reverend clergy of Europe to act their part in, who have so much the possession of princes and people too. May they recommend and labor this pacific means I offer, which will end blood, if not strife; and then reason, upon free debate, will be judge, and not the sword. So that both right and peace, which are the desires and fruit of wise governments and the choice blessings of any country, seem to succeed the establishment of this proposal.

The third benefit is that it saves money, both to the princes and people, and thereby prevents those grudgings and misunderstandings between them that are wont to follow the devouring expenses of war, and enables both to perform public acts for learning, charity, manu- factories, etc., the virtues of government and ornaments of countries. Nor is this all the advantage that follows to sovereignties upon this head of money and good husbandry, to whose service and happiness this short discourse is dedicated, for it saves the great expense that frequent and splendid embassies require and all their appanages of spies and intelligence, which in the most prudent governments have devoured mighty sums of money, and that not without some immoral practices also, such as corrupting of servants to betray their masters by revealing their secrets—not to be defended by Christian or old Roman virtue. But here, where there is nothing to fear, there is little to know, and therefore the purchase is either cheap or may be wholly spared. I might mention pensions to the widows and orphans of such as die in wars and of those that have been disabled in them, which rise high in the revenue of some countries.

Our fourth advantage is that the towns, cities, and countries that might be laid waste by the rage of war are thereby preserved, a blessing that would be very well understood in Flanders and Hungary and in- deed upon all the borders of sovereignties, which are almost ever the stages of spoils and misery, of which the stories of England and Scot- land do sufficiently inform us without looking over the water.

The fifth benefit of this peace is the ease and security of travel and traffic, a happiness never understood since the Roman Empire has been broken into so many sovereignties. But we may easily conceive the comfort and advantage of traveling through the governments of Europe by a pass from any of the sovereignties of it, which this league and state of peace will naturally make authentic. They that have traveled Germany, where is so great a number of sovereignties, know the want and value of this privilege by the many stops and examinations they meet with by the way, but especially such as have made the great tour of Europe. This leads to the benefit of a universal monarchy without the inconveniences that attend it, for when the whole was one empire, though these advantages were enjoyed, yet the several provinces that now make the kingdoms and states of Europe were under some hardship from the great sums of money remitted to the imperial seat and the ambition and avarice of their several proconsuls and governors and the great taxes they paid to the numerous legions of soldiers that they maintained for their own subjection, who were not wont to entertain that concern for them (being uncertainly there and having their fortunes to make) which their respective and proper sovereignties have always shown for them. So that to be ruled by native princes or states with the advantage of that peace and security that can only render a universal monarchy desirable is peculiar to our proposal, and for that reason it is to be preferred.

Another advantage is the great security it will be to Christians against the inroads of the Turk in their most prosperous fortune. For it had been impossible for the Porte[17] to have prevailed so often and so far upon Christendom but by the carelessness or willful connivance, if not aid, of some Christian princes. And for the same reason why no Christian monarch will adventure to oppose or break such a union, the Grand Seignior[18] will find himself obliged to concur for the security of what he holds in Europe, where, with all his strength, he would feel it an overmatch for him. The prayers, tears, treason, blood, and dev-

[17] The Sublime Porte, the government of the Turkish Empire.
[18] The Sultan of Turkey.

astation that war has cost in Christendom for these two last ages especially must add to the credit of our proposal and the blessing of the peace thereby humbly recommended.

The seventh advantage of a European imperial diet, parliament, or estates is that it will beget and increase personal friendships between princes and states, which tends to the rooting up of wars and planting peace in a deep and fruitful soil. For princes have the curiosity of seeing the courts and cities of other countries as well as private men, if they could as securely and familiarly gratify their inclinations. It were a great motive to the tranquillity of the world that they could freely converse face to face and personally and reciprocally give and receive marks of civility and kindness. A hospitality that leaves these impressions behind it will hardly let ordinary matters prevail to mistake or quarrel one another. Their emulation would be in the instances of goodness, laws, customs, learning, arts, buildings, and in particular those that relate to charity, the true glory of some governments, where beggars are as much a rarity as in other places it would be to see none.

Nor is this all the benefit that would come by this freedom and interview of princes; for natural affection would hereby be preserved, which we see little better than lost from the time their children or sisters are married into other courts. For the present state and insecurity of princes forbid them the enjoyment of that natural comfort which is possessed by private families, insomuch that from the time a daughter or sister is married to another crown, nature is submitted to interest, and that, for the most part, grounded not upon solid or commendable foundations but ambition or unjust avarice. I say this freedom, that is the effect of our pacific proposal, restores nature to her just right and dignity in the families of princes and then to the comfort she brings, wherever she is preserved in her proper station. Here daughters may personal[ly] entreat their parents and sisters their brothers for a good understand[ing] between them and their husbands, where nature, not crushed by absence and sinister interests but active by the sight and lively entreaties of such near relations, is almost sure to prevail. They cannot easily resist the most affectional addresses of such powerful solicitors as their children and grandchildren and their sisters, nephews, and nieces, and so backwards from children to parents and sisters to brothers, to keep up and preserve their own families by a good understanding between their husbands and them.

To conclude this section, there is yet another manifest privilege that follows this intercourse and good understanding, which methinks should be very moving with princes; viz., that hereby they may choose wives for themselves, such as they love, and not by proxy merely to gratify interest, an ignoble motive, and [that] rarely begets or continues that kindness which ought to be between men and their wives—a satisfaction very few princes ever knew and to which all other pleasures ought to resign. Which has often obliged me to think that the advantage of private men upon princes by family comforts is a sufficient balance against their great power and glory, the one being more in imagination than real, and often unlawful, but the other natural, solid, and commendable. Besides, it is certain, parents' loving well before they are married, which very rarely happens to princes, has kind and generous influences upon their offspring, which, with their example, makes them the better husbands and wives in their turn. This in great measure prevents unlawful love and the mischief of those intrigues that are wont to follow them: what hatred, feuds, wars, and desolations have in divers ages flowed from unkindness between princes and their wives? what unnatural divisions among their children and ruin to their families, if not loss of their countries by it? Behold an expedient to prevent it, a natural, an efficacious one, happy to princes and happy to their people also. For nature, being renewed and strengthened by these mutual pledges and endearments [I] have mentioned, will leave those soft and kind impressions behind in the minds of princes that court and country will very easily discern and feel the good effects of it, especially if they have the wisdom to show that they interest themselves in the prosperity of the children and relations of their princes. For it does not only incline them to be good, but engage those relations to become powerful suitors to their princes for them, if any misunderstanding should unhappily arise between them and their sovereigns.

Thus ends this section. It now rests to conclude the discourse, in which, if I have not pleased my reader or answered his expectation, it is some comfort to me I meant well, and have cost him but little money and time; and brevity is an excuse if not a virtue, where the subject is not agreeable or is but ill prosecuted.

The Conclusion

I will conclude this my proposal of a European sovereign or imperial diet, parliament, or estates with that which I have touched upon before, and which falls under the notice of everyone concerned, by coming home to their particular and respective experience within their own sovereignties, that the same rules of justice and prudence by which parents and masters govern their families, and magistrates their cities, and estates their republics, and princes and kings their principalities and kingdoms, Europe may obtain and preserve peace among her sovereignties. For wars are the duels of princes; and as government in kingdoms and states prevents men being judges and executioners for themselves, overrules private passions as to injuries or revenge, and subjects the great as well as the small to the rule of justice, that power might not vanquish or oppress right, nor one neighbor act an independency and sovereignty upon another, while they have resigned that original claim to the benefit and comfort of society, so this being soberly weighed in the whole and parts of it, it will not be hard to conceive or frame nor yet to execute the design I have here proposed.

And for the better understanding and perfecting of the idea I here present to the sovereign princes and estates of Europe for the safety and tranquillity of it, I must recommend to their perusal Sir William Temple's *Account of the United Provinces*,[19] which is an instance and answer upon practice to all the objections that can be advanced against the practicability of my proposal; nay, it is an experiment that not only comes up to our case but exceeds the difficulties that can render its accomplishment disputable. For there we shall find three degrees of sov-

---

[19] *Observations upon the United Provinces of the Netherlands* (London, 1672). Sir William Temple was a distinguished English author and diplomat who served for several years as ambassador to The Hague.

ereignties to make up every sovereignty in the general states. I will reckon them backwards: first, the States-General[20] themselves; then the immediate sovereignties that constitute them, which are those of the provinces, answerable to the sovereignties of Europe that by their deputies are to compose the European diet, parliament, or estates in our proposal; and then there are the several cities of each province, that are so many independent or distinct sovereignties, which compose those of the provinces, as those of the provinces do compose the States-General at The Hague.

But I confess I have the passion to wish heartily that the honor of proposing and effecting so great and good a design might be owing to England of all the countries in Europe, as something of the nature of our expedient was, in design and preparation, to the wisdom, justice, and valor of Henry the Fourth of France, whose superior qualities, raising his character above those of his ancestors or contemporaries, deservedly gave him the style of Henry the Great.[21] For he was upon obliging the princes and estates of Europe to a politic balance, when the Spanish faction for that reason contrived and accomplished his murder by the hands of Ravaillac.[22] I will not then fear to be censured for proposing an expedient for the present and future peace of Europe when it was not only the design but glory of one of the greatest princes that ever reigned in it, and is found practicable in the constitution of one of the wisest and powerfullest states of it. So that to conclude, I have very little to answer for in all this affair, because, if it succeed, I have so little to deserve, for this great king's example tells us it is fit to be done, and Sir William Temple's History shows us by a surpassing instance that it may be done, and Europe by her incomparable miseries makes it now necessary to be done, that my share is only thinking of it at this juncture and putting it into the common light for the peace and prosperity of Europe.

[20] The legislature of the United Provinces.

[21] The so-called "Grand Design" of Henry IV is known to us from the *Memoirs* of his Superintendent of Finance, the Duc de Sully, first published in 1638. The majority of scholars now believe that this peace plan was actually the work of Sully himself.

[22] François Ravaillac, a religious fanatic who stabbed Henry IV to death in 1610.

3
The Final Distillation

The Final Distillation

Though Penn wrote incessantly—he published over a hundred separate works during his lifetime, from broadsides to full-length books—it is possible to distinguish three major periods of creativity in his literary career. The first came between 1668 and 1671. It was during these years that he underwent his most intense suffering for his faith, yet he managed to write, among other books, the first version of *No Cross, No Crown, The Great Case of Liberty of Conscience,* and (insofar as he had a hand in its writing) *The People's Ancient and Just Liberties Asserted.* During the years from 1678 to 1683, the exciting years of his major political activity, he produced the revised and enlarged *No Cross, No Crown,* his great Whig political tracts, his first Frame of Government, and his promotional pamphlets for Pennsylvania. And between 1692 and 1694 he composed *An Essay Towards the Present and Future Peace of Europe, The Rise and Progress of the People Called Quakers,* and *Some Fruits of Solitude.*

This last creative period was neither a time of religious exaltation and personal suffering like the first nor one of intensive mundane activity like the second. It was an interval of enforced leisure, of retirement from the world of action and passion. Out of favor at court, his province in America temporarily removed from his control, he was living a kind of hole-and-corner existence, now in London, now at Worminghurst, his country seat in Sussex. Unable to play either of his chosen roles, as preacher or statesman, in the full light of day, he could give himself up to sustained reflection upon man and nature and God—and address himself for the first time to the problems of the writer. Hitherto most of his writings had been tracts for the times, produced under pressure for an immediate and particular purpose. His style had reflected the conditions under which he wrote: it was the style of a man scribbling at top speed, careless of syntax, copious of language, piling clause upon clause in long, loose, straggling sentences. Now he deliberately adopted a literary form that required conciseness, economy, discrimination in the choice of words, care in the structure of his periods.

The result was *Some Fruits of Solitude,* in which he set down his matured philosophy of life in the form of maxims or aphorisms—droplet of clear wisdom, as it were, distilled from a lifetime of sober thought and dedicated action. Within the next few years he composed and published a further series of maxims, which he called *More Fruits of Solitude* and wrote out a little book of advice to his children, which was published after his death under the title *Fruits of a Father's Love*. His primary concern in these works was not to bring forth new ideas but to clarify and refine those which had formed the staple of his discourse for a quarter-century. In *Some Fruits of Solitude* and its two sequels we have a kind of recapitulation of all the main themes of his thought, subtly transmuted and mellowed.

Here is the ultra-Protestant morality of *No Cross, No Crown* with its Puritan austerity, its emphasis on the bourgeois virtues of diligence and thrift, its distinctive Quaker social consciousness—but purged of its harsh Jeremiac quality (he cautions against censoriousness, for example, and laughs avarice out of court with a humorous reference to the "man who died to save charges.") Here is the old love of liberty, religious and political, but it has become less obsessive: he can even praise conformity "where conscience does not forbid a compliance," as being "at least a civil virtue," and he thinks the man who is overscrupulous in "things of an indifferent nature" is a nuisance to society. (Did some of the minor Quaker testimonies which he had once faithfully borne at such cost in ridicule and social ostracism—the testimony against "capping and kneeing," for instance—now seem like petty scruples?) Here is the old concern with righteousness in politics, with responsible government and the rule of law, but after a decade of dealing with the stiff-necked, contentious people of Pennsylvania, there is a little less of the radical Whig's faith in representative institutions. (The long-suffering Proprietor of Pennsylvania now speaks frankly in the accents of a paternalist; he offers helpful advice to princes, and even permits himself an aside that suggests a touch of cynicism: "Let the people think they govern and they will be governed.") Here is the old fondness for a simple rural existence that had always colored his social and economic views, grown, if anything, more insistent. ("The country life," he writes, "is to be preferred, for there we see the works of God, but in cities little else but the works of men.") And here, finally, is his abiding Quaker faith in inward illumination, a serener, more rational faith, perhaps, than that of the tense, turbulent earlier days, but still strong and clear.

The spirit that Penn breathed into these aphorisms has endeared them to many readers over the two and a half centuries since he set them down. Robert Louis Stevenson came upon a copy of *Some Fruits of Solitude* n a secondhand bookstore in San Francisco in 1879. It was during a period of deep personal distress, when he felt depressed and defeated. But the sane and sanative qualities of "this sweet, dignified, and wholesome book," he has told us, lifted his heart and renewed his courage. "There is not the man living," he thought, "no, nor recently dead—that could put with so lovely a spirit so much honest, kind wisdom into words."

Critics like Logan Pearsall Smith (who finds in Penn's aphorisms "no great profundity of observation or subtlety of thought") and C. E. Vulliamy (who confesses that "a wicked thought is generally more amusing than a good one") have missed the point in comparing *Some Fruits of Solitude* unfavorably with La Rochefoucauld's *Maximes* or Pascal's *Pensées* or Lord Chesterfield's *Letters to His Son*. Penn, after all, as William Wistar Comfort pointed out, "is not a great philosopher, but he is the first of Quaker moralists." The sounder comparison, perhaps, would be with Benjamin Franklin or Ralph Waldo Emerson. Certainly Penn's concern with the humbler, workaday virtues of diligence and thrift foreshadows Poor Richard, though Penn falls as far short of Franklin in pungency and humor as he rises above him in generosity and idealism. Penn's intuitive approach to religion suggests Emerson, and if the Quaker lacks the hyperbolic wit of the Yankee Transcendentalist, his writings are at least not obscured by cloudy metaphysics. But fundamentally Penn was himself in these maxims and reflections of his final period—a religious idealist with a saving salt of practical common sense; a man of the world who refused to become soured or embittered by suffering, misunderstanding, and misfortune; an aristocrat whose social conscience never lost its quick sensitivity; an intellectual who did not shrink from emotional commitment; an imperfect saint, whose very human weaknesses are an encouragement to those who are attracted by the vision of perfection he held before the world.

Some Fruits of Solitude was published anonymously in 1693 and went through seven editions in the next ten years. *More Fruits of Solitude* came out in 1702, and the two parts together have been reprinted upward of forty times during two and a half centuries, besides having been translated into French, German, and Dutch. We have selected approximately a third of the 855 maxims which make up the two parts. *Fruits of a Father's Love* was probably written shortly before Penn embarked for America on his second visit in 1699. It was not published, however, until 1726, in which year two editions appeared.

From Some Fruits of Solitude (1693)

THE PREFACE

READER:

This enchiridion[1] I present thee with is the fruit of solitude, a school few care to learn in, though none instructs us better. Some parts of it are the result of serious reflection, others the flashings of lucid intervals, writ for private satisfaction and now published for a help to human conduct.

The author blesseth God for his retirement, and kisses that gentle hand which led him into it, for though it should prove barren to the world, it can never do so to him.

He has now had some time he could call his own, a property he was never so much master of before, in which he has taken a view of himself and the world, and observed wherein he hath hit and missed the mark, what might have been done, what mended, and what avoided in his human conduct, together with the omissions and excesses of others, as well societies and governments as private families and persons. And he verily thinks, were he to live over his life again, he could not only with God's grace serve Him but his neighbor and himself better than he hath done, and have seven years of his time to spare. And yet perhaps he hath not been the worst or the idlest man in the world, nor is he the oldest. And this is the rather said that it might quicken thee, reader, to lose none of the time that is yet thine.

There is nothing of which we are apt to be so lavish as of time, and about which we ought to be more solicitous, since without it we can do nothing in this world. Time is what we want most, but what, alas, we use worst, and for which God will certainly most strictly reckon with us when time shall be no more.

[1] Handbook.

It is of that moment to us in reference to both worlds that I can hardly wish any man better than that he would seriously consider what he does with his time, how and to what ends he employs it, and what returns he makes to God, his neighbor, and himself for it. Will he never have a ledger for this—this, the greatest wisdom and work of life?

To come but once into the world and trifle away our true enjoyment of it and of ourselves in it is lamentable indeed. This one reflection would yield a thinking person great instruction. And since nothing below man can so think, man in being thoughtless must needs fall below himself. And that, to be sure, such do as are unconcerned in the use of their most precious time.

This is but too evident if we will allow ourselves to consider that there's hardly anything we take by the right end or improve to its just advantage.

We understand little of the works of God, either in nature or grace. We pursue false knowledge and mistake education extremely. We are violent in our affections, confused and immethodical in our whole life, making that a burden which was given for a blessing, and so of little comfort to ourselves or others, misapprehending the true notion of happiness, and so missing of the right use of life and way of happy living.

And till we are persuaded to stop and step a little aside, out of the noisy crowd and encumbering hurry of the world, and calmly take a prospect of things, it will be impossible we should be able to make a right judgment of ourselves or know our own misery. But after we have made the just reckonings which retirement will help us to, we shall begin to think the world in great measure mad, and that we have been in a sort of bedlam[2] all this while.

Reader, whether young or old, think it not too soon or too late to turn over the leaves of thy past life, and be sure to fold down where any passage of it may affect thee, and bestow thy remainder of time to correct those faults in thy future conduct, be it in relation to this or the next life. What thou wouldst do if what thou hast done were to

[2] A madhouse.

do again, be sure to do as long as thou livest, upon the like occasions.

Our resolutions seem to be vigorous as often as we reflect upon our past errors, but alas, they are apt to flat[3] again upon fresh temptation to the same things.

The author does not pretend to deliver thee an exact piece, his business not being ostentation but charity. 'Tis miscellaneous in the matter of it and by no means artificial[4] in the composure. But it contains hints that may serve thee for texts to preach to thyself upon, and which comprehend much of the course of human life, since whether thou art parent or child, prince or subject, master or servant, single or married, public or private, mean or honorable, rich or poor, prosperous or unprosperous, in peace or controversy, in business or solitude, whatever be thy inclination or aversion, practice or duty, thou will find something not unsuitably said for thy direction and advantage. Accept and improve what deserves thy notice; the rest excuse, and place to account of good will to thee and the whole creation of God.

IGNORANCE

It is admirable to consider how many millions of people come into and go out of the world ignorant of themselves and of the world they have lived in.

If one went to see Windsor Castle or Hampton Court,[5] it would be strange not to observe and remember the situation, the building, the gardens, fountains, etc., that make up the beauty and pleasure of such a seat; and yet few people know themselves—no, not their own bodies, the houses of their minds, the most curious structure of the world, a living, walking tabernacle; nor the world of which it was made and out of which it is fed, which would be so much our benefit, as well as our pleasure, to know. We cannot doubt of this when we are told that the invisible things of God are brought to light by the things that are seen,

---

[3] Slacken, droop.
[4] Artful, skillful.
[5] Windsor Castle in Berkshire was the principal residence of English rulers from the time of William the Conqueror. Hampton Court on the Thames, southwest of London, was built by Cardinal Wolsey in 1515 and taken over as a palace by Henry VIII.

and consequently we read our duty in them, as often as we look upon them, to Him that is the great and wise author of them, if we look as we should do.

The world is certainly a great and stately volume of natural things, and may be not improperly styled the hieroglyphics of a better. But alas, how very few leaves of it do we seriously turn over! This ought to be the subject of the education of our youth, who, at twenty, when they should be fit for business, know little or nothing of it.

EDUCATION

We are in pain to make them scholars but not men, to talk rather than to know, which is true canting.

The first thing obvious to children is what is sensible,[6] and that we make no part of their rudiments.

We press their memory too soon, and puzzle, strain, and load them with words and rules, to know grammar and rhetoric and a strange tongue or two, that it is ten to one may never be useful to them, leaving their natural genius to mechanical and physical or natural knowledge uncultivated and neglected, which would be of exceeding use and pleasure to them through the whole course of their life.

To be sure, languages are not to be despised or neglected, but things are still to be preferred.

Children had rather be making of tools and instruments of play, shaping, drawing, framing, and building, etc., than getting some rules of propriety of speech by heart; and those also would follow with more judgment and less trouble and time.

It were happy if we studied nature more in natural things, and acted according to nature, whose rules are few, plain, and most reasonable.

Let us begin where she begins, go her pace, and close always where she ends, and we cannot miss of being good naturalists.

The creation would not be longer a riddle to us. The heavens, earth, and waters with their respective, various, and numerous inhabitants, their productions, natures, seasons, sympathies, and antipathies, their

---

[6] Perceived through the senses.

use, benefit, and pleasure, would be better understood by us; and an eternal wisdom, power, majesty, and goodness very conspicuous to us through those sensible and passing forms, the world wearing the mark of its Maker, Whose stamp is everywhere visible and the characters very legible to the children of wisdom.

And it would go a great way to caution and direct people in their use of the world that they were better studied and knowing in the creation of it.

For how could men find the confidence to abuse it while they should see the great Creator stare them in the face in all and every part thereof?

Their ignorance makes them insensible, and that insensibility hardy in misusing this noble creation, that has the stamp and voice of a deity everywhere and in everything to the observing.

It is pity therefore that books have not been composed for youth by some curious and careful naturalists and also mechanics, in the Latin tongue, to be used in schools, that they might learn things with words—things obvious and familiar to them, and which would make the tongue easier to be attained by them.

Many able gardeners and husbandmen are yet ignorant of the reason of their calling, as most artificers are of the reason of their own rules that govern their excellent workmanship. But a naturalist and mechanic of this sort is master of the reason of both, and might be of the practice too, if his industry kept pace with his speculation, which were very commendable, and without which he cannot be said to be a complete naturalist or mechanic.

Finally, if man be the index or epitome of the world, as philosophers tell us, we have only to read ourselves well to be learned in it. But because there is nothing we less regard than the characters of the Power that made us, which are so clearly written upon us and the world He has given us and can best tell us what we are and should be, we are even strangers to our own genius, the glass in which we should see that true, instructing, and agreeable variety which is to be observed in nature, to the admiration of that wisdom and adoration of that Power which made us all. . . .

CENSORIOUSNESS

We are apt to be very pert at censuring others, where we will not endure advice ourselves. And nothing shows our weakness more than to be so sharp-sighted at spying other men's faults and so purblind about our own.

When the actions of a neighbor are upon the stage, we can have all our wits about us, are so quick and critical we can split a hair, and find out every failure and infirmity; but are without feeling or have but very little sense of our own.

Much of this comes from ill-nature, as well as from an inordinate value of ourselves, for we love rambling better than home, and blaming the unhappy rather than covering and relieving them.

In such occasions some show their malice and are witty upon misfortunes; others their justice, they can reflect apace; but few or none their charity, especially if it be about money matters.

You shall see an old miser come forth with a set gravity and so much severity against the distressed to excuse his purse that he will, ere he has done, put it out of all question that riches is righteousness with him. This, says he, is the fruit of your prodigality (as if, poor man, covetousness were no fault) or of your projects, or grasping after a great trade, while he himself would have done the same thing but that he had not the courage to venture so much ready money out of his own trusty hands, though it had been to have brought him back the Indies in return. But the proverb is just: vice should not correct sin.

They have a right to censure that have a heart to help; the rest is cruelty, not justice.

BOUNDS OF CHARITY

Lend not beyond thy ability,[7] nor refuse to lend out of thy ability, especially when it will help others more than it can hurt thee.

If thy debtor be honest and capable, thou hast thy money again, if not with increase, with praise. If he prove insolvent, don't ruin him to

---

[7] Means, estate.

get that which it will not ruin thee to lose, for thou art but a steward, and Another is thy owner, master, and judge.

The more merciful acts thou dost, the more mercy thou wilt receive; and if with a charitable employment of thy temporal riches thou gainest eternal treasure, thy purchase is infinite: thou wilt have found the art of multiplying indeed. . . .

DISCIPLINE

If thou wouldst be happy and easy in thy family, above all things observe discipline.

Everyone in it should know their duty, and there should be a time and place for everything; and whatever else is done or omitted, be sure to begin and end with God.

INDUSTRY

Love labor, for if thou dost not want it for food, thou mayest for physic. It is wholesome for thy body and good for thy mind. It prevents the fruits of idleness, which many times comes of nothing to do and leads too many to do what is worse than nothing.

A garden, a laboratory, a workhouse, improvements, and breeding are pleasant and profitable diversions to the idle and ingenious. For here they miss ill company and converse with nature and art, whose variety are equally grateful and instructing and preserve a good constitution of body and mind.

TEMPERANCE

To this a spare diet contributes much. Eat therefore to live and do not live to eat. That's like a man, but this below a beast.

Have wholesome but not costly food, and be rather cleanly than dainty in ordering it.

The recipes of cookery are swelled to a volume, but a good stomach excels them all, to which nothing contributes more than industry and temperance.

It is a cruel folly to offer up to ostentation so many lives of creatures as make up the state of our treats, as it is a prodigal one to spend more in sauce than in meat.

The proverb says that "enough is as good as a feast," but it is certainly better, if superfluity be a fault, which never fails to be at festivals.

If thou rise with an appetite, thou art sure never to sit down without one.

Rarely drink but when thou art dry; nor then, between meals, if it can be avoided.

The smaller the drink, the clearer the head and the cooler the blood, which are great benefits in temper and business.

Strong liquors are good at some times and in small proportions, being better for physic than food, for cordials than common use.

The most common things are the most useful, which shows both the wisdom and goodness of the great Lord of the family of the world.

What therefore He has made rare, don't thou use too commonly, lest thou shouldst invert the use and order of things, become wanton and voluptuous, and thy blessings prove a curse.

"Let nothing be lost,"[8] said our Saviour; but that is lost that is misused.

Neither urge another to that thou wouldst be unwilling to do thyself, nor do thyself what looks to thee unseemly and intemperate in another.

All excess is ill, but drunkenness is of the worst sort: it spoils health, dismounts the mind, and unmans men; it reveals secrets, is quarrelsome, lascivious, impudent, dangerous, and mad. In fine, he that is drunk is not a man, because he is so long void of reason, that distinguishes a man from a beast.

APPAREL

Excess in apparel is another costly folly: the very trimming of the vain world would clothe all the naked one.

Choose thy clothes by thine own eyes, not another's. The more

[8] John vi. 12.

plain and simple they are, the better—neither unshapely nor fantastical, and for use and decency, and not for pride.

If thou art clean and warm, it is sufficient, for more doth but rob the poor and please the wanton.

It is said of the true church, "The King's daughter is all glorious within."[9] Let our care therefore be of our minds more than of our bodies, if we would be of her communion.

We are told with truth that meekness and modesty are the rich and charming attire of the soul, and the plainer the dress, the more distinctly and with greater luster their beauty shines.

It is great pity such beauties are so rare and those of Jezebel's forehead are so common, whose dresses are incentives to lust but bars instead of motives to love of virtue.

RIGHT MARRIAGE

Never marry but for love, but see that thou lovest what is lovely.

If love be not thy chiefest motive, thou wilt soon grow weary of a married state and stray from thy promise to search out thy pleasures in forbidden places.

Let not enjoyment lessen but augment affection, it being the basest of passions to like when we have not what we slight when we possess.

It is the difference betwixt lust and love that this is fixed, that volatile. Love grows, lust wastes by enjoyment; and the reason is that one springs from a union of souls, and the other from a union of sense.

They have divers originals, and so are of different families: that inward and deep, this superficial; this transient, and that permanent.

They that marry for money cannot have the true satisfaction of marriage, the requisite means being wanting.

Men are generally more careful of the breed of their horses and dogs than of their children.

Those must be of the best sort for shape, strength, courage, and good conditions; but as for these, their own posterity, money shall answer all things. With such, it makes the crooked straight, sets squint-eyes right, cures madness, covers folly, changes ill conditions, mends the

[9] Psalms xiv. 13.

skin, gives a sweet breath, repairs honors, makes young, works wonders.

O how sordid is man grown! Man, the noblest creature of the world, as a god on earth and the image of Him that made it, thus to mistake earth for heaven, and worship gold for god!

AVARICE

Covetousness is the greatest of monsters as well as the root of all evil. I have once seen the man that died to save charges. What! Give ten shillings to a doctor and have an apothecary's bill besides, that may come to I know not what? No, not he, valuing life less than twenty shillings. But indeed such a man could not well set too low a price upon himself, who, though he lived up to the chin in bags,[10] had rather die than find in his heart to open one of them to help to save his life.

Such a man is *felo de se*,[11] and deserves not Christian burial.

He is a common nuisance, a weir across the stream that stops the current, an obstruction to be removed by a purge of the law. The only gratification he gives his neighbors is to let them see that he himself is as little the better for what he has as they are. For he always looks like Lent—a sort of lay-minim.[12] In some sense he may be compared to Pharoah's lean kine, for all that he has does him no good. He commonly wears his clothes till they leave him, or that nobody else can wear them. He affects to be thought poor to escape robbery and taxes, and by looking as if he wanted an alms, excuses himself from giving any. He ever goes late to markets to cover buying the worst, but does it because that is cheapest. He lives off the offal. His life were an insupportable punishment to any temper but his own, and no greater torment to him on earth than to live as other men do. But the misery of his pleasure is that he is never satisfied with getting and always in fear of losing what he cannot use.

How vilely has he lost himself that becomes a slave to his servant, and exalts him to the dignity of his maker: gold is the God, the wife, the friend of the moneymonger of the world.

[10] Moneybags.
[11] A suicide.
[12] A friar belonging to the mendicant order founded by St. Francis of Paula.

But in marriage do thou be wise; prefer the person before money, virtue before beauty, the mind before the body. Then thou hast a wife, a friend, a companion, a second self, one that bears an equal share with thee in all thy toils and troubles.

Choose one that measures her satisfaction, safety, and danger by thine, and of whom thou art sure, as of thy secretest thoughts—a friend as well as a wife, which indeed a wife implies, for she is but half a wife that is not, or is not capable of being, such a friend.

Sexes make no difference, since in souls there is none; and they are the subjects of friendship.

He that minds a body and not a soul has not the better part of that relation, and will consequently want the noblest comfort of a married life.

The satisfaction of our senses is low, short, and transient; but the mind gives a more raised and extended pleasure, and is capable of a happiness founded upon reason, not bounded and limited by the circumstances that bodies are confined to.

Here it is we ought to search out our pleasure, where the field is large and full of variety and of an enduring nature, sickness, poverty, or disgrace being not able to shake it, because it is not under the moving influences of worldly contingencies.

The satisfaction of those that do so is in well-doing and in the assurance they have of a future reward—that they are best loved of those that love most, and that they enjoy and value the liberty of their minds above that of their bodies, having the whole creation for their prospect: the most noble and wonderful works and providences of God, the histories of the ancients, and in them the actions and examples of the virtuous, and, lastly, themselves, their affairs and family to exercise their minds and friendship upon.

Nothing can be more entire and without reserve, nothing more zealous, affectionate, and sincere, nothing more contented and constant than such a couple, nor no greater temporal felicity than to be one of them.

Between a man and his wife nothing ought to rule but love. Authority is for children and servants, yet not without sweetness.

As love ought to bring them together, so it is the best way to keep them well together.

Wherefore use her not as a servant, whom thou wouldst perhaps have served seven years to have obtained.

A husband and wife that love and value one another show their children and servants that they should do so too. Others visibly lose their authority in their families by their contempt of one another, and teach their children to be unnatural by their own examples.

It is a general fault not to be more careful to preserve nature[13] in children, who, at least in the second descent, hardly have the feeling of their relation, which must be an unpleasant reflection to affectionate parents.

Frequent visits, presents, intimate correspondence, and intermarriages within allowed bounds are means of keeping up the concern and affection that nature requires from relations.

FRIENDSHIP

Friendship is the next pleasure we may hope for, and where we find it not at home, or have no home to find it in, we may seek it abroad. It is a union of spirits, a marriage of hearts, and the bond thereof, virtue.

There can be no friendship where there is no freedom. Friendship loves a free air, and will not be penned up in strait and narrow enclosures. It will speak freely and act so too, and take nothing ill where no ill is meant; nay, where it is, 'twill easily forgive, and forget too, upon small acknowledgments.

Friends are true twins in soul; they sympathize in everything, and have the [same] love and aversion.

One is not happy without the other, nor can either of them be miserable alone. As if they could change bodies, they take their turns in pain as well as in pleasure, relieving one another in their most adverse conditions.

What one enjoys the other cannot want. Like the primitive Chris-

[13] Affection.

tians, they have all things in common, and no property but in one another.

QUALITIES OF A FRIEND

A true friend unbosoms freely, advises justly, assists readily, adventures boldly, takes all patiently, defends courageously, and continues a friend unchangeably.

These being the qualities of a friend, we are to find them before we choose one.

The covetous, the angry, the proud, the jealous, the talkative cannot but make ill friends as well as the false.

In short, choose a friend as thou dost a wife, till death separate you.

Yet be not a friend beyond the altar, but let virtue bound thy friendship, else it is not friendship but an evil confederacy.

If my brother or kinsman will be my friend, I ought to prefer him before a stranger, or I show little duty or nature to my parents.

And as we ought to prefer our kindred in point of affection, so too in point of charity, if equally needing and deserving. . . .

RULES OF CONVERSATION

Avoid company where it is not profitable or necessary, and in those occasions speak little and last.

Silence is wisdom where speaking is folly, and always safe.

Some are so foolish as to interrupt and anticipate those that speak, instead of hearing and thinking before they answer, which is uncivil as well as silly.

If thou thinkest twice before thou speakest once, thou wilt speak twice the better for it.

Better say nothing than not to the purpose. And to speak pertinently, consider both what is fit and when it is fit to speak.

In all debates let truth be thy aim, not victory or an unjust interest; and endeavor to gain rather than to expose thy antagonist.

Give no advantage in argument, nor lose any that is offered. This is a benefit which arises from temper.[14]

Don't use[15] thyself to dispute against thine own judgment to show wit, lest it prepare thee to be too indifferent about what is right; nor against another man to vex him, or for mere trial of skill, since to inform or to be informed ought to be the end of all conferences.

Men are too apt to be concerned for their credit more than for the cause.

ELOQUENCE

There is a truth and beauty in rhetoric, but it oftener serves ill turns than good ones.

Elegancy is a good mien and address given to matter, be it by proper or figurative speech; where the words are apt and allusions very natural, certainly it has a moving grace, but it is too artificial for simplicity, and oftentimes for truth. The danger is lest it delude the weak, who in such cases may mistake the handmaid for the mistress, if not error for truth.

'Tis certain truth is least indebted to it, because she has least need of it and least uses it.

But it is a reprovable delicacy in them that despise truth in plain clothes.

Such luxuriants have but false appetites, like those gluttons that by sauces force them, where they have no stomach, and sacrifice to their palate, not their health, which cannot be without great vanity, nor that without some sin. . . .

A COUNTRY LIFE

The country life is to be preferred, for there we see the works of God, but in cities little else but the works of men; and the one makes a better subject for our contemplation than the other.

As puppets are to men, and babies to children, so is man's workmanship to God's: we are the picture, He the reality.

---

[14] Composure, equanimity.
[15] Accustom.

God's works declare His power, wisdom, and goodness; but man's works, for the most part, his pride, folly, and excess. The one is for use, the other chiefly for ostentation and lust.

The country is both the philosopher's garden and his library, in which he reads and contemplates the power, wisdom, and goodness of God.

It is his food as well as study, and gives him life as well as learning.

[It is] a sweet and natural retreat from noise and talk, and allows opportunity for reflection, and gives the best subjects for it.

In short, 'tis an original, and the knowledge and improvement of it man's oldest business and trade, and the best he can be of. . . .

RESPECT

Never esteem any man or thyself the more for money, nor think the meaner of thyself or another for want of it, virtue being the just reason of respecting, and the want of it, of slighting anyone.

A man, like a watch, is to be valued for his goings.

He that prefers him upon other accounts bows to an idol.

Unless virtue guide us, our choice must be wrong.

An able bad man is an ill instrument, and to be shunned as the plague.

Be not deceived with the first appearances of things, but give thyself time to be in the right.

Show is not substance: realities govern wise men.

Have a care therefore where there is more sail than ballast.

HAZARD

In all business it is best to put nothing to hazard, but where it is unavoidable, be not rash, but firm and resigned.

We should not be troubled for what we cannot help, but if it was our fault, let it be so no more. Amendment is repentance, if not reparation.

As a desperate game needs an able gamester, so consideration often would prevent what the best skill in the world cannot recover.

Where the probability of advantage exceeds not that of loss, wisdom never adventures.

To shoot well flying is well, but to choose it has more of vanity than judgment.

To be dextrous in danger is a virtue, but to court danger to show it is weakness. . . .

BALANCE

We must not be concerned above the value of the thing that engages us, nor raised above reason in maintaining what we think reasonable.

It is too common an error to invert the order of things by making an end of that which is a means, and a means of that which is an end.

Religion and government escape not this mischief: the first is too often made a means instead of an end, the other an end instead of a means.

Thus men seek wealth rather than subsistence; and the end of clothes is the least reason of their use. Nor is the satisfying of our appetite our end in eating so much as the pleasing of our palate. The like may also be said of building, furniture, etc., where the man rules not the beast and appetite submits not to reason.

It is great wisdom to proportion our esteem to the nature of the thing, for as that way things will not be undervalued, so neither will they engage us above their intrinsic worth.

If we suffer little things to have great hold upon us, we shall be as much transported for them as if they deserved it.

It is an old proverb, *Maxima bella ex levissimis causis*—The greatest feuds have had the smallest beginnings.

No matter what the subject of the dispute be, but what place we give it in our minds, for that governs our concern and resentment.

It is one of the fatalest errors of our lives when we spoil a good cause by an ill management; and it is not impossible but we may mean well in an ill business, but that will not defend it.

If we are but sure the end is right, we are too apt to gallop over all bounds to compass it, not considering that lawful ends may be very unlawfully attained.

Let us be careful to take just ways to compass just things, that they may last in their benefits to us.

There is a troublesome humor some men have, that if they may not lead they will not follow, but had rather a thing were never done than not done their own way, though otherwise very desirable.

This comes of an over-fulness of ourselves, and shows we are more concerned for praise than the success of what we think a good thing.

POPULARITY

Affect not to be seen, and men will less see thy weakness.

They that show more than they are raise an expectation they cannot answer, and so lose their credit as soon as they are found out.

Avoid popularity. It has many snares and no real benefit to thyself, and uncertainty to others.

PRIVACY

Remember the proverb, *Bene qui latuit, bene vixit*—They are happy that live retiredly.

If this be true, princes and their grandees of all men are the unhappiest, for they live least alone, and they that must be enjoyed by everybody can never enjoy themselves as they should.

It is the advantage little men have upon them: they can be private and have leisure for family comforts, which are the greatest worldly contents men can enjoy.

But they that place pleasure in greatness seek it there, and we see rule is as much the ambition of some natures, as privacy is the choice of others.

GOVERNMENT

Government has many shapes, but 'tis sovereignty, though not freedom, in all of them.

Rex and *Tyrannus* are very differing characters: one rules his people by laws to which they consent, the other by his absolute will and power. That is called freedom, this tyranny.

The first is endangered by the ambition of the popular, which shakes the constitution; the other by an ill administration, which hazards the tyrant and his family.

It is great wisdom in princes of both sorts not to strain points too high with their people, for whether the people have a right to oppose them or not, they are ever sure to attempt it when things are carried too far, though the remedy oftentimes proves worse than the disease.

Happy that king who is great by justice and that people who are free by obedience.

Where the ruler is just he may be strict, else it is two to one it turns upon him, and though he should prevail, he can be no gainer where his people are the losers.

Princes must not have passions in government, nor resent beyond interest and religion.

Where example keeps pace with authority, power hardly fails to be obeyed and magistrates to be honored.

Let the people think they govern and they will be governed.

This cannot fail if those they trust are trusted.

That prince that is just to them in great things and humors them oftentimes in small ones is sure to have and keep them from all the world.

For the people is the politic wife of the prince that may be better managed by wisdom than ruled by force.

But where the magistrate is partial and serves ill turns, he loses his authority with the people and gives the populace opportunity to gratify their ambition, and so lays a stumbling-block for his people to fall.

It is true that where a subject is more popular than the prince, the prince is in danger. But it is as true that it is his own fault, for nobody has the like means, interest, or reason to be popular as he.

It is an unaccountable thing that some princes incline rather to be feared than loved, when they see that fear does not oftener secure a prince against the dissatisfaction of his people than love makes a subject too many for such a prince.

Certainly service upon inclination is like to go farther than obedience upon compulsion.

The Romans had a just sense of this when they placed *optimus* before *maximus* to their most illustrious captains and Caesars.

Besides, experience tells us that goodness raises a nobler passion in the soul and gives a better sense of duty than severity.

What did Pharaoh get by increasing the Israelites' task? Ruin to himself in the end.

Kings, chiefly in this, should imitate God: their mercy should be above all their works.

The difference between the prince and the peasant is in this world, but a temper ought to be observed by him that has the advantage here because of the judgment of the next.

The end of everything should direct the means; now that of government being the good of the whole, nothing less should be the aim of the prince.

As often as rulers endeavor to attain just ends by just mediums, they are sure of a quiet and easy government, and as sure of convulsions where the nature of things are violated and their order overruled.

It is certain, princes ought to have great allowances made them for faults in government, since they see by other people's eyes and hear by their ears. But ministers of state, their immediate confidants and instruments, have much to answer for if to gratify private passions they misguide the prince to do public injury.

Ministers of state should undertake their posts at their peril. If princes overrule them, let them show the law and humbly resign. If fear, gain, or flattery prevail, let them answer it to the law.

The prince cannot be preserved but where the minister is punishable, for people, as well as princes, will not endure *imperium in imperio*.[16]

If ministers are weak or ill men and so spoil their places, it is the prince's fault that chose them; but if their places spoil them, it is their own fault to be made worse by them.

It is but just that those that reign by their princes should suffer for their princes, for it is a safe and necessary maxim not to shift heads in

_____

[16] A sovereignty within a sovereignty.

government while the hands are in being that should answer for them.

And yet it were intolerable to be a minister of state if everybody may be accuser and judge.

Let therefore the false accuser no more escape an exemplary punishment than the guilty minister.

For it profanes government to have the credit of the leading men in it subject to vulgar censure, which is often ill grounded.

The safety of a prince therefore consists in a well-chosen council, and that only can be said to be so where the persons that compose it are qualified for the business that comes before them.

Who would send to a tailor to make a lock or to a smith to make a suit of clothes?

Let there be merchants for trade, seamen for the admiralty, travelers for foreign affairs, some of the leading men of the country for home business, and common and civil lawyers to advise of legality and right, who should always keep to the strict rules of law.

Three things contribute much to ruin governments: looseness, oppression, and envy.

Where the reins of government are too slack, there the manners of the people are corrupted; and that destroys industry, begets effeminacy, and provokes Heaven against it.

Oppression makes a poor country and a desperate people, who always wait an opportunity to change.

He that ruleth over men must be just, ruling in the fear of God, said an old and a wise king.[17]

Envy disturbs and distracts government, clogs the wheels, and perplexes the administration. And nothing contributes more to this disorder than a partial distribution of rewards and punishments in the sovereign.

As it is not reasonable that men should be compelled to serve, so those that have employments should not be endured to leave them humorously.

Where the state intends a man no affront, he should not affront the state.

[17] II Samuel xxiii. 3.

A PRIVATE LIFE

A private life is to be preferred, the honor and gain of public posts bearing no proportion with the comfort of it. The one is free and quiet, the other servile and noisy.

It was a great answer of the Shunamite woman, "I dwell among my own people."[18]

They that live of their own neither need nor often list[19] to wear the livery of the public.

Their subsistence is not during pleasure, nor have they patrons to please or present.

If they are not advanced, neither can they be disgraced; and as they know not the smiles of majesty, so they feel not the frowns of greatness or the effects of envy.

If they want the pleasures of a court, they also escape the temptations of it.

Private men in fine are so much their own that, paying common dues, they are sovereigns of all the rest.

A PUBLIC LIFE

Yet the public must and will be served, and they that do it well deserve public marks of honor and profit.

To do so men must have public minds as well as salaries, or they will serve private ends at the public cost.

Governments can never be well administered but where those entrusted make conscience of well discharging their places. . . .

RELIGION

Men may tire themselves in a labyrinth of search and talk of God, but if we would know Him indeed, it must be from the impressions we receive of Him; and the softer our hearts are, the deeper and livelier those will be upon us.

If He has made us sensible of His justice by His reproof, of His

[18] II Kings iv. 13.
[19] Wish.

patience by His forbearance, of His mercy by His forgiveness, of His holiness by the sanctification of our hearts through His spirit, we have a grounded knowledge of God. This is experience, that speculation; this enjoyment, that report. In short, this is undeniable evidence with the realities of religion, and will stand all winds and weathers.

As our faith, so our devotion should be lively. Cold meat won't serve at those repasts.

It is a coal from God's altar must kindle our fire. And without fire, true fire, no acceptable sacrifice.

"Open thou my lips, and then," said the royal prophet, "my mouth shall praise God."[20] But not till then.

The preparation of the heart as well as answer of the tongue is of the Lord. And to have it our prayers must be powerful and our worship grateful.

Let us choose therefore to commune where there is the warmest sense of religion, where devotion exceeds formality, and practice most corresponds with profession, and where there is at least as much charity as zeal. For where this society is to be found, there shall we find the church of God.

As good, so ill men are all of a church, and everybody knows who must be Head of it.

The humble, meek, merciful, just, pious, and devout souls are everywhere of one religion, and when death has taken off the mask, they will know one another, though the divers liveries they wear here makes them strangers.

Great allowances are to be made for education and personal weaknesses, but 'tis a rule with me, that man is truly religious that loves the persuasion he is of for the piety rather than ceremony of it.

They that have one end can hardly disagree when they meet; at least their concern in the greater moderates their value and difference about the lesser things.

It is a sad reflection that many men hardly have any religion at all, and most men have none of their own, for that which is the religion

[20] Psalms li. 15.

of their education and not of their judgment is the religion of another and not theirs.

To have religion upon authority and not upon conviction is like a finger watch—to be set forward or backward as he pleases that has it in keeping.

It is a preposterous thing that men can venture their souls where they will not venture their money; for they will take their religion upon trust, but not trust a synod about the goodness of half a crown.

They will follow their own judgment when their money is concerned, whatever they do for their souls.

But to be sure, that religion cannot be right that a man is the worse for having.

No religion is better than an unnatural one.

Grace perfects but never sours or spoils nature.

To be unnatural in defense of grace is a contradiction.

Hardly anything looks worse than to defend religion by ways that show it has no credit with us.

A devout man is one thing, a stickler is quite another.

When our minds exceed their just bounds, we must needs discredit what we would recommend.

To be furious in religion is to be irreligiously religious.

If he that is without bowels is not a man, how then can he be a Christian?

It were better to be of no church than to be bitter for any.

Bitterness comes very near to enmity, and that is Beelzebub, because the perfection of wickedness.

A good end cannot sanctify evil means, nor must we ever do evil that good may come of it.

Some folks think they may scold, rail, hate, rob, and kill too, so it be but for God's sake.

But nothing in us unlike Him can please Him.

It is as great presumption to send our passions upon God's errands as it is to palliate them with God's name.

Zeal dropped in charity is good, without it good for nothing, for it devours all it comes near.

They must first judge themselves that presume to censure others; and such will not be apt to overshoot the mark.

We are too ready to retaliate rather than forgive or gain by love and information.

And yet we could hurt no man that we believe loves us.

Let us then try what love will do. For if men do once see we love them, we should soon find they would not harm us.

Force may subdue, but love gains, and he that forgives first wins the laurel.

If I am even with my enemy, the debt is paid; but if I forgive it, I oblige him forever.

Love is the hardest lesson in Christianity, but for that reason it should be most our care to learn it. *Difficilia quae pulchra.*[21]

It is a severe rebuke upon us that God makes us so many allowances and we make so few to our neighbor, as if charity had nothing to do with religion, or love with faith, that ought to work by it.

I find all sorts of people agree, whatsoever were there animosities, when humbled by the approaches of death. Then they forgive, then they pray for and love one another, which shows us that it is not our reason but our passion that makes and holds up the feuds that reign among men in their health and fullness. They therefore that live nearest to that which they should die, must certainly live best.

Did we believe a final reckoning and judgment or did we think enough of what we do believe, we would allow more love in religion than we do, since religion itself is nothing else but love to God and man.

He that lives in love lives in God, says the beloved disciple,[22] and to be sure, a man can live nowhere better.

It is most reasonable men should value that benefit which is most durable. Now tongues shall cease, and prophecy fail, and faith shall be consummated in sight, and hope in enjoyment, but love remains.

Love is indeed heaven upon earth, since heaven above would not be heaven without it; for where there is not love, there is fear, but

[21] The best things are hardest to come by.
[22] I John iv. 16

perfect love casts out fear.[23] And yet we naturally fear most to offend what we most love.

What we love we'll hear, what we love we'll trust, and what we love we'll serve, aye, and suffer for too. "If you love me," says our blessed Redeemer, "keep my commandments." Why? Why, then He'll love us; then we shall be His friends; then He'll send us the Comforter; then whatever we ask we shall receive; and then, where He is we shall be also, and that forever.[24] Behold the fruits of love, the power, virtue, benefit, and beauty of love!

Love is above all; and when it prevails in us all, we shall all be lovely and in love with God and one with another.

From More Fruits of Solitude (*1702*)

OF THE RULE OF JUDGING

In all things reason should prevail. 'Tis quite another thing to be stiff than steady in an opinion.

This may be reasonable, but that is ever willful.

In such cases it always happens that the clearer the argument, the greater the obstinacy, where the design is not to be convinced.

This is to value humor[1] more than truth, and prefer a sullen pride to a reasonable submission.

'Tis the glory of a man to vail[2] to truth, as it is the mark of a good nature to be easily entreated.

Beasts act by sense, man should by reason, else he is a greater beast than ever God made. And the proverb is verified, the corruption of the best things is the worst and most offensive.

---

[23] I John iv. 18.
[24] St. John xiv. 23, 26; xv. 7, 10, 14–15.
[1] Whim, caprice.
[2] To bare the head in respect.

A reasonable opinion must ever be in danger, where reason is not judge.

Though there is a regard due to education and the tradition of our fathers, truth will ever deserve, as well as claim, the preference.

If, like Theophilus and Timothy, we have been brought up in the knowledge of the best things, 'tis our advantage; but neither they nor we lose by trying their truth, for so we learn their, as well as its, intrinsic worth.

Truth never lost ground by inquiry because she is most of all reasonable.

Nor can that need another authority that is self-evident.

If my own reason be on the side of a principle, with what can I dispute or withstand it?

And if men would once consider one another reasonably, they would either reconcile their differences or more amicably maintain them.

Let that therefore be the standard that has most to say for itself, though of that let every man be judge for himself.

Reason, like the sun, is common to all, and 'tis for want of examining all by the same light and measure that we are not all of the same mind, for all have it to that end, though all do not use it so. . . .

OF THE INTEREST OF THE PUBLIC IN OUR ESTATES

Hardly anything is given us for ourselves but the public may claim a share with us. But of all we call ours we are most accountable to God and the public for our estates; in this we are but stewards, and to hoard up all to ourselves is great injustice as well as ingratitude.

If all men were so far tenants to the public that the superfluities of gain and expense were applied to the exigencies thereof, it would put an end to taxes, leave never a beggar, and make the greatest bank for national trade in Europe.

It is a judgment upon us as well as a weakness, though we won't see it, to begin at the wrong end.

If the taxes we give are not to maintain pride, I am sure there would be less if pride were made a tax to the government.

I confess I have wondered that so many lawful and useful things are excised by laws and pride left to reign free over them and the public.

But since people are more afraid of the laws of man than of God, because their punishment seems to be nearest, I know not how magistrates can be excused in their suffering such excess with impunity.

Our noble English patriarchs as well as patriots were so sensible of this evil that they made several excellent laws, commonly called sumptuary, to forbid, at least limit, the pride of the people, which, because the execution of them would be our interest and honor, their neglect must be our just reproach and loss.

'Tis but reasonable that the punishment of pride and excess should help to support the government, since it must otherwise inevitably be ruined by them.

But some say it ruins trade and will make the poor burdensome to the public. But if such trade in consequence ruins the kingdom, is it not time to ruin that trade? Is moderation no part of our duty and temperance an enemy to government?

He is a Judas that will get money by anything.

To wink at a trade that effeminates the people and invades the ancient discipline of the kingdom is a crime capital, and to be severely punished instead of being excused by the magistrate.

Is there no better employment for the poor than luxury? Miserable nation!

What did they before they fell into these forbidden methods? Is there not land enough in England to cultivate, and more and better manufactures to be made?

Have we no room for them in our plantations,[3] about things that may augment trade without luxury?

In short, let pride pay and excess be well excised. And if that will not cure the people, it will help to keep the kingdom. . . .

THE CONFORMIST

It is reasonable to concur where conscience does not forbid a compliance, for conformity is at least a civil virtue.

[3] Colonies.

But we should only press it in necessaries; the rest may prove a snare and temptation to break society.

But above all, it is a weakness in religion and government, where it is carried to things of an indifferent nature, since besides that it makes way for scruples, liberty is always the price of it.

Such conformists have little to boast of, and therefore the less reason to reproach others that have more latitude.

And yet the latitudinarian that I love is one that is only so in charity, for the freedom I recommend is no skepticism in judgment, and much less so in practice. . . .

OF CHARITY

Charity has various senses, but is excellent in all of them.

It imports, first, the commiseration of the poor and unhappy of mankind, and extends a helping hand to mend their condition.

They that feel nothing of this are at best not above half of kin to [the] human race, since they must have no bowels,[4] which makes such an essential part thereof, who have no more nature.[5]

A man and yet not have the feeling of the wants or needs of his own flesh and blood! A monster rather! And may he never be suffered to propagate such an unnatural stock in the world.

Such an uncharitableness spoils the best gains, and two to one but it entails a curse upon the possessors.

Nor can we expect to be heard of God in our prayers that turn the deaf ear to the petitions of the distressed amongst our fellow creatures.

God sends the poor to try us as well as He tries them by being such, and he that refuses them a little out of the great deal that God has given him lays up poverty in store for his own posterity.

I will not say these works are meritorious, but dare say they are acceptable and go not without their reward; though to humble us in our fullness and liberality too, we only give but what is given us to give as well as use, for if we are not our own, less is that so which God has entrusted us with.

[4] Compassion.
[5] Affection, kindness.

Next, charity makes the best construction of things and persons, and is so far from being an evil spy, a backbiter, or a detractor that it excuses weakness, extenuates miscarriages, makes the best of everything, forgives everybody, serves all, and hopes to the end.

It moderates extremes, is always for expediencies, labors to accommodate differences, and had rather suffer than revenge, and so far from exacting the utmost farthing that it had rather lose than seek her own violently.

As it acts freely, so zealously too, but 'tis always to do good, for it hurts nobody.

A universal remedy against discord and a holy cement for mankind.

And lastly, 'tis love to God and the brethren which raises the soul above all worldly considerations, and, as it gives a taste of heaven upon earth, so 'tis heaven in the fullness of it hereafter to the truly charitable here.

This is the noblest sense charity has, after which all should press as that more excellent way.

From Fruits of a Father's Love published (1726)

Not knowing how long it may please God to continue me amongst you, I am willing to embrace this opportunity of leaving you my advice and counsel with respect to your Christian and civil capacity and duty in this world. And I both beseech and charge you, by the relation you have to me and the affection I have always shown to you and indeed received from you, that you lay up the same in your hearts as well as your heads with a wise and religious care.

I will begin with that which is the beginning of all true wisdom and happiness: the holy fear of God.

Children, fear God; that is to say, have a holy awe upon your minds to avoid that which is evil and a strict care to embrace and do that which is good, the measure and standard of which knowledge and duty is the light of Christ in your consciences, by which (as in John iii. 20, 21) you may clearly see if your deeds, aye, and your words and thoughts too are wrought in God or not. (For they are the deeds of the mind and for which you must be judged.) I say, with this divine light of Christ in your consciences, you may bring your thoughts, words, and works to judgment in yourselves, and have a right, true, sound, and unerring sense of your duty toward God and man. And as you come to obey this blessed light in its holy convictions, it will lead you out of the world's dark and degenerate ways and works and bring you unto Christ's way and life, and to be of the number of His true self-denying followers, to take up your cross for His sake, that bore His for yours, and to become the children of the Light, putting it on, as your holy armor by which you may see and resist the fiery darts of Satan's temptations and overcome him in all his assaults. . . .

Above all things, my dear children, as to your communion and fellowship with Friends, be careful to keep the unity of the faith in the bond of peace. Have a care of reflectors, detractors, backbiters, that undervalue and undermine brethren behind their backs or slight the good and wholesome order of Truth for the preserving things quiet, sweet, and honorable in the church. Have a care of novelties and airy, changeable people, the conceited, censorious, and puffed up, who at last have always shown themselves to be the clouds without rain and wells without water, that will rather disturb and break the peace and fellowship of the church where they dwell than not have their wills and ways take place. I charge you, in the fear of the living God, that you carefully beware of all such; mark them, as the apostle says (Romans xvi. 17). And have no fellowship with them but to advise, exhort, entreat, and finally to reprove them (Ephesians v. 11). For God is and will be with His people in this holy dispensation we are now under and which is now amongst us unto the end of days; it shall grow and increase in gifts, graces, power, and luster, for it is the last and unchangeable one. And blessed are your eyes if they see it and your ears if they hear it and your hearts if they understand it, which I pray that you may to God's glory and your eternal comfort.

Having thus expressed myself to you, my dear children, as to the things of God, His truth and kingdom, I refer you to His light, grace, spirit, and truth within you and the Holy Scriptures of truth without you, which from my youth I loved to read and were ever blessed to me, and which I charge you to read daily: the Old Testament for history chiefly, the Psalms for meditation and devotion, the prophets for comfort and hope, but especially the New Testament for doctrine, faith, and worship; for they were given forth by holy men of God in divers ages as they were moved of the Holy Spirit, and are the declared and revealed mind and will of the Holy God to mankind under divers dispensations and they are certainly able to make the man of God perfect through faith unto salvation. . . . I say, having thus expressed myself in general, I refer you, my dear children, to the light and spirit of Jesus that is within you and to the Scriptures of truth without you and such other testimonies to the one same eternal truth as have been borne in our day, and shall now descend to particulars that you may more directly apply what I have said in general, both as to your religious and civil direction in your pilgrimage upon earth.

I will begin here also with the beginning of time, the morning. So soon as you wake, retire your mind into a pure silence, from all thoughts and ideas of worldly things, and in that frame wait upon God, to feel His good presence, to lift up your hearts to Him, and commit your whole self into His blessed care and protection. Then rise, if well, immediately. Being dressed, read a chapter or more in the Scriptures, and afterward dispose yourselves for the business of the day, ever remembering that God is present, the overseer of all your thoughts, words, and actions; and demean yourselves, my dear children, accordingly, and do not you dare to do that in His holy all-seeing presence which you would be ashamed a man, yea a child, should see you do. And as you have intervals from your lawful occasions, delight to step home, within yourselves, I mean, and commune with your own hearts, and be still; and (as Nebuchadnezzar said on another occasion) one like the Son of God[1] you shall find and enjoy with you and in you, a treasure the world knows not of, but is the aim, end, and diadem of the children of God. This will bear you up against all temptations, and carry you sweetly and evenly through your day's business, supporting you under disappointments and moderating your satisfaction in success and prosperity. The evening come, read again the Holy Scripture, and have your times of retirement before you close your eyes, as in the morning, that so the Lord may be the Alpha and Omega of every day of your lives. And if God bless you with families, remember good Joshua's resolution: "But as for me and my house, we will serve the Lord."[2]

Fear God; show it in desire, refraining, and doing. Keep the inward watch, keep a clear soul and a light heart. Mind an inward sense upon doing anything. When you read the Scripture, remark the notablest places, as your spirits are most touched and affected, in a commonplace book, with that sense or opening which you receive, for they come not by study or in the will of man, no more than the Scripture did, and they may be lost by carelessness and over-growing thoughts and businesses of this life; so in perusing any other good or profitable book. Yet rather meditate than read much. For the spirit of a man knows the things of a man, and with that spirit, by observation of the tempers and actions of men you see in the world, and looking into your own spirit and meditating thereupon, you will have a deep and strong judgment of men and things. For from what may be, what should be, and what is most probable or likely to be, you can hardly miss in your judgment of human affairs; and you have a better spirit than your own in reserve for a time of need to pass the final judgment in important matters.

In conversation mark well what others say or do, and hide your own mind, at least till last; and then open it as sparingly as the matter will let you. A just observance and reflection upon men and things give wisdom; those are the great books of learning, seldom read. The

[1] See Daniel iii. 25.
[2] Joshua xxiv. 15.

laborious bee draws honey from every flower. Be always on your watch, but chiefly in company; then be sure to have your wits about you and your armor on. Speak last and little, but to the point. Interrupt none, anticipate none. . . . Be quick to hear, slow to speak. . . . It gives time to understand and ripens an answer. Affect not words but matter, and chiefly to be pertinent and plain. Truest eloquence is plainest, and brief speaking (I mean brevity and clearness, to make yourselves easily understood by everybody and in as few words as the matter will admit of) is the best. . . .

Return no answer to anger unless with much meekness, which often turns it away; but rarely make replies, less rejoinders, for that adds fuel to the fire. It is a wrong time to vindicate yourselves, the true ear being then never open to hear it. Men are not themselves, and know not well what spirits they are of. Silence to passion, prejudice, and mockery is the best answer, and often conquers what resistance inflames.

Learn and teach your children fair writing and the most useful parts of the mathematics and some business when young, whatever else they are taught.

Cast up your income and live on half; if you can, one-third, reserving the rest for casualties, charities, portions.

Be plain in clothes, furniture, and food, but clean, and then the coarser the better; the rest is folly and a snare. Therefore, next to sin, avoid daintiness and choiceness about your person and houses. For if it be not evil in itself, it is a temptation to it, and may be accounted a nest for sin to brood in. . . .

Have very few acquaintance and fewer intimates, but of the best in their kind.

Keep your own secrets, and do not covet others'; but if trusted, never reveal them, unless mischievous to somebody, nor then, before warning to the party to desist and repent. . . .

Trust no man with the main chance, and avoid to be trusted. . . .

Choose God's trades before men's; Adam was a gardener, Cain a plowman, and Abel a grazier or shepherd. These began with the world, and have least of snare and most of use. When Cain became murderer, as a witty man said,[3] he turned a builder of cities and quitted his husbandry. Mechanics, as handicrafts, are also commendable, but they are but a second brood and younger brothers. If grace employ you not, let nature and useful arts; but avoid curiosity here also, for it devours much time to no profit. I have seen a ceiling of a room that cost half as much as the house—a folly and sin too.

Have but few books, but let them be well chosen and well read, whether of religious or civil subjects. Shun fantastic opinions. Measure both religion and learning by practice; reduce all to that, for that brings a real benefit to you; the rest is a thief and a snare. And indeed reading many books is but a taking off the mind too much from meditation. Reading yourselves and nature in the dealings and conduct of men is the truest human wisdom. The spirit of a man knows the things of man, and more true knowledge comes by meditation and just reflection than by reading, for much reading is an oppression of the mind and extinguishes the natural candle, which is the reason of so many senseless scholars in the world. . . .

The wisdom of nations lies in their proverbs, which are brief and pithy; collect and learn them; they are notable measures and directions for human life; you have much in little; they save time and speaking, and upon occasion may be the fullest and safest answers. . . .

Meddle not with government; never speak of it, let others say or do as they please. But read such books of law as relate to the office of a justice, a coroner, sheriff, and constable, also the doctor and student; some book of clerkship,[4] and a treatise of wills, to enable you about your own private business only or a poor neighbor's. For it is a charge I leave with you and yours: meddle not with the public, neither business nor money, but understand how to avoid it and defend yourselves upon occasion against it. For much knowledge brings sorrow, and much

[3] In *The Garden* Abraham Cowley wrote: "God the first garden made, and the first city Cain."

[4] Penmanship and orthography.

doings more. Therefore know God, know yourselves, love home, know your own business and mind it, and you have more time and peace than your neighbors. . . .

Diligence is another virtue useful and laudable among men: it is a discreet and understanding application of one's self to business, and avoids the extremes of idleness and drudgery. It gives great advantages to men: it loses no time, it conquers difficulties, recovers disappointments, gives dispatch, supplies want of parts, and is that to them which a pond is to a spring: though it has no water of itself, it will keep what it gets and is never dry. Though that has the heels, this has the wind, and often wins the prize. Nor does it only concern handicrafts and bodily affairs; the mind is also engaged, and grows foul, rusty, and distempered without it. It belongs to you throughout your whole man; be no more sauntering in your minds than in your bodies. And if you would have the full benefit of this virtue, don't balk[5] it by a confused mind. Shun diversions; think only of the present business till that be done. Be busy to purpose, for a busy man and a man of business are two different things. Lay your matters right, and diligence succeeds them, else pains is lost. How laborious are some to no purpose? Consider your end well, suit your means to it, and then diligently employ them, and you arrive where you would be, with God's blessing. Solomon praises diligence very highly. First, it is the way to wealth: "The diligent hand makes rich" (Proverbs x. 4). "The soul of the diligent shall be made fat" (Chap. xiii. 4). There is a promise to it, and one of another sort to the sluggard (Chap. xxiii. 21). Secondly, it prefers men: "Seest thou a man diligent in his business? He shall stand before kings" (Chap. xxii. 29). Thirdly, it preserves an estate: "Be thou diligent to know the state of thy flocks, and look well to thy herd, for riches are not forever" (Chap. xxvii. 23, 24). There is no living upon the principal; you must be diligent to preserve what you have, whether it be acquisition or inheritance, else it will consume. In short, the wise man advises: "Whatsoever thy hand finds to do, do it with thy might" (Ecclesiastes ix. 10). As it mends a temporal state, no spiritual one can

5 Frustrate.

be got or kept without it. Moses earnestly presses it upon the Israelites (Deuteronomy iv. 9 and vi. 7). The apostle Paul commends it in the Corinthians, and Titus to them for that reason (II Corinthians viii. 7, 22). So he does Timothy to the Philippians on the same account, and urges them to work out their salvation (Philippians ii. 12, 20, 21). Peter also exhorts the churches to that purpose: "Wherefore the rather, brethren," says he, "give diligence to make your calling and election sure: for if you do these things you shall never fail"[6] (II Peter i. 10). And in Chap. iii. 13, 14: "Wherefore, beloved, seeing that you look for such things [the end of the world and last judgment] be diligent that you may be found of him in peace, without spot and blameless." Thus diligence is an approved virtue. But remember, that is a reasonable pursuit or execution of honest purposes, and not an over-charging or oppressive persecution, to mind or body, of most lawful enterprises. Abuse it not, therefore, to ambition or avarice. Let necessity, charity, and conveniency govern it, and it will be well employed, and you may expect prosperous returns.

Frugality is a virtue too, and not of little use in life—the better way to be rich, for it has less toil and temptation. It is proverbial, "A penny saved is a penny got"; it has a significant moral, for this way of getting is more in your own power and less subject to hazard as well as snares, free of envy, void of suits, and is beforehand with calamities. For many get that cannot keep, and, for want of frugality, spend what they get, and so come to want what they have spent. But have a care of the extreme; want not with abundance, for that is avarice, even to sordidness. It is fit you consider children, age, and casualties, but never pretend those things to palliate and gratify covetousness. As I would have you liberal but not prodigal, and diligent but not drudging, so I would have you frugal but not sordid. If you can, lay up one-half of your income for those uses, in which let charity have at least the second consideration, but not Judas's, for that was in the wrong place. . . .

I have chosen to speak in the language of the Scripture, which is that of the Holy Ghost, the spirit of truth and wisdom, that wanted no art or direction of man to speak by and express itself fitly to man's

[6] The King James Version, which Penn seems to be quoting, reads *fall*.

understanding. But yet that blessed principle, the eternal Word I began with to you and which is that light, spirit, grace, and truth I have exhorted you to in all its holy appearances or manifestations in yourselves, by which all things were at first made and man enlightened to salvation, is Pythagoras's great light and salt of ages, Anaxagoras's divine mind, Socrates's good spirit, Timaeus's unbegotten principle and author of all light, Hieron's God in man, Plato's eternal, ineffable, and perfect principle of truth, Zeno's maker and father of all, and Plotin[us'] root of the soul;[7] who, as they thus styled the eternal Word, so for the appearance of it in man they wanted not very significant words. A domestic God or God within, say Hieron, Pythagoras, Epictetus, and Seneca; genius, angel, or guide, say Socrates and Timaeus; the light and spirit of God, says Plato; the divine principle in man, says Plotin[us]; the divine power and reason, the infallible, immortal law in the minds of men, says Philo; and the law and living rule of the mind, the interior guide of the soul and everlasting foundation of virtue, says Plutarch. Of which you may read more in the first part of *The Christian Quaker*[8] and in *The Confutation of Atheism* by Dr. Cudworth.[9] These were some of those virtuous gentiles commended by the apostle (Romans ii. 13, 14, 15) that, though they had not the law given to them as the Jews had, with those instrumental helps and advantages, yet doing by nature the things contained in the law, they became a law unto themselves.

[7] Here Penn calls the roll of the ancient Greek philosophers and attributes to each of them a recognition of the principle of the Inward Light. It is not clear whom he has in mind in his reference to Hieron. There were two Greek tyrants of that name, both rulers of Syracuse, but neither is remembered as a philosopher.

[8] *The Christian Quaker* (1674) by William Penn and George Whitehead was an answer to an attack on Quakerism by Thomas Hicks, a Baptist preacher. The first part, for which Penn was responsible, was a study of "Gentile Divinity"; i.e., the religious ideas of those who had not had the benefit of Christ's revelation. In this work Penn develops at greater length the ideas outlined here on the universality of the Light Within.

[9] Ralph Cudworth was a member of the group known as the Cambridge Platonists. The reference here is to his great work *The True Intellectual System of the Universe, Wherein All the Reason and Philosophy of Atheism Is Confuted* (1678).

Bibliographical Note

The personality and career of William Penn have attracted the attention of more than forty biographers since Joseph Besse published the first memoir in 1726. No one has yet produced a really definitive treatment of this many-sided man, but several of his biographers have written books that illuminate aspects of his genius. Perhaps the most nearly complete biography is Catherine Owens Peare's *William Penn* (Philadelphia: Lippincott, 1957), a reliable and readable book, though stronger on his domestic and personal life than on his religious and intellectual development. The best brief sketch is William Wistar Comfort's *William Penn: A Tercentenary Estimate* (Philadelphia: University of Pennsylvania Press, 1944), written by a Friend and stressing Penn's Quakerism. Most useful for reference purposes because of its schematic arrangement is William I. Hull's scholarly *William Penn: A Topical Biography* (New York: Oxford University Press, 1937). Of the older books, Mabel Brailsford's *Making of William Penn* (London: Longmans, 1930), Bonamy Dobrée's *William Penn* (Boston and New York: Houghton Mifflin, 1932), and C. E. Vulliamy's *William Penn* (New York: Scribner, 1934) can be recommended. Samuel M. Janney's *Life of William Penn* (Philadelphia, 1852), though written more than a century ago, is still valuable for its extensive quotations from original documents. Elizabeth Janet Gray's *Penn* (New York: Viking, 1938) is an excellent biography for younger readers.

Penn the writer and thinker tends to be slighted in most of the biographies, but there are a few books and articles which deal helpfully with special aspects of his thought. Edward C. O. Beatty's *William Penn as Social Philosopher* (New York: Columbia University Press,

1939) is a study of his social, economic, and political ideas. J. H. Powell, "William Penn's Writings: An Anniversary Essay," in *Pennsylvania History*, XI (1944), 239–259, is a briefer and somewhat sharper analysis of those ideas with some appreciative comments on Penn's qualities as a writer. Irvin Goldman's "Deviation Toward Ideas of Natural Ethics in the Thought of William Penn," *Philological Quarterly*, XVII (1939), 337–352, discusses his tendency in his later works to blur the distinction between the Inward Light and reason. The *Pennsylvania Magazine of History and Biography* in 1944 (Vol. LXVIII, No. 4) published a group of thoughtful essays on various aspects of Penn's thought: "William Penn's Religious Background" by William Wistar Comfort, "Persecution and Religious Liberty" by Henry J. Cadbury, "William Penn's Experiment in Race Relations" by Thomas E. Drake, and "William Penn and City Planning" by William E. Lingelbach. Mary Maples' "William Penn: Classical Republican," *Pennsylvania Magazine of History and Biography*, LXXXI (1957), is a useful commentary on his political ideas. Fulmer Mood's "William Penn and English Politics in 1680–81," *Journal of the Friends' Historical Society*, XXXII (1935), 3–21, places the founding of Pennsylvania in its historical context.

There has never been a complete edition of Penn's writings. The closest approximation is *A Collection of the Works of William Penn*, published in two thick folio volumes under the editorship of Joseph Besse in London in 1726. A more limited selection appeared in a huge royal folio in 1771 under the title of *Select Works of William Penn*, these selections were reprinted in five volumes in 1782 and again in three volumes in 1825. Only a few of his writings have been republished in the past century. There have been good editions of *Some Fruits of Solitude* and the *Essay Towards the Present and Future Peace of Europe; No Cross, No Crown*, has been kept in print by the London and Philadelphia Yearly Meetings of Friends; and his promotional tracts for Pennsylvania are included in *Narratives of Early Pennsylvania, West New Jersey, and Delaware*, edited by Albert Cook Myers (New York: Scribner, 1912). But for the most part Penn's writings can only be found in the early editions in libraries.

A few general books useful in illuminating the background of Penn's writings may be listed. The best account of early Quakerism is to be found in two books by William Charles Braithwaite: *The Beginnings of Quakerism* (London: Macmillan, 1912; 2nd edition, revised by Henry J. Cadbury, Cambridge: Cambridge University Press, 1955), and *The Second Period of Quakerism* (London: Macmillan, 1919). The history of the "holy experiment" in Pennsylvania can be followed in Book V (by Isaac Sharpless) of Rufus M. Jones *et al.*, *The Quakers in the American Colonies* (London: Macmillan, 1911). *Meeting House and Counting House* by Frederick B. Tolles (Chapel Hill: University of North Carolina Press, 1948) shows how some of Penn's ideas —on business, education, and science, for instance—were carried on into American life by the Quaker merchants of colonial Philadelphia.